C000195885

From Asgard to Valhalla

For Ellen, Tom and Josie:
the next generation

From Asgard to Valhalla

THE REMARKABLE HISTORY OF THE NORSE MYTHS

HEATHER O'DONOGHUE

I.B. TAURIS
LONDON · NEW YORK

Published in 2007 by I.B.Tauris & Co. Ltd
6 Salem Road, London W2 4BU
175 Fifth Avenue, New York NY 10010
www.ibtauris.com

In the United States and Canada distributed by Palgrave Macmillan,
a division of St. Martin's Press, 175 Fifth Avenue, New York NY 10010

ISBN 978 1 84511 357 5

A full CIP record for this book is available from the British Library
A full CIP record for this book is available from the Library of Congress
Library of Congress catalog card: available

Typeset in Sabon by Dexter Haven Associates Ltd, London
Printed and bound in Great Britain by CPI Bath

CONTENTS

LIST OF PLATES

Carving on a Viking-age stone from Ramsund, in Sweden.

The Hørdum Stone from Thy, in Denmark.

Viking-age figurine of Thor, perhaps holding his hammer, from Northern Iceland.

One of the eastern fjords of Iceland.

The Oseberg Ship, the sarcophagus of a royal woman buried in southern Norway in the ninth century.

The first leaf of the *Codex Regius*, the manuscript of the *Poetic Edda*.

A Viking-age picture stone from the island of Gotland, Sweden.

Henri Fuseli: *Thor Battering the Midgard Serpent* (1790).

Odin summons the sibyl: one of William Blake's illustrations for Gray's *The Descent of Odin*.

William Blake's illustration for the title page of Gray's poem *The Fatal Sisters*.

Rune gymnastics. Drawing by Siegfried Adolf Kummer.

Poster for Peter Jackson's film of *The Lord of the Rings: The Return of the King* (2003).

Amalie Materna as Brünnhilde in the first Bayreuth production of Wagner's *Die Walküre* in 1876.

'Brisings' Ruff', a piece of contemporary jewellery by Lori Talcott.

The Mighty Thor, as pictured by Marvel Comics.

Cover of the album *Hammerheart*, by Swedish Viking metal band Bathory.

ACKNOWLEDGEMENTS

I would like to thank all the students who came to my lectures and classes on Norse myth. Whether they made comments, asked questions, looked interested or looked bored, they all contributed to the writing of this book, and I am grateful to them. A number of people offered invaluable specialist advice: David Clark, Antje Frotscher, Alastair Hird, Carolyne Larrington, Phil Lavender, Josephine McDonagh, Tom O'Donoghue, Alex Sarll, Emma Smith and Beth Tovey. Particular thanks go to Tara Stubbs, who gave me an enormous amount of expert help with pictures and proof-reading, and to Alex Wright at I.B.Tauris, who has been unfailingly supportive from the very beginning. The idea for this book came to us both, separately but simultaneously.

A NOTE ON PROPER NAMES

I have anglicized many of the Norse proper names, especially those which have been picked up and used by later writers in English. This has often involved substituting special characters, and removing accents and the final 'r' from names such as Olaf (Old Norse Óláfr), or Frey (Old Norse Freyr). Sometimes, however, that final 'r' has been retained by later writers – for instance, Balder is a common form of the Old Norse Baldr. In cases such as this, and others, I have retained it. No doubt there will be inconsistencies; my aim has been ease of usage and readability, rather than strict regularity.

Introduction

Myth is a notoriously slippery term. It derives from the Greek word *muthos*, 'something said' (as opposed to 'something done'), but derivation is more useful in showing us what words once used to mean than in helping with present usage. Today the commonest meaning of the word 'myth' is of something said which is simply not true. But as a glance at the (very) long list of books whose titles include the word 'myth' – from *The Myth of America* through *The Myth of Motherhood, of Masculinity* or *of the Master Race*, to *The Myth of the Welfare State* – will show, whether or not myths are 'true', they are certainly significant. They have an agenda, a purpose, and seem to be of such powerful or fundamental relevance, either for society or for the individual, that they demand a response. And while the works which try to dispel these myths are the products of specific, often individual authors, the myths themselves are less easy to source. They have, somehow, crept up on us, taken shape and hold in mysterious and unaccountable ways. They represent 'something believed'.

The kinds of myths most Western readers are most familiar with – classical myths, say, or the Norse myths which are the subject of this book – belong to the distant past. They can be most easily defined as *stories about the gods*. But both parts of this definition need some discussion. The word *story*, for instance, should not be passed over lightly. 'Something said' is not necessarily a *story* (and only in the loosest possible terms could the sort of modern myths I've referred to be called

1

stories). But mythology – in the sense of a body of myths – has traditionally come down to us in narrative form. In fact, it has been suggested that myths began simply as entertaining tales, and only gradually acquired significance and deeper meanings. This leads us to the second part of the definition: are myths necessarily *sacred* stories? Many people would see the relationship between myths and gods as absolutely fundamental – indeed, would see myths as in some sense the 'script', or 'screenplay', of actual religious practice, part of a ritual of worship. As it happens, some of the most celebrated 'myths' in the classical tradition do not have gods as their central characters: Oedipus, for example, is a legendary king of the historical city of Thebes. Nonetheless, the story of *Oedipus Rex* takes place in a world in which the supernatural – in the form of oracles, monsters like the Sphinx, or Fate itself – plays its part in an otherwise historical, human context. Whether myths are set in the distant past, or in the realm of the gods, the key point is that it is always a world apart from our own everyday one, a world which might physically resemble our own, but one in which we may encounter gods, heroes or monsters, and which is governed by strange potent forces, where anything at all might happen: both the bafflingly unpredictable, and, with the mysterious logic of dreams, the utterly inevitable.

If myths are about the pagan gods, then a modern reader might think it stands to reason that they are untrue. But does this mean that contemporary religions can have no mythologies? We are likely to find phrases such as 'Christian mythology' or 'Islamic mythology' uncomfortable, or even offensive. Perhaps for this very reason, most of the work done on the relationship between myth and religion has focussed on past societies – or on so-called 'primitive' societies, distanced from us in time or geographical space, or both. Myths are stories which *other people* – not 'people like us' – held (or hold) to be true. These sorts of myths are interesting to scholars, because it seems that having been passed down in story form, they can encode information about past or distant religions. The theory goes that either religious rituals give rise to accompanying stories – that is, mythology; or that the stories themselves somehow provoke actions on the part of the listeners – that is, rituals. The supposed function of these rituals is to make the stories – perhaps stories about fertility or rebirth, violence or apocalypse – happen (or not!). Either way, with the extant mythology, scholars aim to work either backwards or forwards to find out about the religious ritual.

Similarly, myths can be seen as encoding if not the religious beliefs of societies, then beliefs of almost equal, or perhaps related, significance (in some ways like the modern myths mentioned earlier). Myths are understood as stories which serve to legitimate certain ways of organizing society, certain sexual practices, or gender roles. They may reflect the cultural preoccupations of societies. For instance, it has been said that the Navajo people of North America are notably hypochondriac, and their myths, being largely concerned with healing and curing, reflect this (though it might be difficult to distinguish cause and effect!). Or myths may act as vents for anxieties which concern particular societies at particular times: fear of invasion, of social disorder, of the assimilation of immigrant groups. On a political level, myths have been understood as societal responses to 'the hurt of history' – an attempt to cover up the unacceptable aspects of the formation of societies or nations, of social hierarchies or methods of production. It has seemed, therefore, that properly, sensitively decoded – if that were only possible! – myths might act as a window on to past societies. The important feature of this approach to myths is that they are treated as functional – as if they serve a social purpose. But it still tends to treat myths as historical or anthropological curiosities: again, as how *other people* in other times and places have understood the mysteries and difficulties of existence.

There is, however, a large body of opinion which argues for the relevance of myths for 'people like us'. Myths can be understood as narrative responses to the universal human condition: creation, fertility, the struggle for life, and death. Myths confront the most difficult questions. What was here before? How did we come into existence? How can we ensure survival? What happens when we die? How will the world end? These are questions which all of us face, and questions which all mythologies address. An explanation for this is that these questions are not only part of our social existence, but also part of our individual experience of life – of our psychology. Sigmund Freud's interpretation of the myth of Oedipus – that the story of Oedipus presents a scenario in which men's repressed sexual desires, to kill the father and sleep with the mother, are symbolically, and therefore safely, enacted – is perhaps the most celebrated. Carl Jung held that the remarkable similarities between myths of different times and places testify to the human mind's capacity to produce what he called 'archetypal symbols' – the building blocks of myth. And Claude Lévi-Strauss reduced the multiplicity and variety of mythic narratives to a set of basic polarities – oppositions – which might reflect the unchanging and unchanged structure of the human mind itself.

By now, the intimate relationship between myth, religion, science, psychology and philosophy will have become evident. But perhaps more importantly, we can see that different aspects of life's mysteries seem to have been best addressed by different disciplines. Thus, creation is still down to religion: the 'big bang' theory does not explain where the primeval atom which first went 'bang' came from, and evolutionary science has no purchase on it, for it begins (with the *development* of life) at a point later than the one we want to know about (that is, how did anything at all ever come into existence?). Fertility, both human and agricultural, has been dealt with by science in a completely satisfactory way. The conduct of life between birth and death has been, in different ways, the concern of all the disciplines: religion, science, history, philosophy and political science. But the escatology of human existence – the status of the very last things – illustrates, in today's society at least, the surprising similarity of the responses of science, religion and mythology. Science speaks of global warming (or, by contrast, an extended ice age), or an asteroid hitting the earth and exploding in a ball of fire, or a nuclear war. Religion – for instance, contemporary Christianity – speaks of a conflagration: Armageddon, the final battle in the Book of Revelation. Norse mythology tells us of *fimbulvetr*, the monstrous winter with no summers in between, and of Ragnarök, the last battle of the gods and the giants, fought against a backdrop of a world in flames which reach up to the heavens themselves.

Myths have come down to us in literary form – usually, in the form of stories. We are most likely to encounter literary myths at a very late stage in the re-telling process: myths collected, ordered, tidied up, perhaps re-told for children. Norse mythology has been processed in just this way, but in fact most of the work had been done for modern editors and story-re-tellers by the thirteenth century, in Iceland, by an Icelandic antiquarian and scholar called Snorri Sturluson.

The connection between Iceland and Norse mythology is a very basic one. At the beginning of the so-called Viking age – from, roughly, the beginning of the ninth century AD to the end of the eleventh – Iceland, which had been uninhabited, was settled by Scandinavians from Norway, and people of mixed Celtic and Scandinavian parentage from Ireland and Scotland. Some of these people were already Christians; most were pagan. Together they established a remarkable new nation, with a sophisticated legal system and a surprisingly democratic parliament. Life must have been very harsh for them in material terms; there were food shortages, bad weather and – as is still the case, of course – winter nights so long that the sun barely rises at midday. But in intellectual and literary terms, Iceland was rich. To begin with, Icelanders would have recited the poetry and told the stories which they had brought with them to their new land. But around the year 1000 AD, Icelanders adopted Christianity, and Christian laws, and with this came literacy, the power to write down and record a great mass of material: all those oral traditions they had preserved in verse and prose, together with the necessary texts of their nation – laws, Christian literature, historical records. And early on, new forms began to flourish: pre-eminently, family sagas – long, naturalistic, fictionalized chronicles of the lives of the first settlers. By the thirteenth century, literary production in Iceland was coming to its height, and this was when Snorri Sturluson undertook his treatise on Norse mythology.

Snorri's work – usually known nowadays as *The Prose Edda*, or Snorri's *Edda* – is a synthesis of Norse myths, a re-telling of material from many different sources. Some of these sources are likely to have been oral ones, of unknowable, and perhaps very great, age. Others were already in literary form, mostly as poems. Snorri collected an enormous amount of material, sometimes quoting directly, sometimes paraphrasing, probably sometimes inventing. He imposed on all this material narrative form, and all the other things which come with a story: the onward drive of cause and effect, characters, motive and consistency.

Snorri's sources include poems describing mythic scenes apparently originally illustrated on objects such as shields or tapestries. Though these objects have not themselves survived, there are prehistoric or Viking-age rock carvings which depict scenes we can recognize from the poems, or from Snorri's accounts of them. But what we call myths are always *representations* of the thing itself, which is tantalizingly out of reach, always absent. To try to reach back to or reconstruct some 'original' myth is fruitless. Nonetheless, it will be important to distinguish earlier and later versions of Snorri's material, for Snorri was a thirteenth-century Christian scholar whose own thoughts and beliefs were both similar to and, crucially, different from those of his ancestors. And we must then move forward, to later re-tellings of Norse mythology. This move needs some explanation of the power of myth, which, in the case of Norse mythology, has long outlasted any worship of or belief in the gods it depicts.

An obvious explanation of the enduring significance of mythologies is the argument put forward by the psychologists: that myths reflect the deepest preoccupations of the human mind. This would readily explain their appeal – not only the pleasure people have in hearing or reading them, but also, and more significantly, why writers and artists keep repeating them. In fact, this may even lead us to formulate another definition of myth: that is, a story which holds such appeal or signifi- cance that it is typically told and re-told throughout history. On the other hand, it has been argued, as we have seen, that myths reflect not universal preoccupations, but the particular concerns of particular societies. Perhaps we can understand myths as having a double perspective: embodying both fundamental, universal, concerns and, in each successive re-telling, being elaborated with details which relate the basic story to the society which has recycled it. It is after all only to be expected that re-tellings of ancient myths may update all kinds of detail – one might compare modern-dress productions of Shakespeare plays, or cinematic adaptations of classic novels in a contemporary idiom. And this process may be carried on indefinitely: thus, for example, we have not only Wagner's re-use of Norse mythology for his operatic *Ring* cycle, but also continuing re-interpretations of the operas, with, for instance, the Norse god Odin – Wagner's Wotan – figured as a malevolent capitalist factory owner. Perhaps one of the most celebrated literary adaptations of a mythic theme is James Joyce's novel *Ulysses*, in which the wanderings of Leopold Bloom, in Dublin on one day in June, seem, unexpectedly, to mirror those of the Greek hero Ulysses in Homer's *Odyssey*.

Many mythologies also have the sort of structure which can accom- modate almost any number of additional stories. For example, between setting out and returning home, Ulysses can have limitless numbers of adventures within the basic structure of the *Odyssey*. King Arthur has twelve knights at his Round Table, each one with his own set of adventures. Norse mythology, with its pantheon of gods, tells of many encounters between them and their old adversaries, the giants. The possibilities are endless – and there is always the option of attaching to the mythic base stories which might have come from anywhere: fairy tales, folk tales, bits of history, Bible stories, even improvisations by the latest re-teller. A mythology may in this way contain material from many times and places. Even when an author seems to be neutrally collecting mythic material, the very action of collecting and ordering it may involve developing links from one scene to another, implying sequence and causality, and tending to smooth away jumps and discontinuities evident in an earlier version.

The continuing literary or artistic life of a myth need not have much to do with its supposed spiritual or psychological content. Re-telling may be undertaken for a whole host of reasons. For example, it has been suggested that it was because Norse mythology somehow 'spoke' to the historical condition of thirteenth-century Iceland that Snorri Sturluson took on the immense labour of collecting all his material into a great mythological compendium. This may well have some truth in it. But it is at least as likely that Snorri acted for antiquarian reasons: that he wanted to preserve a major element in the formative culture of his own young nation, the pagan mythology, knowledge of which must have been dim-inishing after Iceland's conversion to Christianity. And whether he meant to or not, a thirteenth-century Christian like Snorri would inevitably re-cast his material in the light of his own spiritual and cultural norms. It may be that Richard Wagner recognized in Norse mythology some timeless psychological archetypes. Conversely, he may have been attracted by its striking topicality for the proto-Fascist politics and philosophy of his day. But the connection was probably more complex than this: at the time, many Germans were passionately interested in what they saw as the prehistory of their race, and believed that Norse mythology was their window on to it. It was not solely the content of the myth which inspired men like Wagner – let alone its transcendental or immanent meaning – but also its cultural identity, historical identity, and ultimately, of course, its supposed racial identity. But in re-telling the myths, authors and artists inevitably (or purposefully) imprinted on them the concerns of their own time.

A mythology may acquire a desirable status quite independent of its original function – and this has obviously been the case throughout almost the whole history of English literature with regard to classical – Greek and Roman – mythology. For English authors, allusions to and reworkings of classical myths established their credentials as educated people. This has only begun to fade relatively recently: the poet Philip Larkin, for instance, referred scathingly to the 'myth-kitty', this bank of classical allusion, which poets have drawn on. On the other hand, there are other good reasons – unconnected with the original function of myths – why later authors might rework them: either the original significance of the material, or its universal appeal, will naturally have meant that the most gifted authors and artists represented it. Myths are 'good stories' re-represented by the best practitioners: they have become great art and great literature. Finally, it may be that the reasons for re-presenting myth are simply too complex to be reconstructed. A good example might be this very book: as its author, I neither believe in the Norse gods, nor am persuaded by the explanatory possibilities of the mythology's accounts of creation and apocalypse. I'm certainly not interested in disseminating Aryan propaganda. I am, though, moved by the imaginative reach of the myths, by the high quality of the literature which expresses them, and by their enduring appeal over so many centuries. But there are a host of other accidental forces, at once too slight and too various – academic, commercial, personal – to set out, which have led to this particular representation of Norse mythology. Who is to say that the motivation behind any other representation of any mythology was not equally complex?

Norse mythology as it has come down to us cannot be confined to a single society or a single time. Throughout its early history of telling and re-telling, for all the reasons given above, it may have both changed its original forms, and gathered to itself material very widely, both in time and geographical space. As we shall see, some of its elements may not be Scandinavian at all, but borrowed from near neighbours the Finns, or northern Slavic pagans, or even the Anglo-Saxons. It is very likely that Scandinavian paganism was early influenced by Christianity. Snorri's great thirteenth-century compendium, in addition to encompassing all these possibilities, must itself have reflected Snorri's own Christian faith, and the very process of turning his material into narrative must have had its own effect. The first part of this book, therefore, will examine in turn the four great phases of Norse mythology – Creation and the Cosmos; the Gods and the Giants; Heroes and Humans; and Afterlife and Apocalypse. We shall see how the various elements of these phases have been represented in other, earlier forms: poetry, prehistoric art, classical sources. The second part of the book will look forward from this first, medieval, synthesis to later versions of Norse myth, in a dazzling variety of forms: not only literature and art, but also music, politics, and even, to come round full circle, religion.

PART ONE

THE EARLIEST
SOURCES OF
OLD NORSE
MYTHOLOGY

CHAPTER 1

Creation and Cosmos

Iceland, as I explained in the introduction, was settled by a mixed population – Celtic and Scandinavian, Christian and pagan – bringing with them, no doubt, a wide range of literary traditions and backgrounds. But all these stories and poems were oral: nothing was written down. However, in pre-Christian mainland Scandinavia, memorial inscriptions, and sometimes even scraps of early poetry, were carved on wood, bone or stone – particularly gravestones – in the old Germanic alphabet: runes.

The origins of the runic alphabet are mysterious, but it may have been used as early as the first century AD. The alphabet is sometimes called the 'futhark' after its first six letters: F U Þ (the equivalent of English 'th') A R K, and the stiff angularity in the shape of these runic letters is usually explained as a stylistic adaptation to the difficulties of carving on wood, with its pronounced grain. There is no runic language: runic inscriptions are found in various early Germanic languages, including Anglo-Saxon, but especially in the early Scandinavian used all over mainland Scandinavia before the settlement of Iceland. Christian gravestones with pious runic inscriptions are also quite common; it has sometimes been claimed that runes were somehow magical, or even divinatory (as in the modern journalistic cliché 'reading the runes' to mean making an educated guess about the political or financial future). But although, as we shall see, runes play a fascinating role in Old Norse mythology, in historical reality they were used for all sorts of purposes, even everyday ones, as a recent find of runic messages on scraps of wood and bark in Norway makes clear: we have here shopping lists, grocery prices – even a demand from a disgruntled housewife that her husband come back from the pub. It may even be the case that runes were sometimes used for decorative purposes, without any regard for possible meaning. It has been tempting for runologists to interpret obscure sequences of letters as magical formulae; it is more likely that they are either incompetent inscriptions, practice runs by apprentice rune-carvers, or simply idle decoration.

For whatever reason, no evidence of runic inscriptions has been found in Iceland – nor, indeed, any examples of figurative or symbolic rock carvings such as are also found in mainland Scandinavia. No literary trace of pre-Christian Iceland remains. It is almost as if the national conversion to Christianity in the year 1000 AD – when Iceland, at its legal and parliamentary assembly, the Althing, decided, in the very secular and legalistic interests of the unity of the nation, to adopt Christian laws (perhaps the most non-spiritual conversion in human history) – released a dammed-up flood of literary endeavour as the new nation filled sheets and sheets of vellum with laws, saints' lives, translations of devotional texts, sagas, poems and histories. The literary inscription of a new nation had begun. Even so, the first surviving manuscripts are from the twelfth century, and the high point of literary production seems to have begun in the thirteenth century. It was in this century that the manuscript now known as the *Codex Regius* was produced: it comprises a collection of mythological poems of varying date and provenance and authorship. This collection is usually known as the *Poetic Edda*, and the poems in it, together with a handful of similar poems in other manuscripts, as Eddaic verse. The poems are not attributed to any named poets – perhaps because they had long outlived the impress of an individual creator, and had passed into collective anonymity. But the poems have been ordered with meticulous care, the mythological giving way to heroic, and the collection opening with the mighty and most difficult text: *Völuspá*.

Völuspá: the title of the poem means 'the sibyl's prophecy'. But the sibyl's words are not only a prophecy of what is to come, but also an immense and authoritative recall of times immemorial – and these powerful words are presented as a response to the god Odin (here called *Valföðr*, 'the father of the slain'). They are, the sibyl tells us, 'the world's old news'. And the sibyl's first memory is of giants.

It is unfortunate that giants have a fairy-tale connotation in modern English, and that what is now conjured up by the term giant is a great, lumbering, half-witted creature, gratifyingly and often lethally outwitted by smaller, younger and smarter persons like Jack the Giantkiller. (Elves too have a very different character in children's literature from the chillingly shadowy beings of Norse mythology, as we shall see in due course.)

The sibyl of *Völuspá* remembers as far back as it is possible to go. She was, she says, brought up by giants, and she calls to mind nine giantesses in nine realms. Her other powerfully evocative memory is of the great World Tree, Yggdrasill, the centre of the cosmos, envisaged as the pillar which holds up these mysterious layered worlds. But she remembers a time so far back that mighty Yggdrasill was itself still underground, a seed waiting to sprout up into life.

When the sibyl recalls this pre-primeval emptiness, before earth and sky existed, she describes it as a time so early that the only living thing then was the first giant himself: Ymir, a 'frost-giant' or 'rime-thurs'. Ymir lived even before the earth was created, and preceded both gods and men. There was only the great void, the *ginnunga gap* – James Joyce's brilliant, oddly sinister 'Grinning Gap'. And then, suddenly, and again allusively, the sibyl introduces the sons of Burr: they create the earth by lifting it out of the sea. These are the gods, the powers who form the earth and then people it with humans. But where did they come from? And how did Ymir himself, the primeval being, come into existence? However, the sibyl, or her creator, the poet of *Völuspá*, is moving swiftly onward now, not back.

Völuspá is not the only poem about the beginning of the world. Odin has other sources of wisdom – one of them a giant called Vafthrudnir. According to the poem *Vafþrúðnismál* ('What Vafthrudnir Had to Say'), Odin – in spite of the anxious entreaties of his wife, Frigg – sets out to visit Vafthrudnir: he wants to find out about 'ancient matters', and therefore the obvious source is one of the giants, the most ancient race. God and giant engage in a wisdom competition: who can ask the most difficult question? And the loser will forfeit his life. According to *Vafþrúðnismál*,

From Ymir's flesh the earth was shaped,
and the mountains from his bones;
the sky from the skull of the frost-cold giant
and the sea from his blood.

13

The corpse of this primeval giant has been recycled into our earth. The same idea is recounted in another Eddaic poem, *Grímnismál* ('What Was Said by Grimnir' – the Masked One, that is, Odin). In this poem, Odin sets out to visit a king called Geirrod, who, not realizing Odin's real identity, has him tortured with starvation and fire. Odin speaks a long monologue about mythological matters, repeating Vafthrudnir's claim that the earth was made from Ymir's dead body, with some extra details, such as Ymir's brain forming the clouds.

But if the earth came from Ymir, where did Ymir come from? And how did he die? In *Vafþrúðnismál*, Odin digs deeper, and Vafthrudnir comes up with a mysterious genealogy of giants who existed before the earth was made – and therefore, one supposes, before Ymir: Bergelmir, his father Thrudgelmir, and his grandfather, Aurgelmir. Odin presses further: where then did Aurgelmir come from? Now Vafthrudnir tells Odin about a strange spring, Élivágar ('snowstorm waves'), which spat out poison droplets; these came together to form the first frost-giant. But how, asks Odin, did the dynasty continue, if there were no giantesses?

By parthenogenesis, replies Vafthrudnir; or rather:

> They said that under the frost-giant's arms
> a girl and boy grew together;
> one foot with the other, of the wise giant,
> begot a six-headed son.

Odin finally asks what Vafthrudnir's own earliest memory is. The giant – described in the poem as 'all-wise' – remembers a time when Bergelmir, the grandson of the most ancient frost-giant, was laid on a *lúðr*. But no-one knows for certain what the word *lúðr* means. It is tempting to assume that it was either a cradle or a coffin, so that the giant Vafthrudnir is remembering the beginning or end of this ancient creature's life. But other interpretations have included a boat or even a part of a wooden flour mill. How are we to make sense of these allusive, contradictory and patchy poetic sources?

Snorri Sturluson's synthesis of all these traditions – and some more – is one part of a large work which has come to be known as the *Prose Edda*, or *Snorri's Edda*. The opening section of the whole work is called *Gylfaginning* – the deluding, or fooling, of Gylfi. Gylfi is a legendary king of Sweden who, in disguise, like Odin himself, turns up at the court of the Æsir – a race of people who have apparently migrated north from

Asia – asking questions about creation and cosmos, the gods and the giants, heroes and humans, afterlife and apocalypse. Presenting himself as a wanderer called Gangleri, Gylfi begins at the beginning: 'What was the beginning? And how did things start? And what was there before?' A strange threesome answers him on behalf of the Æsir. A figure called Har ('the High One') responds with a quotation from the beginning of *Völuspá* about the *ginnunga gap*, but there is no mention of Ymir: this was a time 'when nothing was' – no Ymir, no nothing. The first world, according to Snorri's second speaker, Jafnhar ('Just-as-High'), is Niflheim – 'the dark, or foggy, realm' – from which flow the rivers which Vafthrudnir called the Élivágar, and which Snorri names individually. But then Snorri's third speaker, Thridi (Third-one), butts in: the first world was Muspell, a realm of burning fire to the south of Niflheim, presided over by Surtr, a great fire-giant with a flaming sword.

Like the poet of *Vafþrúðnismál*, Snorri describes how Ymir was created from coagulated river water, but only after a bafflingly complex series of chemical and physical reactions: as the Élivágar flow, their waters gradually harden – 'like the clinker that comes from a furnace' – or, one might speculate, like lava flow in a volcanic island like Iceland, which would first flow and then harden into fantastic shapes. But Snorri's account is more elaborate than this. The flow from the Élivágar turned to ice, and poisonous vapours rising off it turned into frost, or soot, which coated the whole of the *ginnunga gap*. But on the far side of the *ginnunga gap* is the fiery realm of Muspell, and when the warmth from Muspell interacted with the frost from Niflheim, it was this resulting condensation which dripped into the form of our primeval frost-giant, Ymir. This quasi-scientific sequence is an elaborate version of the old and widespread idea that life arises from contraries: heat and cold, ice and fire, frost and flame. Snorri has one final loose end to tie up: Ymir is just a different name for Aurgelmir, so that Snorri's account of creation now tallies with what Odin is told in *Vafþrúðnismál*.

Snorri's questioner Gangleri pursues a highly practical agenda: satisfied with this account of the creation of Ymir/Aurgelmir, he next wants to know where Ymir lived (since all this was before the creation of the earth) and indeed what he lived on. Snorri (unsupported by any poetic source) introduces the cow Audumbla, the next creature to be formed from the melted frost. Ymir drinks Audumbla's milk – she acts as a sort of wet-nurse, though, significantly enough, no female has so far been involved in the conception or birth of these primeval figures. Audumbla, as well as nursing the frost-giant Ymir, licks the blocks of ice, and from them, freed up by the licking, emerges Buri: handsome, big and strong. Buri's son Bor marries a giantess, Bestla, and from this point on, pro-creation is apparently more conventional. Their three sons – Odin, Vili and Ve – are the gods who create heaven, earth and mankind. But their first act is destructive: they murder their maternal relative – perhaps their uncle – the frost-giant Ymir, and, as we have seen, create the world from his corpse. Ymir's blood loss is so monstrous that it causes a flood, and all the frost-giants are drowned – except for Bergelmir, who with his wife is saved by climbing up on to his *lúðr*, just as Vafthrudnir has explained.

No-one knows what sources Snorri might have used for some of these details – for example, the cow Audumbla – or indeed if he simply invented some of them. And finally, we have no real idea of the original dates of the various mythological elements he used. The poems them-selves are usually believed to date from some time between the ninth and the thirteenth centuries AD, but even if we allow the earliest of these dates, there's no knowing how ancient the traditions are on which the poems are based. Mythology, as I explained in the introduction, has come down to us in literary form: we may be a long way removed from 'actual' myth (whatever that might be).

Two relatively fixed points are worth remembering. Firstly, the latest thinking on *Völuspá* dates it to the years just before the conversion of Iceland to Christianity – seeing it as a pagan response to Christian theology. As such, it would be not only an affirmation of the complex, weighty, time-honoured truths of the old religion, but also a claim for neck-and-neck rivalry – and crucially, comparable sophistication – with the new Christianity, especially in its exposition of creation and apocalypse. Secondly, Snorri Sturluson, as we know, was a thirteenth-century Christian, and although it seems that unlike his European contemporaries he was happy, indeed proud, to represent the pagan mythology of his ancestors without undue moralizing, mockery or allego-rical interpretations, nonetheless it is inevitable that he would have understood some of the events and concepts through the lens of his own beliefs, giving them what we might now call a Christian spin. We have no evidence that is certainly pre-Christian about any of these creation myths.

Aside from the Eddaic poems mentioned here, there are two other references to Ymir's body in early Norse poetry. One describes the sky as the ancient skull of Ymir; the poet in this case lived in the eleventh century (after the conversion of Iceland), although he may well have been using an archaic kind of poetic diction deriving from an earlier period. More telling is a poem by Iceland's most celebrated pagan poet, Egill Skalla-Grímsson, who lived in the tenth century. Egill is presented in the saga named after him (*Egils saga*) as a devotee of the god Odin, and when both of his sons die before him, the saga represents him as composing an extraordinarily touching and powerful lament about his bereavements – in fact, a memorial to his own grief. In this poem, entitled *Sonatorrek* ('On the Loss of Sons'), Egill questions Odin's loyalty to him (especially given his own devotion to the god) but gradually, as the poem itself progresses, he comes to find that the process of poetic composition is itself a healing process, and this reconciles him to Odin, the god of poetry who gave the gift of poetry to men, and to his own death. One of Egill's two sons was drowned, and Egill calls the sea 'the resounding wounds of the giant's neck'. It has to be said that the saga about Egill might have been composed by Snorri himself – though it would be going too far to try to claim that the poems quoted in it are elaborate thirteenth-century forgeries by Snorri or his associates. What is interesting is that the verse refers to the blood as flowing from Ymir's neck: an appropriately bloody severed artery, and a distinctly sacrificial wound.

The earth which is described as having been formed from Ymir's corpse is very plainly the physical world we ourselves recognize: mountain, valleys, rivers, seas and plains. But throughout Old Norse mythology, a wider cosmos is envisaged, although it takes different forms in different sources. Sometimes, it is comfortingly concentric: Asgard, the strong-hold of the gods, securely central, surrounded by Midgard, the human realm (or the protective wall around the home of the gods), and the realm of the giants around the outer edges, between the margin of the known world and the unbounded ocean. We might contrast with this the more familiar 'vertical' cosmos, with the heavens above, the underworld, naturally, below, and our own earth between the two. It is this vertical arrangement which lends itself to the organizing principle of the World Tree: in Norse, Yggdrasill; this is a central feature in any number of Northern Eurasian and North American civilizations.

The name Yggdrasill means 'Odin-steed' – Yggr, literally, 'the terrifier', being a synonym for the god Odin, and *drasill* being a poetic word for horse – akin to the English word 'steed'. In *Völuspá*, Yggdrasill is a great

17

ash tree, which nourishes the world with the dew that falls from it. According to the Eddaic poem *Grímnismál*, the gods gather each day beneath it to pass their judgements. But this poem also offers a haunting picture of a vulnerable tree: a serpent gnaws its roots, while deer graze on its higher branches, and a squirrel scuttles up and down the trunk relaying messages from top to bottom. The tree, the poet tells us, 'suffers agony'. But worse is to come. At the end of the world, the tree will shudder and creak: it will be old then, having spanned the time from when the sibyl first spotted it sprouting under the soil. The earth is figured not as an inert ball of rock, but as an organic thing, subject to a natural life cycle.

According to this cosmological plan, the various realms are situated along the three great roots of the tree: Hel, the goddess of the under-world, under one; the frost-giants under another; and mankind under the third. Snorri Sturluson echoes this arrangement, but places the gods, and not mankind, under the third root, as if to replant the tree in an imaginary cosmos, not in a world which would be an extension of our own. The roots reach down to deep springs: the wells of fate. Odin himself, in the Eddaic poem *Hávamál* ('What the High One Had to Say'), hangs for nine nights on a windswept tree: paradoxically sacrificed to himself, he learns in this way the wisdom of the dead. His tree has no known roots, and must surely be Yggdrasill, the Odin-steed, which he rides just as criminals were said to 'ride' the gallows tree. The place of the great ash tree at the centre of the universe is unexpectedly echoed in the Norse account of the creation of mankind. According to Snorri, three gods, strolling along the seashore, find two pieces of driftwood: Ask and Embla – ash, and, perhaps, elm, or vine. The poem *Völuspá* describes Ask and Embla as 'little capable of anything', and 'lacking destiny'. The gods imbue these lifeless objects with human qualities: breath, spirit and living flesh. They are the Norse Adam and Eve, from whom all mankind, living in Midgard, is descended.

This brings us to the historic present. Everything is in place: gods, humans, shadowy giants, the earth and heavens. Before moving on to the series of dramatic encounters between the gods and the giants, we must pause a moment to reflect on the possible significances of all this material, to put it in some sort of context. What are we to make of such a detailed, even confused, account?

Many aspects of the material offer striking parallels with Judaeo-Christian traditions. In the Book of Genesis, for example, we are told of the formless abyss which existed before God's first creative act, and of the darkness on the waters. Further on in Genesis, we learn of the giants who roamed the world in those days, and who were drowned, like the Norse giants, in a great flood. Of humankind, only Noah was saved, aboard his ark – which floated on the waters like Bergelmir's *lúðr*. In Genesis we learn too of miscegenation: of giants and humans producing offspring. In fact, the question and answer format is distinctly reminiscent of – and perhaps actually derived from – Christian catechism. And the detail of Surtr's flaming sword may well owe something to the archangel Michael.

And just as it is unlikely that the myth and religion of Scandinavians were uninfluenced by Christian thought – whether by Snorri's spin, or through contact between pagans and Christians in the early period – it is only natural that Norse mythology might also have been influenced by the mythology and religion of the neighbours of the Norse: the hunter-gatherer Finns, and the present-day Northern Siberian Saami people, whose shamanistic beliefs still echo Norse traditions: shape-shifting (assuming animal form) and, perhaps most strikingly, a world tree, stretching up to the heavens, balancing the whole world around its central axis, like the fixed point which is the North Star. The closest parallels to Odin's sacrifice on the tree are not only the crucifixion of Christ, but also the action of the Northern shaman, whose mystical trance involves climbing a tree out of this world into the spirit world to gather wisdom. In fact, it would be a mistake to assume a single unified body of thought called 'Norse mythology': there would certainly have been variations – and probably significant differences – among the beliefs and practices of the various early Scandinavian peoples which constitute the body of material written down in medieval Iceland, and which we for that reason call 'Norse'.

Parallels with other Indo-European mythologies are many. The prominent role of Audumbla the cow naturally brings to mind ancient Indian traditions, and the continuing veneration of cattle. The name of Ymir, the primeval being whose corpse provided the material for our earth, has been linked with Iranian and Sanskrit creation myths, in which the first man is called 'Yima', or 'Yama', which means twin, providing another link with the Norse Ymir, who produced offspring without a partner. The Roman historian Tacitus, who described the Germanic tribes in Europe in his *Germania*, written in the first century AD, reports that they trace their ancestry back to a god called Tuisto – whose name has also been

19

interpreted as twin. The alternative creation story – that, according to the sibyl in *Völuspá*, the sons of Burr lifted the earth out of the sea – has been linked to Indo-European myths about the earth rising from water: themselves interpreted as the way flooded land seems to rise as monsoon floodwaters gradually subside.

The disconcerting tendency of mythologies widely separated in time and space to echo each other – sometimes with startlingly detailed and precise parallels – is sometimes explained, rather romantically, as the result of an astounding conservatism in oral tradition: that archaic stories, patterns and ideas can be transmitted through any number of centuries to much more recent societies – such as that of the Norse in the Viking age. According to this theory, all Indo-European mythologies can be traced back to an infinitely distant point of origin in India, or the Near East. (If this sounds like an improbable idea, however, we need to remember that it is still the model used to explain the similarities between words and sentence structures in the Indo-European family of languages. Readers of George Eliot's *Middlemarch* may remember that the desiccated scholar Casaubon was himself fruitlessly working on a mammoth tome called *The Key to all Mythologies*, in which he hoped to explain all these echoes and similarities through the theory of common descent from a 'tradition originally revealed'; whether that original revelation was Christian or not, Eliot does not reveal to us.)

An alternative theory to explain these coincidences is the much more down-to-earth idea that the later societies had simply heard about the older traditions – sometimes even in the usual modern way: they had read about them. Thus the parallels which have been noted between Ymir's body as a microcosm of the earth itself, and Plato's theories of the world as a macrocosm of the human body, could be due to the popularity of neo-Platonic learning in the Middle Ages. In other words, the story of Ymir's corpse does not derive from unimaginably ancient Sanskrit belief, or even have its origins in native Germanic tradition. It is, according to iconoclasts, an attractive idea which Snorri Sturluson or his immediate predecessors picked up from a book.

As I outlined in the introduction, broader parallels may be explained as universal responses to the human condition. If it is the fate of all humans to die, then one would expect mythologies to deal with resurrection. Evident elemental oppositions – warmth–cold, fire–ice, water–air – have universally been seen as generative contrasts, perhaps provoked by the direct experience of two flints producing a spark; it is worth remembering at this point that modern scientific theories about the origin of life have involved the action of sunlight on water (the so-called 'primeval soup') or even the collision of comets or asteroids.

It has also been argued that vegetation myths, as generated perhaps by the first farming societies in the Neolithic period, have been based on human wonder at the apparently non-sexual reproduction of crops and other food-providing plants. Here we may recall the claim in Eddaic verse that Aurgelmir produced offspring from his armpits. Some theorists have made the startling claim that the hairy armpit is a sort of transferred genital area. But it is also striking that many plants produce new shoots from the point at which side branches grow out from the main stem – the plant's 'armpit', so to speak. Could it be feasible that the six-headed son which Aurgelmir produced from rubbing one foot against another is an anthropomorphic representation of an ear of corn or barley, with its fat round grains, plump with potential flour? After all, the element *aur-* in his name means, in Norse, mud, or soil, and it could be that *Bergelmir's* name is related to the word for '*bar*ley'. The mysterious word *lúðr*, on which Bergelmir was laid, which a common-sense reading of the Norse story might interpret as cradle or coffin, Snorri, under Christian influence, seems to have understood as something like an ark. But most plausibly, at least in linguistic terms, it is the word for the frame around a flour mill, so that we might see the giants Aurgelmir, Thrudgelmir and Bergelmir as figures representing different stages in the production of flour, the most basic Western European foodstuff, but perhaps even more significant, culturally, as the element which so radically distinguished the Mesolithic hunter-gatherers in Europe, nomadic people at the mercy of the elements, from the later Neolithic farmers – settled people who planted crops to harvest grain: the foundation of what we call civilization. Even more speculatively, might we see in the primeval opposition between the older giants and the new generation of gods a representation of a prehistoric conflict between different species – different physically as well as culturally – of early humans in Europe or beyond?

Myths, then, can be interpreted in a vast range of ways, and these interpretations are of course directly linked to the functions that modern scholars suppose any mythology to have served for its society. Was the re-telling of the story of the killing of Ymir used as a celebration of how one group of humans established dominance over another? More sensationally,

21

was that dominance celebrated and re-lived through an accompanying sacrifice of an Ymir-figure? Or rather, was the hope or gratitude for a new season's harvest expressed through a collective re-telling of the saving of Bergelmir on his *lúðr*? Was the story of the creation of the earth through the killing of Ymir a collective justification for the violence which characterizes all human society? Or, as the sceptics would have it, is it merely a good idea borrowed from classical authors?

Finally, we must think about topical relevance – that is, what meaning this mythology, or parts of it, might have had for medieval Icelanders or their nearest ancestors. Here we might note the strikingly inferior status of the female element in Snorri's composite creation myth, and the initial absence of the female in the process of procreation. We might see a dramatic reflection of internecine feud in the killing of the giant Ymir by his nephews, gods whose mother was a giantess herself. We might notice that while the gods marry giantesses (a theme which will become more evident in the next section, concerning the long-running feud between gods and giants) giants do not marry goddesses (though again, as we shall see, they try very hard to get hold of the gods' women). All these aspects of the creation myth seem to reflect aspects of what we know of early Norse society, and, perhaps even more significantly, Old Norse and Old English literature, in which the instability of the family – especially the uncertain loyalty of nephews to the patriarch – is a pervasive weakness in the struggle against rival clans. In the Old Norse sagas, and in heroic poems such as the Anglo-Saxon *Beowulf*, the danger of disaffected nephews, and the vital importance of a politically advantageous marriage, are fundamental themes on which the narrative is built.

The place of creation myths in any belief system is a special one. Creation demands explanation; mythology, in providing this, fulfils a basic human need. In the next section, I want to turn to a series of mythological episodes which do not, in the same way, answer this basic need for explanation, but which may still reflect the concerns and deepest anxieties of the societies which both produced and transmitted them. Having outlined the Norse accounts of creation and cosmos, we must move on to the entertaining, dramatic, and occasionally still cryptic stories of the hostile encounters of gods and giants.

CHAPTER 2

Gods and Giants

Old Norse mythology imagined its gods and goddesses in human form. Sometimes, these representations are unforgettably vivid: old Odin with one eye, his hat pulled down over his face; Thor with his fearsome frown and mighty hammer; Frigg weeping over the death of her son Baldr. Sometimes, no more than a name remains in the literary record, or the slightest hint of a shadowy role or function in the great scheme of things. But the humanity of the gods extends beyond physical form: they also act like humans, motivated by emotions familiar to us, such as anger, jealousy, love and even, as we shall see, fear and apprehension. Their human feelings bring with them human failings. Odin's mastery of the arts of language facilitates oath-breaking and betrayal; Thor's anger is hasty and destructive; Frigg's love for her son leads to incapacitating grief. Eventually, these flawed gods face annihilation at Ragnarök. But much is to happen before this last battle. The gods – equipped with supernatural powers and attributes, but hampered by their quasi-human natures – are engaged in a constant struggle against the giants. This struggle is sometimes serious, sometimes farcical, but invariably violent, in the tradition of the very first encounter between the two groups: the killing of the primordial giant Ymir.

ODIN

The whole pantheon of Old Norse divinities is organized like human society: there are husbands and wives, sons and daughters, brothers and sisters. The god Odin is described as *Alföðr*, 'the father of all', and as *Valföðr* – 'the father of the slaughtered'. These two names reflect his position at the head of the Old Norse pantheon, and also his dual role as god of war, and of the dead. But in the beginning, Odin is not the chief of all the gods, but only of one tribe of them, the Æsir, for the Norse gods also reflect human society in that there are even, it seems, two separate races: the Æsir and the Vanir. Several Old Norse sources mention – in tantalizingly incomplete or allusive detail – the 'first war in the world', between the Æsir and the Vanir. As with the Norse creation myths, the poem *Völuspá* offers an account which may pre-date Norse Christianity. Near the beginning of her speech, shortly after her account of creation, the sibyl tells of the coming of two mysterious women: Gullveig, whose name means 'golden liquor', and Heid, brightness herself. Gullveig is tortured by the Æsir – studded with spears, and burned – but is reborn each time, like strong drink triple distilled, or gold repeatedly melted and refined. Heid seems to present the Æsir with competition: she is a sorceress, who is welcomed into people's homes as a prophetess who only prophesies good fortune. In consternation, the Æsir call a meeting to decide how to respond to this challenge, and Odin starts the first war in the world with a shot of his spear. But in spite of Odin's reputation as a god of battle and victory, the Æsir he leads are not triumphant. Though the fighting is not described, a violent conflict is implied: the walls of the gods' stronghold, Asgard, are broken down. But the opponents of the Æsir – only now identified by the poet of *Völuspá* as the Vanir – are not defeated. The key to their success is their indestructible life-force. Gullveig (and perhaps Heid too) must have been their emissary, because like her they seem to hold the secret of endless regeneration.

The war, then, is a stalemate. In this, it resembles another mythic war in Old Norse: the battle of the Hjadningar. The most naturalistic version of this story is told by Snorri Sturluson, when he is explaining why one of the many poetic names for battle might be 'the storm of the Hjadningar'. Hild, the daughter of King Högni, is abducted by Hedinn, a warrior whose followers are called the *Hjaðningar*, the people of Hedinn. Högni at once pursues Hedinn (to the Old Man of Hoy, in the

Hebrides, as the story goes), and his daughter Hild is sent to him with a peace offering. She is no diplomat, however, and only manages to incite each side against the other. They fight all day, but Hild magically restores to life all the dead warriors and makes whole all the damaged weapons, so the battle continues for ever – at least until Ragnarök, the end of the world.

Snorri refers us to an old poem which recounts, though rather cryptically, this interminable battle. Its author, Bragi, is the first named poet in Norse tradition, and the author of what is probably the earliest poem to have survived from the pre-Christian period, *Ragnarsdrápa* ('The Lay of Ragnarr'), in which four mythological scenes said to have been painted on a shield are described in its verses. In one scene, Hild – whose name means 'battle': she is perhaps to be seen as the very person-ification of conflict – is portrayed as a malevolent figure whose powerful desire for bloodshed causes her to prolong the fighting indefinitely. In Snorri's more naturalistic account, one might infer that Hild keeps the battle going because she is so divided in her loyalties that she cannot bear either side to have victory over the other. But the poet Bragi revels in the paradox that bringing the warriors to life to fight each new day is both infinitely merciful and infinitely cruel. Hild is described as a goddess who dries up veins too much: but are her warriors' veins dry because she has caused so much bloodshed, or because she has, in a more traditionally feminine role, staunched their wounds, only in this case over and over again?

The motif of warriors brought back to life to die another day is echoed in allusions to Odin's hall, Valhalla (*Valhöll*, 'the hall of the slaughtered'). Valhalla, as will become clear in later chapters, is one of the elements in Old Norse mythology which has most fascinated later readers. According to various Norse sources it is a magnificent great hall, roofed with golden shields, accessed by hundreds of doors, and filled with hundreds of the *einherjar* – warriors who have died on the battlefield and enjoy an everlasting afterlife of drinking mead and fighting in Valhalla. These are Odin's troops, to be called into their final battle at Ragnarök.

Clearly, it was the intriguing idea of the never-ending deadlock which engaged the poets. Neither Bragi nor the sibyl (or her poet) has any interest in the political manoeuvrings necessary to break the equilibrium. We must turn as always to Snorri, and not to his mythological scholarship –

Gylfaginning, in which he recounts creation myths – but to his great historical compilation, *Heimskringla*, to find out what happens next.

The name *Heimskringla* is taken from the first two words of this lengthy thirteenth-century history of the Norwegian kings. Snorri begins it by locating Scandinavia on the globe, the earth's sphere – in Norse, *kringla heimsins*. His history reaches way back, as far as the legendary founders of the Scandinavian royal dynasty, the Ynglings, who were descended from Odin. Odin, in Snorri's history, is a great battle chieftain and ruler of a people who originated in Asia: the Æsir (an irresistible piece of wordplay for medieval scholars). Eventually, Snorri's Odin will lead a great national migration northward, from Asia to the Scandinavian lands. But this is after he takes his people into battle against his neighbours, the Vanir, in Snorri's version of the first war in the world.

Snorri, like the poet of *Völuspá*, represents this war as a stalemate: now one side, now the other, takes the victory. But as befits a work of political history, Snorri details the peace treaty: hostages are exchanged. The Vanir offer their most prominent figures: Njörd (a male god in Norse tradition whose name nevertheless corresponds exactly to the mother-earth goddess Tacitus describes as the chief deity of the Germanic tribes) and his son Frey, whose name means 'lord'. According to Snorri, they are accompanied by Kvasir, the cleverest of all the Vanir. It is worth noting that elsewhere Snorri reports that Kvasir was formed from the blended spittle of the Æsir and the Vanir, as part of the peace treaty itself. His name has very suggestive echoes of Indo-European words for 'drink' (for instance, the Russian word 'kvass', meaning beer, or even the familiar English 'squash', as in the children's fruit drink). As we shall see, Kvasir comes to a horrible end as part of the myth about the origins of poetry.

But the Vanir themselves do not fare so well. The Æsir send in exchange Hœnir, an obscure figure in Old Norse mythology, and perhaps understandably so, since the Vanir soon discover that Hœnir, though extremely good-looking, is like a ventriloquist's dummy. He cannot function without his companion, the second hostage, wise Mimir. As Snorri drily notes, if asked for an opinion, Hœnir replies evasively: 'That's for others to decide'. The Vanir are so incensed by this unfair exchange that they cut off Mimir's wise head and send it back. Odin embalms it, and preserves it as an oracle for his own use. The upshot of this extraordinary story is that the Æsir are greatly fortified by the incorporation of the highest-ranking

Vanir, and their only loss is the dysfunctional Hœnir; they even get back Mimir, though on somewhat bizarre terms.

It has been argued that the war of the Æsir and the Vanir is a mythic representation of a cult war, as the deities (or adherents) of two religions represent their rivalry, and eventually their unification. Some mythographers have argued that the story is a mythic transformation of a half-remembered actual war which happened far back in time. On the other hand, it is possible that the story of the war is a way of explaining how a religious system might have come to embody contrasting aspects of the essentials of human life – in this case, warmaking and fertility, or more grandly, the metaphysical and the material. All of these accounts of everlasting battles suggest a deep concern with the double aspect of all life on earth: individual death, with the possibility of resurrection, or the endlessly repeating cycles of the natural world.

As Snorri's pseudo-historical narrative progresses, we see how its legendary figures come to assume the status of gods among the peoples they rule over. Njörd succeeds Odin, and is succeeded in turn by Frey – Ingvi-Frey, after whom the dynasty is named. The Swedes, Snorri informs us, had sacrificed to Odin, and finally deified Frey. This process of interpreting pagan gods as originally historical or legendary figures is known as euhemerism, and Snorri's trick is to present others – the subjects of this early dynasty – as having brought about the original transformation. Given that the gods are in all the sources portrayed in human forms and social contexts, Snorri is now quite free to recount Norse mythology without becoming entangled in the theological status of his subject matter – that is, without having to condemn the pagan gods as demons, which is what Christian doctrine insisted. The elements of Snorri's 'biography' of Odin – his magical skills as a sorcerer, his invincibility in battle, his mastery of poetry and learning – match the pagan mythological references from pre-Christian Norse poetry to Odin as the god of war, of poetry, and of the arcane wisdom of the underworld.

To see just how a continuous narrative by Snorri relates to the mass of often obscure allusions in Old Norse mythological poetry, we can take his account of the myth of poetry as a case in point.

THE MYTH OF POETRY

The second part of Snorri's great treatise on mythology is called *Skáldskaparmál* ('The Art of Poetic Diction'). Like *Gylfaginning*, it is presented in dialogue form. In this case, a figure called Ægir comes to Asgard to visit the Æsir, and falls into conversation with a god called Bragi (whose name, interestingly enough, is the same as that of the first Norse poet whose work has come down to us). In response to Ægir's question about the origins of poetry, Bragi recounts one of the most famous of the Norse myths.

He begins with Kvasir, the giant formed from the peace-spittle of the Æsir and Vanir. Kvasir is murdered by a pair of malevolent dwarves, who drain off his blood into three containers, Son, Bodn and Odrœrir. They brew a kind of mead out of this blood, and Bragi explains that it turns anyone who drinks it into a poet or a scholar. In a bizarre aside, the dwarves are said to explain away Kvasir's disappearance by telling the rest of the Æsir that he suffocated in his own cleverness because the other dwarves were not able to supply him with questions which he might have answered, thus venting, as it were, the pressure of his learning. The dwarves' next victim is a giant called Gilling, whom they drown. In a chilling sequel, they become so irritated by Gilling's wife's loud lamenting that they drop a rock on her head. But the giant Suttung, hearing of his parents' killing, takes vengeance, stranding the two dwarves on a tidal rock. In exchange for rescue, and as compensation for their crimes, they give the mead of poetry, in its three containers, to the giant Suttung, who stores it in a place called Hnitbjörg, in the care of his daughter Gunnlöd.

At this point in the story, Bragi notes that the narrative, with its plethora of names, has provided the basis for a whole series of poetic terms for poetry. In Old Norse, the most striking characteristic of skaldic verse – the name is derived from the Norse word for a court poet, a *skáld* – is the riddling periphrases which colourfully but cryptically vary the terms with which objects can be denoted. These poetic terms are called 'kennings'. Thus, as Bragi explains, instead of referring to poetry by its normal names, skaldic poets can call it 'the blood of Kvasir', 'the drink of the dwarves', 'the contents of Odrœrir', 'Suttung's mead' or 'Hnitbjörg's liquid'. From our own point of view, the situation is reversed: kennings in skaldic verse can seem to offer us a vast amount of information about the mythology which, Bragi claims, gave rise to them. In fact, it has been argued that Snorri himself spun his mythological narrative from the kennings – we might imagine a process something like the game called 'Consequences', in which one must invent a narrative which twists and turns to accommodate a series of random, and apparently disconnected, individual names or words. On the other hand, it seems commonsensical to suppose that verses with completely opaque kennings could scarcely have survived without some accompanying knowledge of the myths these terms refer to. Perhaps the answer lies somewhere between the two: that Snorri, for instance, may have known a myth of poetry in broad outline, which he elaborated or extended on the evidence of kennings which suggested to him additional incidents or characters. This would explain, for instance, the existence in his account of *three* containers for the poetic mead, or the repeated changes in its guardianship.

But the mead of poetry has not nearly finished its to-ing and fro-ing. At this point, the god Odin steps in. He kills some slaves belonging to Baugi, Suttung's brother, and then offers himself to Baugi, in the guise of a travelling labourer called Bölverk ('Evil-Doer'), as their replacement. For payment, he requests a drink of Suttung's mead. Suttung refuses. Odin gets Baugi to drill through a rock wall to the mead, and, magically turning himself into a serpent, he squeezes through the hole and (presumably having shifted shape back again) sleeps with Gunnlöd for three nights. This earns him three sips of the mead, which he takes as monstrous draughts which empty all three containers. Shape-shifted again, this time into an eagle, he flies back to Asgard, hotly pursued by Suttung (also in the form of an eagle), and empties up the mead into containers which the Æsir have put out for the purpose. But he is so near to being caught by Suttung that in his fright he defecates a small amount just before he flies into Asgard: this is the source of the inferior, debased kind of poetic inspiration which is directly available to humans, rather than what is passed down to poets through divine inspiration – via, one supposes, intoxication. And as Bragi points out, this narrative provides material for a further series of kennings for poetry: Odin's loot, or find, or drink or gift, or the drink of the Æsir. He does not offer any more examples, for which the myth obviously provides plenty of justification, especially given the multiple transformations of the mead of poetry from or into most of the most unpleasant bodily fluids: spit, blood, vomit and faeces.

It is evident from this myth why some Norse poets believed that their poetic powers were the result of a special relationship with the god. But the myth shows us more about Odin than simply his links with poets and poetry. We can see the underlying structure of a contest with the giants to obtain an intellectual prize – in this case, the art of poetry – which is repeated in various forms throughout Old Norse myth as part of the continuing struggle between gods and giants. We might also note this instance of Odin's sexual success with giantesses. It is perhaps surprising that Odin did not need to pay or bribe Gunnlöd for access to either her sexual favours or the poetic mead: he seems to have overcome both her resistances at once. This raises the issue of a dubious kind of magic, associated with Odin, called in Norse *seiðr* (sorcery). According to Snorri's biography of Odin (in which he is presented as having originally been a human war leader), he had mastered the art of *seiðr*, and the magical powers it gave him included knowledge of the future, and the ability to cause sickness and even death. But Norse sources are reticent, not to say coy, about the details of *seiðr*. Snorri himself notes that it was associated with 'shameful behaviour' if men practised it – in Norse this usually means something to do with effeminacy or homosexuality – and that it was really the preserve of priestesses. It is the sorcery attributed to the figure called Heid who in *Völuspá* presented the original challenge to the Æsir by being so enthusiastically welcomed by 'bad women'. And one brief mention of it by a tenth-century Icelandic poet attributes Odin's seduction of the giantess Rind to his exercise of *seiðr*.

The most famous source for how Odin managed to master the magical arts is the Eddaic poem *Hávamál* ('What the High One Had to Say'). This poem is a strange miscellany of pieces of wise advice – ranging from the engagingly sensible (eat before any social occasion, so that hunger doesn't distract you from behaving sociably; no point lying awake worrying, because in the morning your worry will still be there but you'll be tired) to the elegantly touching (no matter how far away a good friend lives, it will always seem an easy journey). But the anonymous voice of such time-honoured pieces of wisdom gives way to a more personal, autobiographical voice, in which Odin himself describes his experiences. Odin confesses that he counts himself among those who have been made fools of by women, and tells the story of his encounter with the daughter of a giant called Billing. Driven wild by the sight of her, 'on the bed/sleeping, sun-radiant', Odin agrees to her suggestion that they meet later, in secret. But when he returns, full of anticipation and confidence, he finds the place full of armed guards, and later still, at dawn, when the guards are asleep, he finds, in crude mockery of his desire, a bitch tethered to her empty bed. Perhaps it was to overcome such humiliations that Odin took up *seiðr*, or perhaps it was to avoid being the object of Odin's magic that Billing's clever daughter gave him the slip. Certainly, Odin is very much more successful with Gunnlöd, though their encounter in this poem is slightly different from Snorri's prose narrative.

The wisdom set out in *Hávamál* moves from the social to the supernatural. A figure called Loddfafnir is offered several significant pieces of wisdom, and this paves the way for the most dramatic sequence in the poem, in which Odin describes his own acquisition of what seem to be sacred mysteries:

> I know that I hung on a windy tree
> nine long nights,
> wounded with a spear, dedicated to Odin,
> myself to myself, on that tree of which no man knows
> from where its roots run.
>
> No bread did they give me nor a drink from a horn,
> downwards I peered;
> I took up the runes, screaming I took them,
> then I fell back from there.
>
> Nine mighty spells I learnt from the famous son
> of Bölthor, Bestla's father,
> and I got a drink of the precious mead,
> poured from Odrœrir.

We learn from these extraordinary verses that Odin has accessed the wisdom of the underworld, of the dead, and to do this he made an Odinic sacrifice of himself, hanged and pierced with a spear. He learns too, painfully and drainingly, either the secret of writing in runes, or the magic associated with them. From his ancestors the giants he learns powerful spells, and he gets to drink the mead of poetry. Every kind of inspirational and occult wisdom imaginable is now his, after this experience of what is clearly an ecstatic ritual. A number of names for Odin in early Norse poetry now become clear: the god of hanged men; the burden of the gallows; the dangling, or swaying one.

Odin's sacrifice on the tree has of course struck very many scholars with its echoes of the crucifixion of Christ. It has been suggested that

Snorri never alludes to this sacrifice in his own work precisely because he was made uncomfortable by the parallels. On the other hand, the motif of the hanged god is not uncommon in other cultures. And the hanged man is one of the major tarot cards, and he is most often portrayed as hanging upside down from a living tree, with an expression of ecstatic inspiration. In addition, the practice of shamanism among northern Siberian tribes such as the Saami involves the ascent of a tree (or a stylized representation of it) to gain the wisdom of otherworld spirits; while the ritual takes place, the shaman may collapse as if unconscious or dead, while, as his followers suppose, his spirit journeys more widely. It is impossible to be definite about the relationships between all these rituals, but it is clear that Odin as we know him from Norse sources is the fount of all wisdom, and that his sources for it are the world of the dead and the world of the giants.

The most mysterious episode in Norse accounts of how Odin sought for otherworldly wisdom involves again the strange figure of Mimir, who was a hostage in the war between the Æsir and the Vanir, and whose head – so Snorri tells us – Odin embalmed in order to use as an oracle. Snorri has perhaps derived this story from the poem *Völuspá*, in which Odin is said to confer with Mimir's head (though the form of the name is a little different) when Ragnarök threatens. But earlier in the poem, the sibyl herself alludes to a different story about Odin and Mimir. She boasts mockingly that she knows how Odin came to lose one of his eyes: that he hid it in the well of Mimir, apparently in exchange for wisdom, for Mimir is associated with wisdom in early Norse poetry. The sibyl's words are obscure, but the image of a single eye – perhaps the reflection of the sun or moon – glaring up from the bottom of a deep well is a vivid one, and Odin himself is invariably represented as one-eyed in later versions of Old Norse myth. It becomes his single most characteristic feature, which identifies him even when he attempts to disguise himself.

What, we may ask, drives Odin to seek out more and more arcane secrets, challenging giants in their own halls, giving up one of his eyes, or risking his life by tasting death? The most compelling answer to this question belongs, strictly, in the final section of this chapter: Odin is constantly checking on the likelihood of what he most fears, which is that his precious son Baldr is fated to die, the first act in the great drama of Ragnarök, when all the gods will perish.

Odin's role as the god of war is not much represented in Old Norse mythological narratives about the conflicts of gods and giants, even though most of the kennings applicable to war in skaldic poetry take it for granted. In skaldic verse, battle may be 'the storm of Odin'; a sword, 'the fire of Odin'; or more elaborately, a warrior, a tree battered by the storm of Odin, or blood as the special liquid of Odin's bird (a raven, picking at human carrion on a battlefield). But of course war is an evidently human activity, and in many heroic narratives and poems, which I shall consider shortly, Odin is said to intervene, determining according to his or his valkyries' whim the course of the battle, to which side the victory, and which of the dead warriors should be transported to Valhalla. All of this, then, belongs to a later discussion of the affairs of gods and men. For more adventures of gods and giants, we must turn to the god Thor, a single-handed giant-killer.

THOR

Snorri Sturluson describes the god Thor as the mightiest of the Æsir, and second only to Odin in status. He drives a chariot, drawn by goats, and carries a great hammer, Mjöllnir, whose name is related to other European words for 'lightning', such as the Russian word *molnja*. Thor's imagined progress across the skies seems to represent the sights and sounds of a terrifying thunderstorm, and indeed Thor's own name belongs to a set of related Germanic words for 'thunder' – for example, the Anglo-Saxon form of the word and of his name, Thunor. Thor's role is to defend Asgard, the home of the Æsir, and Midgard, the home of mankind, against their old enemies, the giants. Some of the earliest Norse sources about Thor's exploits are skaldic verses which simply list his victims, such as the short verse by a tenth-century Icelandic poet, Vetrliði Sumarliðason, who praises Thor because he 'broke Leikn's legs / leathered Thrivaldi / felled Starkad / and finished off Gjalp'. As this list makes clear, giantesses were also fair game, for Gjalp ('the yelper') was the daughter of a giant called Geirrød, and Thor's adventures with him are the subject of one of the most difficult of all Old Norse mythological poems, the *Þórsdrápa* ('Skaldic Poem about Thor').

The author of the *Þórsdrápa* was one of the chief poets of a fiercely pagan tenth-century Norwegian chieftain, Earl Hakon. The poem begins by describing how Loki (a strangely ambivalent creature, part god and part giant, who often accompanies Thor on his exploits, and whose most notorious role in Old Norse myth concerns his part in the killing of the god Baldr) persuades a far from unwilling Thor to visit the giant Geirrød at home. Snorri Sturluson, who also tells this story, has Loki trick Thor into leaving behind his hammer, or his magic belt of strength. On his way to meet the giant, Thor spends the night with a friendly giantess, who lends him her magic staff and belt instead. The next day, having resumed his journey, Thor is nearly drowned by a river in full flood – but looking upstream he sees that the floodwaters are being swelled by Geirrød's daughter, Gjalp; the liquid is either urine, or menstrual blood. To stem this unruly flow, Thor hurls a stone at Gjalp; and he picks his precise target on her body with some care, declaring that a river must be stemmed 'at its source'. Once at Geirrød's, Thor is given humiliatingly mean lodgings, and when he sits down on the only seat, he finds himself being pushed up to the ceiling; the giant's two daughters are under the chair, lifting him up. He forces the chair down, with the help of the friendly giantess's magic staff, and breaks the daughters' backs. Finally, he and Geirrød throw lumps of molten metal at each other, and Thor kills Geirrød. In the poem *Þórsdrápa*, in which Thor is not tricked out of leaving his hammer behind, he kills the giant with it.

This bizarre series of events is only just discernible from the highly cryptic and allusive poetic style of the poem, and Snorri's interpretation is only one way of understanding them. Loki, for instance, is referred to as 'the pathway of the vulture', a kenning for 'air' (that is, the medium through which vultures travel) because the Norse word for air, *lopt*, is also a nickname for Loki. Thor is called 'the stronghold-visitor of Idi', which makes sense if you already know that Idi is the name of a(nother) giant. And Giantland is called 'the family seat of the race of Ymsi' – straightforward enough if you recognize the name Ymsi as a variant of Ymir, the primeval giant. These examples are all from one stanza of the poem; they are never used again, for the poet coins fresh puzzles for each mention of almost every item and character in the poem. But even a broad-brush paraphrase of *Þórsdrápa* makes it clear that the poem is dealing with serious myths in which Thor's physical superiority over the terrifying threats posed by giants, and, more especially, their female counterparts, must be established. And just as Thor himself may be associated with the most powerful forces in the known world – thunder and lightning – so the giants and giantesses have been understood as representing the dangers of the natural world – or, indeed, of the opposite sex – which need a hero to keep them in check.

Snorri has often been praised for re-telling old myths without subverting them, or distorting them to accord with his own Christian ideology. But translating poetic sources in which these dark and powerful myths are treated allusively and cryptically, as if for a highly committed audience, into more or less coherent narratives, as Snorri does, almost always involves some diminution of seriousness, or reduction of drama. The story of Thor's fight with the giant Hrungnir is a case in point. According to Snorri, Odin and Hrungnir tangle over who has the faster horse; Hrungnir pursues Odin, so fast that he cannot rein in his horse and gallops right into Asgard. The Æsir rather coolly invite him in for a drink, and he becomes boastful and obnoxious, grandly threatening to take away Freyja and Sif, the Æsir's chief goddesses, and kill the rest of the Æsir. The gods, more irritated than really afraid, call for Thor, who fights a duel with Hrungnir, and kills him with the hammer Mjöllnir. Thor is victorious even though Hrungnir has a bizarre helper. The giants have created a huge figure made out of clay – *Mökkurkálfi*, 'Cloud-Calf'. But they have given him the heart of a mare, and so in spite of his mighty stature, the clay giant is a coward, and wets himself in fright at the sight of Thor. As we shall see, it is possible that J.R.R. Tolkien picked up on this strange story when he came to create one of his most celebrated characters in *The Lord of the Rings*.

In a tenth-century poem which describes the fight between Thor and Hrungnir – but not the run-up to it – it was such a cataclysmic encounter that even mountains shook; rocky cliffs shattered, and heaven burned. Thor is referred to in the poem as 'the son of Earth' – he is elsewhere described as the son of the goddess Jörd, whose name means earth, so it is not clear whether this is simply wordplay, or meaningful cosmic imagery. But Snorri's account is most memorable for its entertainingly naturalistic picture of the drunken Hrungnir with his wild boasts. This giant is no mighty and mysterious force of nature but a tedious bar-room bore.

Thor's most celebrated encounter was not with a giant, but with an even more awe-inspiring foe: the World Serpent, or *Miðgarðsormr*. The episode is told in several Old Norse sources. According to Snorri, Thor has been bettered by the World Serpent and is looking for revenge. But in Bragi's poem *Ragnarsdrápa*, in which mythological scenes painted on a shield are apparently described by the poet, the confrontation is described as taking place 'early on' in Thor's career. Snorri rather craftily accommodates this detail by having his vengeful Thor disguise himself as a young man; this allows for a good deal of quiet comedy as the giant Hymir, whom Thor has persuaded to take him far out to sea to fish for the World Serpent, pretends that his reluctance is due not to his own fear of these dangerous waters, but rather to concern about the young boy (as he supposes) in his boat. Thor baits his fishing line with the head of a huge ox called Himinhrjótr ('the skyscraper') and soon gets a bite.

The story can be easily pieced together from the various sources. The World Serpent, hooked on Thor's fishing line, is gradually pulled out of the water, and for a moment the great monster and the mightiest of the Æsir (elsewhere described as being possessed of a quite terrifying frown) hold each other's gaze. They are held apart – and together – by a fishing line alone. The giant Hymir panics; he cuts the line, and the World Serpent disappears back down into the ocean. Thor throws Hymir overboard in his frustration, and, having put his foot through the bottom of the boat in his struggle to land the monster, wades ashore.

Was this encounter, then, a failure on Thor's part? Was he again bettered by the World Serpent? Early poetic allusions suggest that Thor killed the monster. For example, the Icelander Ulf Uggason was commissioned by a wealthy Icelandic farmer Olaf the Peacock to compose and recite a poem on the occasion of his daughter's wedding in 985 AD; Ulf's *Húsdrápa* ('Skaldic Poem about the Hall') describes scenes depicted in the elaborate carvings with which Olaf's magnificent hall was decorated, including the episode of Thor and the World Serpent. In Ulf's poem, the fatal blow is struck by Thor's fist, against the World Serpent's 'place of hearing' – in effect, a massive box on the ears which knocks the serpent's head clean off, a hearty, if unsubtle, strike which, one might imagine, Ulf's audience might greatly enjoy. Elsewhere, though, it is left ambiguous as to whether this blow was actually fatal or not: Thor strikes, and the serpent sinks back down into the sea. Crucially, it was not in Snorri's narrative interests to have the World Serpent killed off at this stage, because it is to be one of the major players in the great confrontation at Ragnarök, as our best authority, the sibyl of *Völuspá*, makes quite clear. So although Snorri acknowledges that it has been claimed that Thor killed the monster, he puts forward his own preferred reading: that Thor boxed the giant's ears, and the World Serpent survives.

The heart of this episode – the moment of stasis as god and monster stare each other down – plainly caught the imagination not only of poets, but also of artists: Scandinavian rock carvings depict the scene with extraordinary economy and drama. The most arresting is a Danish rock carving, the Stone of Hørðum, which depicts with wonderful clarity a helmeted figure in a boat, braced at a dangerously steep angle, and held there by a single taut line: Thor and his fishing line. There is an indistinct representation of what may be another figure in the boat – probably the giant Hymir – and the World Serpent itself is not clearly carved. Quite unmistakable, though, is Thor's foot, poking through the bottom of the boat. A tenth-century carving from Gosforth, in Cumbria, is less clear, but the figure which is taken to be Hymir seems to be about to use his knife – presumably, as in Snorri's version of the myth, to end the terrifying stand-off by cutting the line.

This version of the encounter between Thor and the World Serpent offers a dramatic version of the archetypal battle between the forces of good and evil, represented in so many cultures as a fight between a hero and a monster. The World Serpent is referred to in the riddling diction of skaldic poetry as 'the belt of the world' – most obviously, a monstrous snake, but, in more cosmic terms, perhaps understood as the belt, or girdle, which holds the whole world together. Thor, unimaginably mighty, even early on in his life, rashly takes on a force far more powerful than simply a Leviathan-like creature. In hooking the World Serpent, Thor puts the stability of the whole cosmos at risk: our world literally hangs by a thread: the fishing line which the giant Hymir thankfully cuts. Their next encounter really will herald the end of the world. It is this pivotal moment which so gripped early poets and artists.

The uncomfortable implication of this reading of the myth, of course, is that Thor is mighty but dangerous in his irresponsibility: he is potentially a force for chaos himself. At this point, we may recall that although he put paid to the giant Geirrød and his two daughters, Thor was actually tricked by Loki into visiting Geirrød in the first place. A picture is emerging of a god who is both rash and slow-witted. Snorri's prose account of Thor's adventures in the home of a giant called Utgarda-Loki powerfully reinforces this impression.

Thor, together with three companions (one of them the ambivalent half-god half-giant, Loki), sets off (Snorri offers no particular reason) for Giantland. On the way, they stay the night in a most peculiar house: its doorway is as wide as the main hall itself, and there is a side chamber halfway down one side. During the night, there are deafening noises, and an earthquake, and at dawn they discover a giant, Skrymir, whose snoring has been the cause of the disturbance. This enormous creature makes Thor and his companions look comically diminutive. In fact, their night lodgings were the giant's glove. A series of further humiliations is in store for Thor. When the giant next falls asleep, Thor makes three attempts to strike him with his thunderbolt hammer Mjöllnir: Skrymir supposes that the three blows are the result of a leaf, then an acorn and, finally, bird-droppings, falling on his head from the tree above him. When Thor at length arrives at the magnificent stronghold of Utgarda-Loki (who is, of course, the giant Skrymir himself), Thor is again belittled, though now he is represented as not quite as tiny as the Tom Thumb figure of earlier episodes, but as a child-like weakling. Challenged in the giant's hall to a series of physical feats, one of his companions under-standably fails to run faster than Utgarda-Loki's thought, and Loki fails to eat meat as fast as Utgarda-Loki's champion, whose name gives him away: Logi means wildfire, and he eats the meat and its container as well. Thor himself is made a complete fool of in his contests. To the giant's mock astonishment, Thor fails to finish off a yard of ale, or even to lift a cat off the floor. He claims to be a great fighter, but Utgarda-Loki is sceptical, and calls an old woman on to the hall floor to provide a suitable opponent. It is a hard-fought contest, but eventually the old woman seems to be getting the upper hand, and Utgarda-Loki calls off the fight to prevent further embarrassment to Thor.

But all is not what it has seemed in the hall of Utgarda-Loki, as the giant explains. The yard of ale was so enormous that Thor couldn't see how the giant had tipped the far end of it into the ocean. Thor's mighty drinks naturally failed to empty it, but certainly caused the tide to ebb. The cat, which arched its back when Thor tried to lift it, was the World Serpent itself; Utgarda-Loki and his companions had watched in great terror as Thor managed not to lift it clean up, but to raise one of its paws from the ground. And the old woman was Old Age, against whom no-one can successfully contend. Thor had lived up to his reputation after all. Ostensibly, the point is that not even Thor could have prevailed over those the giant offered as his opponents, and he actually performed terrifyingly well. Except, of course, that every reader or listener's abiding impression of this story is the comedy of little Thor, mad with frustration, failing the tasks, and subject to the sly patronage of the giant's pretended surprise at his poor performance. Thor is tricked; he fails to see through the giant's magical illusions; his strength is no proof against the giant's cunning. And there is in addition a strong element of coarse comedy throughout the whole tale, but especially in the eating and drinking competitions.

No-one knows where Snorri got these stories from, and it is theoretically possible that he invented some of them, although the episode of Thor hiding in the giant's glove is mentioned elsewhere in Old Norse tradition. It is of course hard to imagine a religious system in which one of the chief divinities was a figure of fun. Perhaps Snorri's source, if he had one, did not present as comical a picture of Thor as Snorri's prose does. But maybe the mockery of Thor is not Snorri's own spin on the story. We should turn now to the Eddaic poem *Þrymskviða* ('Thrym's Poem'), which further reinforces this picture of Thor as a powerful buffoon, strong on vigour, but weak on imagination and wit.

In *Þrymskviða*, Thor wakes up one morning to find his hammer missing. Loki borrows the goddess Freyja's feather coat and flies off into Giantland to track it down. He learns that a giant called Thrym has stolen the hammer and hidden it, but will return it to Asgard in exchange for Freyja herself, as his bride. Loki reports this bad news back to the Æsir, who hit on a daring plan: Thor shall dress up as Freyja and go to Giantland to get his hammer back. Thor immediately objects to this plan, protesting:

The Æsir will call me a pervert,
if I let you put a bride's veil on me.

But Loki rudely tells him to be quiet:

The giants will be settling in Asgard
unless you get your hammer back!

Thor's subsequent disguise is a very thorough one. He is provided with a veil, with the bunch of keys which were the mark of a Scandinavian housewife, and Freyja's most precious and characteristic treasure, the necklace of the Brisings, made for her by the dwarves in exchange for her sexual favours. It is, as it were, the symbol of her generous sexuality. Thor might be imagined as a flamboyant pantomime dame.

Once in the hall of the giant Thrym, Loki, who has accompanied Thor in the guise of a sort of bridesmaid, engages in a series of broadly comic

– one might almost say pantomimic – exchanges with the giant. In a manner reminiscent of the story of Red Riding Hood and the Big Bad Wolf, the giant enquires anxiously about the gross appetite of his 'bride', who has eaten and drunk the whole wedding feast at one go. Loki reassures him; 'Freyja' has been so excited at the prospect of this marriage that she has not eaten or drunk for a week. Lifting her veil, the giant recoils in surprise from Thor's celebrated glaring eyes. But again Loki is on hand to explain; 'Freyja' has been so excited that she has not slept for a week. Fooled, and his suspicions overcome by his own excitement, Thrym calls for the hammer Mjöllnir, which is to be used – presumably because of its phallic connotations – to consecrate the marriage. Thor need contain himself no longer: he snatches up the hammer, and kills Thrym and all his companions, including his unfortunate sister, who was about to accept a wedding gift from her new sister-in-law.

The two chief male gods in the Old Norse pantheon are represented as having demeaned themselves by dressing as women, or playing a woman's part: a hugely transgressive act in Old Norse society. But the contexts are completely different. Odin is engaged in the mastery of the sinister magic called *seiðr*, in which stretching or overturning the boundaries of gender has a disturbing and perhaps liberating function; the usual rules can no longer be relied upon. By contrast, Thor is involved in a comic burlesque episode, in which his dignity is overturned. Odin acquires more wisdom, while Thor just gets his hammer back, and is the butt of the whole joke.

The degree to which any religion can tolerate open mockery of its divinities is still a matter of debate among theologians and mythographers. It may well be that the practitioners of highly respectful religions (such as Christianity, or Islam, say) underestimate how much transgression – religious or social – might be allowable. One need only think of the Roman festival of Saturnalia, in which slaves changed places with their masters, and which had its later Christian counterparts in such customs as the appointment of a Christmas Lord of Misrule, or the Boy Bishop, who, dressed in full bishop's robes, took over the functions of the bishop for a period in December. Nevertheless, the suspicion remains that stories in which the god Thor was openly mocked might belong to a period when belief in these pagan deities was either declining, or over. However, it seems that such mockery was indeed a deep-seated aspect of Old Norse mythology, as we can see from, for instance, the poem *Harbarðzljóð*

('The Song of Harbard'). Here too Thor is mocked, but Odin is not. Disguised as a ferryman, Odin refuses to row Thor over the water, and the two engage in a string of insulting exchanges which systematically demonstrate Thor's slow-wittedness, and Odin's far superior cunning (including a reminder of Thor's humiliating time spent in the giant's glove). Thor is all stupid bluster. He is no match for his opponent, who neatly points out what may well be the crucial difference between the two of them:

> Odin has the nobles who fall in battle
> and Thor has the breed of serfs.

Here we might suppose not a general decline in pagan religious belief, but an assertion of one divinity's precedence over another. And it is only to be expected that Odin, the god of poetry, is more favourably represented by his devotees than Thor.

But no account of Norse traditions in which the gods are treated with disrespect can overlook *Lokasenna* ('Loki's String of Insults'). Here all the gods are mocked – but the mockery is not funny. Loki's allusive slanders against the gods are not the stuff of knockabout comedy, but telling accusations of perversion, bestiality, dishonesty and betrayal, which, significantly enough, the gods do not attempt to deny, although they do try to silence Loki. But their human weaknesses are ruthlessly exposed. Loki begins by accusing Odin of disloyalty – of granting success in battle to those who do not deserve it (this is, of course, an inevitable result of Odin's practice of gathering to himself in Valhalla the best warriors; it is in his interests therefore to kill off the bravest, and Loki has swiftly exposed this deep-rooted irony). But when Odin responds by viciously accusing Loki of having given birth, like a woman (in fact, we hear elsewhere in Old Norse tradition that Loki gave birth to Odin's eight-legged horse, Sleipnir), Loki retorts with a slander we already know: that Odin took part in the 'shameful' practice of *seiðr*. This silences Odin. Thor is Loki's last target. Before Loki has a chance to slander him, Thor steps up and threatens Loki with his hammer Mjöllnir. But Loki's task is far too easy. He at once reminds Thor of his humiliations at the hands of Utgarda-Loki, and all Thor's hammer-waving threats are not enough to shut him up, because, of course, there are lots of humiliations to hurl at him. Loki, though, is not careless of the real physical threat Mjöllnir offers, and Thor, while himself utterly routed in verbal terms, is the only one of the Æsir who is able to drive out Loki, by force. On the other hand, Loki is not permanently disempowered, because, bizarrely, he is the father of both the World Serpent, and the monstrous wolf Fenrir; they will be the deaths of both Thor and Odin at Ragnarök.

THE VANIR

The Vanir, it will be remembered, were the tribe who were opposed to the Æsir in the first war in the world, and who, according to Snorri, did so very badly in the exchange of hostages following the stalemate in the hostilities. As well as the mysterious Kvasir, the cleverest of the Vanir, there were their most important men, Njörd and his son Frey. In Snorri's quasi-historical account, Odin, leader of the Æsir, appointed Njörd and Frey to be his 'sacrificial priests', and when Odin dies, it is Njörd who succeeds to the kingdom of the Æsir, and he in his turn is succeeded by Frey. Njörd's triumph as king was the peace and the good harvests which characterized his reign – so remarkable that the Swedes over whom he ruled believed, Snorri tells us, that their king actually had power over the fertility of the land. Frey too was blessed with good harvests, and thus it was that his subjects began to worship him as a god. His wife was called Gerd, the daughter of Gymir, and from his alternative name – Yngvi, or Yngvi-Frey – the Swedish royal dynasty, the Ynglings, is named, and is descended. This is fairly straightforward legendary genealogy.

But the Vanir are stranger than this. As we have seen, Snorri's pseudo-history is a good way of incorporating the gods of Old Norse mythology into a plausible history of the Scandinavian royal house, and of allowing stories about the gods to take their place in a Christianized history. But it is clear even from Snorri's euhemerized account that the Vanir were gods of fertility, and of the sacrifices which were believed necessary to induce it. Not only did they possess the secret of the scandalous magic called *seiðr*, they also indulged in incest – for Njörd, their patriarch, had his sister for a wife, and their children were Frey, a son, and also Freyja, a daughter. Freyja is without question the most prominent of the Old Norse goddesses: her arena is love and sex.

The name Frey means 'lord', and Freyja, 'lady'. When the hostages from the Vanir were handed over to the Æsir, Snorri makes no mention of Freyja, but only of her brother and father. It has been suggested that the women (or woman with two names) who caused such chaos among the Æsir – Heid/Gullveig – were perhaps Freyja, especially given their associations with *seiðr*. But it is not anywhere explained why or how Freyja – if it was indeed her – came to practise her magic arts among the Æsir, causing them such consternation, and indeed the great war itself. There is just the faintest shadow of that old situation characteristic of so much Old English and Old Norse literature: the woman in the enemy hall, stolen and held by a rival tribe, a little like Hild, who was abducted and found herself impossibly caught between husband and father. In any event, we learn that Freyja was the daughter of Njörd, and taught the Æsir this secret magic, which, in its links with sexual practices, is clearly linked to the enhanced fertility and prosperity characteristic of the Vanir. But Snorri is clear on one point: the custom of incest – the marriage of a brother and sister – which characterized the Vanir, was forbidden among the Æsir, so when the Vanir were incorporated into Asgard, Njörd and Frey took non-sibling wives: and thereby hang two tales.

The first concerns Njörd, whose sister was the mother of Frey and Freyja. Njörd as a patriarch is a puzzling figure in Old Norse, because his name in Norse – *Njörðr* – corresponds precisely to the god whom the Roman historian Tacitus, writing in the first century AD, names as the chief deity of the Germanic tribes known as the Angles. But this deity, Nerthus, is female – and indeed Tacitus is extremely clear about this: he writes of the worship of 'Nerthus, that is, *Terra mater* ("Mother Earth")'. Several explanations have been put forward to explain this odd gender change. Perhaps an old goddess cult was replaced by a newer patriarchal religion. Perhaps, as has recently been suggested, Tacitus misunderstood just what the Angles were worshipping, and assumed that the name of a male priest was the name of the female goddess he attended. But whatever the gender of the deity, the important element in his/her identity is that both Nerthus (according to Tacitus) and Njörd (according to Snorri) were associated with peace and fertility. And as befits such a god, originally a member of the Vanir, Njörd's story is all about marriage: not the incestuous union with his unnamed sister, which the Æsir so disapproved of, but marriage with a giantess.

The giantess was called Skadi, but the story of the marriage has a long preamble in Norse tradition. It is the story with which Snorri begins his treatise explaining the kennings in skaldic verse, *Skáldskaparmál*. He based his account on a difficult poem by an early Norwegian poet called

Thjodolf: the poem is called *Haustlöng* ('Autumn-long') – which is usually taken to refer to the time it took Thjodolf to compose it, though it might just as plausibly refer to the time it takes modern readers (and perhaps even a medieval audience) to unravel its meaning. Three gods – Odin, Loki and Hœnir – are apparently cooking an ox, out in the open air. An ancient eagle – actually a giant called Thjazi – demands a share of the meat, and when Loki tries to drive him off with a pole, he himself is carried off by the eagle, still clinging to his pole. Loki begs to be released, and the giant names his price: predictably, given the stories of gods and giants already told, Thjazi tells Loki to bring him the goddess Idunn, the goddess who knows 'the old-age medicine of the Æsir' – that is, apples of immortality. The result is devastating for the Æsir; as Thjodolf puts it:

> The dwellers in bright peaks [the giants] were not despondent;
> it was when Idunn had just arrived from the south
> [that is, from Asgard into Giantland];
> all the people of Yngvi-Frey [the Æsir] discussed what to do;
> the deities were ugly, grey-haired, and old.

Their discussion naturally identifies Loki as the ultimate cause of their hideous ageing, and he borrows Freyja's feather coat again, and rescues the goddess Idunn. He is chased back to Asgard by the giant Thjazi (also shape-shifted into bird form), but the gods light a bonfire which sets light to his wings, and he is killed.

The story does not end here, however. Thjazi has a daughter Skadi, a giantess who is keen to avenge her father, and she turns up to threaten Asgard. The gods offer her compensation (she must have been a formidable woman): her choice of a husband from among them, but to be chosen on the evidence of feet alone. She assumes that the most beautiful feet on view must belong to Odin's son Baldr, and chooses accordingly. But the feet are Njörd's, and thus begins their ill-fated union. What's interesting here, of course, is that we have an intriguing gender swap: so far the pattern has been that the giants demand goddesses, but now a giantess has overturned this, and is in a position to demand one of the Æsir.

Snorri explains that Njörd is the god of fishing, and travelling by sea, and his home is, naturally, by the sea. (It's not clear, incidentally, why he had such beautiful feet, unless it might be the beneficial effects of sea paddling.) But Skadi belongs, like her father and all her kin, to the high mountains. An awkward compromise is put in place: husband and wife will spend alternate periods of nine nights at each other's homes. But it doesn't work. In two snatches of poetry quoted by Snorri, found nowhere else in Old Norse, Njörd complains bitterly about the howling of the wolves in the mountains, and Skadi laments the horrid screaming of seagulls. Their marriage is abandoned.

Njörd, though, has his two children, Frey and Freyja, even if it is not clear just when they were born, or indeed who their mother was. Frey is described by Snorri as one who 'governs sunshine and rain, and the fertility of the earth, to whom one must pray for prosperity and peace'. He is quite evidently a fertility deity. There is only one extended narrative about him, but it is one which powerfully reinforces this identity.

This story is told with great clarity and enormous drama in the Eddaic poem *Skírnismál* ('What Skirnir Had to Say'). Snorri also gives a rather minimalist prose account of it, carefully omitting the most sensational elements. *Skírnismál* opens with the god Frey sitting in Hlidskjalf, a seat belonging to Odin which commanded an extensive view over many realms. Snorri presents this as a daring and transgressive act by Frey: he was sitting where he shouldn't have been, and what he saw paid him back for his temerity. He saw – and at once fell madly in love with – a beautiful giantess. His immediate lovesickness is utterly paralysing, and his mother – here identified as Skadi – calls on his childhood companion and now servant, Skirnir ('the shiner'), to find out what is the matter with him. Frey is, eventually, persuaded to talk about the giantess, and is lyrical about her beauty. Skirnir agrees to ride out to Giantland to woo the giantess, whose name is Gerd, on Frey's behalf.

After a dangerous and difficult journey, Skirnir reaches Gerd and offers her the greatest treasures the Norse gods have: the apples of eternal youth (whose theft by the giant Thjazi caused such a calamity among the Æsir) and the ring Draupnir ('the dripper'), so called because every ninth night, eight rings drop from it – that is, it turns into nine rings, perpetually. These two extraordinary treasures are perfectly apt as gifts from Frey, originally one of the Vanir, traditionally, though it is not at all clear how, or indeed whether, Skirnir has got them in his possession to give. But they provide the best that the Vanir can offer: perpetual youth (and by extension, life) and perpetual prosperity. Gerd, however, is not impressed: she refuses the gifts and Skirnir turns nasty. He threatens first her, and then her father, with Frey's sword, but this only increases her resistance to him. Finally, he threatens her with curses: her fate will be exactly the opposite of the fulfilled sexuality, fertility and prosperity the Vanir represent. She will be hidden from sight, but paradoxically, on constant show, vulnerable to the male gaze which Frey's first, transgressive sighting of her signalled. She will be tormented by all manner of horrible creatures, and suffer either the attentions of a three-headed ogre, or have no husband at all: that is, one might infer, an excess of sexual attention, or none at all. She will be tortured by unsatisfied sexual desire. Skirnir presents her with a vision of a hideous perversion of the role of a married woman: her partner will be a frost-giant, Hrimgrimnir ('the icy masked one'), and in a hall 'down below the bars of the dead' she will be served not mead, but goats' piss. And Skirnir will impose this will of his (or Frey's?) upon her: she will not get what she wants, but what he decrees for her. This imposition of the male will is chillingly reinforced with phallic images of Skirnir 'taming' her with a magic staff. Gerd suddenly capitulates, and restores her actual role as the daughter of a grand giant to blot out the vision of its nightmarish opposite. She formally welcomes Skirnir into her hall, and offers him ancient mead in a crystal cup. So, it would seem, she is overpowered.

But there is a curious epilogue following this dramatic and even shocking denouement. Skirnir insists on following through with his victory, and seeks to make arrangements for their union. Gerd is co-operative – but only up to a point. A place for their tryst is specified, but Gerd will be there in nine nights' time. Skirnir rides back to Frey in triumph, his mission accomplished. Frey, however, is consumed by sexual frustration: how, he wails, can he possibly wait that long? Gerd has, at the last moment, exerted her authority, and condemned Frey to the same kind of torment his emissary threatened her with. Is this – to put it crudely – a feminist or a misogynist strategy? In other words, is it a final triumph for the woman – Gerd – or a taunt at the power of women? And why, we may ask ourselves, is Frey's frustration somehow comic, the 'natural' male sexual urge thwarted, while the curses proposed for Gerd seem unnatural, sinister, even. *Skírnismál* is a poem which unexpectedly challenges the modern-day reader, and perhaps even bears out our introductory definitions of myth as stories which have, in spite of surface strangenesses, universal relevance.

Aside from intuitive responses to the narrative content of *Skírnismál*, how can we 'read' this mythic story? On one level, it seems clear that we are dealing with a fertility myth. That is to say, we can interpret Skirnir – 'the shiner' – as a sunbeam, an emanation of, as Snorri puts it, the god of the seasons and the weather. Skirnir might be seen as the link between the god Frey and the earth, or soil, or field and pasture: the action of spring sunshine on the cold winter ground. Gerd, as the object of his affection, is like the earth: distant, beautiful, and waiting to be awakened by the touch of Frey/spring. Her name is rather like the word for 'enclosure', *garðr*, that is, the ground which has been cultivated by humans. If she refuses the attentions of Frey/Skirnir, then the comforting cycle of fertility and harvest is thrown into chaos: everything is out of kilter, and the world may oscillate perilously between sterility and unfulfilled desire, instead of the steady rhythm of propagation and harvest. This reading of the poem does not in the least stretch its content: in fact, only a serious disruption of the rhythm of the seasons is enough to account for the violence of its rhetoric.

But this is not the only way to read the poem. Frey is not just a vegetative principle: he is a passionate and determined lover, and Skirnir plays the part of his surrogate wooer, winning the lady by a mixture of threats and promises. The poem is full of human interest: Frey's sulky lovesickness; his mother's touching concern; his friend Skirnir's devotion; even Gerd's modest delay about the wedding night, followed by Frey's almost comic protests about that delay. In this sense, the poem is simply 'a story about the gods'; divinities are given human qualities and concerns, as lovers and maidens, as emissaries and parents.

And finally, the poem speaks very directly to us as an allegory of what used to be called the battle of the sexes: Gerd's defiance, Skirnir's disturbingly phallic threats ('I shall tame you with my large stick'), and Gerd's final trump card – the holding back, the fetching (but infuriating) delay. The aspect of the poem which is perhaps most amenable to a modern, theoretical feminist reading is the vulnerability of Gerd to what has been called 'male gaze' – here, Frey's usurpation of Odin's all-seeing seat, Hlidskjalf, which allows him to catch sight of the giantess and send his emissary to threaten and bully her. Hardly less evocative are the terms of Skirnir's curse: that she shall be 'on show', 'stared at', 'gaped at': a spectacle. She is the object of Frey's gaze, and hence the subject of his attentions.

This leads us on to consider the goddess Freyja, whose primary role in Old Norse mythology is also that of the passive desired one: the precious asset of the Æsir, whom the giants covet. We have already come across Freyja in this capacity – mostly as the reason why Thor is called on to fight giants when Freyja has been threatened. So, for instance, when the giant Hrungnir became tediously drunk and boastful, it was Freyja who, of all the Æsir in Asgard, was bold enough to keep serving him drink, but equally it was she whom he threatened to take away with him. As we have seen, in the poem *Þrymskviða* it was Freyja whom the giant Thrym demanded in return for the stolen hammer Mjöllnir. And there is another story about a giant who threatened Asgard, and demanded Freyja as a prize.

Again, this story has a disconcerting ring of relevance to our time. The gods, nicely settled in Asgard, are approached by a builder, cold-calling, who offers to construct a secure defence for them against the depredations of their old enemies, the giants. His stipulated payment is Freyja, and the sun and the moon. This is surely a highly significant package: Freyja is a major prize here. The Æsir suggest something engagingly analogous to what we would now call a penalty clause: if he misses the stated deadline for the completion of the work by even one day, he is to forfeit the agreed payment.

To the gods' increasing consternation, and helped by his stallion Svadilfæri, the giant builder comes very close to completing this magnificent fortification within the agreed period. The gods are terrified of losing Freyja, and they call on Loki to devise a plan to thwart the giant. Loki turns himself into a mare, and manages to distract the giant's stallion so much that the work is delayed. The gods call on Thor, who, as part of the bargain, has been absent, and he kills the giant. The consequences of Loki's plan to distract the giant's helper are still to come: in due course he gives birth to an eight-legged horse: Sleipnir. But Freyja is saved.

Suggested by the kennings in Old Norse poetry, Freyja's various attributes are recorded by Snorri in his *Prose Edda*. She lives in a hall called Sessrumnir, and travels in a chariot drawn by cats. She is, as one might expect of a fertility goddess, constantly associated with sex: her legendary necklace, the Brisingamen, is paid for by sex with the dwarves who made it; in *Lokasenna* Loki accuses her of sleeping with every single one of the elves and the Æsir. Perhaps fittingly as a member of the Vanir, who knew the secret of bringing the battlefield dead back to life, she is described as sharing half of those slain in battle with Odin, though it seems likely that there has been some overlap or confusion here with Odin's wife, Frigg. It may be the result of similar confusion that her husband is called Odr. Freyja is said to weep tears of gold when he is away on his long travels – but we learn elsewhere that Odin himself often went away for long periods, and that his wife Frigg slept with his brothers Vili and Ve while he was away. Freyja and Frigg are also linked together in the Eddaic poem *Oddrúnargrátr* ('Oddrun's Lament'), in which both are invoked as help for a difficult childbirth. It is striking that while Odin and Thor are so very clearly distinguished, the goddesses are almost interchangeable.

Freyja is also associated with treasure: her golden tears; the wondrous necklace of the Brisings; perhaps her identity as Gullveig ('golden liquor'); one of her daughters is called Hnossir ('precious things'). That she is constantly desired by the giants may suggest that she as a goddess is a figure representing what humans most desire: treasure itself. Or perhaps she combines the three most desirable things in the world: continued prosperity, available sex, and, closely connected with both, the continuance of one's family line into the foreseeable future. It is perhaps in this context that we should understand what Snorri calls the greatest catastrophe to have befallen the gods: the death of Odin's son Baldr. Clearly, the deepest concerns of humans are also projected on to the stories of the gods.

CHAPTER 3

Heroes and Humans

The relationship between the gods in their mythic world and real humans in this one – that is, just how mythology relates to religion, to actual religious practice – is an important issue which I will turn to at the end of this section. But before that, we must look at the representation of humans in the mythology itself. And as we shall see in later chapters, it is this interaction between the gods and the giants on the one hand, and legendary heroes on the other, which has proved one of the most compelling aspects of Norse mythology down through the centuries.

The compiler of the anthology we know as the *Poetic Edda* has confidently arranged the individual poems according to a clear scheme: mythological poems first, and then the poems about legendary heroes, female as well as male. These heroic poems follow a clear chronological order, beginning with the exploits of Helgi *Hundingsbani* ('the killer of Hunding'), who is one of the sons of the great legendary hero Sigmund the Volsung. The *Poetic Edda* continues with the story of Sigmund's far more celebrated son, Sigurd, known as *Fafnisbani*, 'the killer of the dragon Fafnir', although the poem about the killing of the dragon consists not of a description of the fight between monster and hero, but of the dying words of Fafnir himself. Having killed Fafnir, Sigurd – as a helpful prose link between the poems, probably supplied by the compiler of the anthology, explains – takes possession of the dragon's immense treasure. It is the story of this hoard which inspired Richard Wagner: he called the treasure *Das Rheingold*, and the hero who won it, Siegfried. From this ethereal gold, according to Wagner, is forged, by magic, the ring: *Der Ring des Nibelungen*, the great ring of his operatic cycle.

Just how Wagner used, adapted and added to the Norse sources which form the basis of his *Ring* cycle will be discussed in a later chapter. The poems of the *Edda*, having celebrated Sigurd's victory over the dragon and his possession of the treasure, move on to the larger-than-life but still tragic human consequences: Sigurd's aborted betrothal to Brynhild; his doomed marriage to Gudrun; and his murder by her brothers. From this point on, in the *Edda*, Gudrun becomes the central character. She subsequently marries Attila the Hun, and when he murders her brothers, she exacts a terrible but classic revenge by killing their own two sons. She sends her sons by her next marriage on a hopeless revenge quest: the Gothic emperor Jörmunrekkr has been led to believe that his own son has slept with his new young bride – the daughter of Gudrun and Sigurd – and when he has her brutally executed (she is trampled to death by carefully trained horses) Gudrun urges them, the last remaining members of her family, to avenge their step-sister, against impossible odds. None of this plays any part in Wagner's operatic work; his interest is in the history of the ring – its origins, the curse on it, and its home in the waters of the Rhine. But our subject here is one which also concerned Wagner very deeply: the relations between gods and heroes.

The heroic section of the *Poetic Edda* opens with the Helgi poems. To look at the mythical prehistory of the Volsung family, whose origins are traced back to Odin, we must turn to *Völsunga saga* ('The Saga of the Volsungs'), which begins further back in legendary time than the poems of the *Edda*.

Völsunga saga is a thirteenth-century Icelandic text which draws on the poems of the *Poetic Edda*; it is in fact largely a prose paraphrase of those poems. But its opening chapters are not based on any poems which have come down to us. Here we learn of a figure called Sigi – his name seems to be related to the Norse word for victory, and he is fittingly identified as the son of Odin. Thus the Volsungs, like the English and Scandinavian royal houses, trace their ancestry back to Odin. Sigi becomes a rich and powerful king, but his wife's brothers kill him, and his son Rerir is caught between the filial duty of revenge for his father, and kinship with his maternal uncles. But in a clear echo of Odin himself as depicted in the creation stories related by Snorri, Rerir kills his maternal uncles, just as Odin, Vili and Ve killed the primeval giant Ymir. Rerir and his wife have no children, but when they pray to Frigg, she prevails on Odin to help, and, after an unnaturally long pregnancy, the first Volsung is born. It seems likely that his name (which becomes the name of the whole dynasty) is related to the Norse word for 'phallus'; a short story in Norse, the *Völsa þáttr* ('The Tale of Völsi'), describes the ribald doings of a family which worships an enormous embalmed horse phallus. Volsung marries the valkyrie sent by Odin to help his mother conceive (she brought an apple which, rather oddly, it seems the father ate), and together they have ten sons and a daughter. One of the sons – Sigmund – and the daughter – Signy – are twins.

The story of the Volsungs is a harsh one. Its early stages contain mythic elements we have come across already: the killing of the maternal uncle; the origins of a royal house in the mixed ancestry of gods and giants; Odin, Frigg and valkyries. Furthermore, the great hall of King Volsung has a massive tree growing in the middle of it, reminiscent of the World Tree, Yggdrasill, and Odin himself appears to Volsung: the familiar figure of an old, one-eyed man with a hood drawn down low over his face. This old man sinks a sword deep into the tree in the hall, and, like King Arthur in Celtic legend, Sigmund the son of Volsung is the only one who can pull it out. Signy, Sigmund's twin, now married to King Siggeir, takes her place among so many women in Germanic myth and legend when she is caught between the warring factions of her husband Siggeir and her brothers, the Volsungs. Her father is killed, and all her brothers are taken prisoner by her husband (and all except Sigmund are eaten by a ferocious wolf who is perhaps Siggeir's mother in disguise). But there are even darker social undercurrents. Sigmund escapes, and his sister Signy sends him her sons by Siggeir to help him in his exile. But both boys, set to the task of baking bread, fail because they become squeamish about something wriggling in the flour. Signy recognizes in them the inferior breeding of her husband Siggeir, and tells Sigmund to kill them. Only one recourse now remains to her. She changes shape with a witch, who sleeps with Siggeir while Signy visits her brother in this disguise, and becomes pregnant by him. Thus is born the hero Sinfjötli: the purity of his Volsung blood is assured since he is the son of twins. This too may have its echoes in the twin or hermaphrodite ancestors of the gods, as Norse creation myths relate, but for our own time it is hard not to see the attraction of this story for those predisposed to value racial purity.

As it happens, the boy Sinfjötli, the son of twins, also encountered something nasty in the flourbin, but kneaded it into the bread. It was a poisonous snake.

It is only to be expected that heroes should rise above mere pain, and Sinfjötli is duly stoical when his mother sews his sleeves tightly at the cuff, to keep in the warmth, but passes the stitches through his skin as well. But Sinfjötli rises above the merely human in other ways too. He and Sigmund dress themselves in wolf skins in their outlawry, and in effect become werewolves, howling to each other like wolves, and even biting each other. When they return to the court of Siggeir, in search of vengeance, the little sons of Signy and Siggeir spot their arrival, and tell their father. Signy orders her brother and son-nephew to kill the children. Sigmund baulks at this, but Sinfjötli never hesitates, and flings their bodies in front of their father Siggeir. Siggeir captures Sigmund and Sinfjötli, and has them buried alive, but they escape, with Signy's help, and burn Siggeir. Signy proudly recounts the terrible things she has done to help her brother avenge their father, and then walks into the flames to her own death. After Sinfjötli's death, his father Sigmund re-marries, and a son, the product of Sigmund's old age, is born after his father's death: Sigurd, the celebrated dragon-slayer, and guardian – for a while – of the Rhinegold.

The early history of the Volsungs is marked by close interaction with Odin, the mythical progenitor of the dynasty. The mysterious boatman who conducts Sinfjötli's body to the otherworld is Odin; Sigmund's death on the battlefield is heralded by his encounter with a familiar one-eyed old man, his hat drawn low over his face. This kind of interaction is set to continue – the young Sigurd meets an old man who gives him a horse descended from Sleipnir – the name of Odin's famous eight-legged steed. And the story of the treasure itself – the ring – begins with Odin. But all this must wait until we come to our discussion of Wagner's transformation of these sources.

Another human hero who is represented as having close relations with Odin is Starkad, whose story is told in the legendary *Gautreks saga*. In fairy-tale fashion Odin bestows gifts on him, while Thor tries to counteract them. So when Odin decrees that Starkad shall be granted three lifespans, Thor's rejoinder is to decree that he will commit a terrible deed in each of them. And the first of these deeds is the sacrifice of his friend and foster-brother, King Vikar, to Odin. While marauding at sea together, Starkad and Vikar try by divination to get a favourable wind. But to their horror, the will of Odin is that Vikar should be sacrificed to him. Starkad's plan is that Vikar should be subjected to a pretend sacrifice: the gallows is to be the flimsiest branch of a fir tree, the rope a soft and slimy length of calf gut, and the spear a floppy reed. But when this 'sacrifice' is set up, and Starkad speaks the ritual words 'Now I give you to Odin', the god's power transforms the mock instruments of murder into real and effective ones, and Vikar is killed.

The most obvious similarity between this sacrifice and the description Odin gives of sacrificing himself on the World Tree is the dual action of hanging and piercing with a spear. But does either bear any relation to actual sacrifice to Odin? This brings us to the final part of this section: the relationship between actual humans in the real world and the gods about whom the stories – our myths – are told.

It has seemed, throughout this chapter, that mythology is really no more than a particular branch of literature, possibly far removed from what anyone, at any time, actually does, or did, governed by its own rules and conventions. Religion, though, might be defined precisely as *practice*, as 'what people actually do'. Although it may be based on religious belief, or personal conviction, the key element of religion is that it involves more than belief: it involves action. Such action is based on a perceived, personal relationship between the deity or deities in question and the believer him- or herself. Put very simply, religion is the enactment of practices which reflect three kinds of relationship with the divine: worship, supplication and propitiation. The two underlying emotions involved here are love and fear. Love leads to the practice of worship; fear to propitiation. Supplication assumes that the divinity might be receptive to human prayer. To believe in a god is to believe that one's actions, in either or both of these spheres, are making a real, actual connection with the divine.

In fact, worship and propitiation are opposite ends of the same spectrum. To worship a deity is to show respect, and to hope for favour: believers may convince themselves that their praise is disinterested, but this is not actually the case. Praying to the divine for help or guidance is a very familiar form of supplication, and is at root the same impulse as, for instance, sacrificing to Norse fertility gods to ensure a good harvest. Less congenial to modern believers is the further end of the spectrum, religious practice born out of fear: the urgent desire to placate an angry or unpredictable god.

In the broadest possible sense, mythology can suggest the outlines of the religion to which it is, or once was, related. For instance, a god of war, fickle and powerful, like Odin, would be an obvious candidate for fearful propitiation, and we might expect such practices as sacrifices to be associated with his devotees. It would be natural to pray to Frey, a fertility god, for good harvests, or personal prosperity, and offerings, perhaps of a less dramatic kind, might seem appropriate. Thor, on the other hand, the guardian of Asgard and Midgard, our defence against giants, might be worshipped.

In fact, such evidence as we have for actual pagan religious practice suggests precisely this division of relationship with humankind. There may also be a two-way process at work: that the stories of mythology helped to shape and refine believers' religious attitudes to their gods. Stories about Odin controlling the battlefield, for instance, may have impressed upon the human mind the urgent and continuing need to placate him. On the other hand, it may be that a knowledge of the mythology – as stories – influenced those who purported to record the religious beliefs of pagans. But mythology can provide scarcely any detail about the actual forms of worship and propitiation. And as we shall see, in the virtual absence of contemporary records – that is, the direct testimony of pagans themselves – the sources on which we must rely are liable to be misleading in lots of ways.

If we hope to learn about the actual practices of real society, then the Icelandic family sagas are an obvious and very valuable resource. They are naturalistic prose narratives which purport to recount the lives of those settlers – mostly pagans – who first came to Iceland in the ninth century, and the generations immediately following them. Their style is sober and unshowy; their authors do not intrude in the narrative, but seem to describe, simply, 'what happened', as historians used to. Nowadays, scholarly opinion is inclined to stress their fictionality, but it is generally accepted that they are set in a plausible recreation of a possible society which may, indeed, record authentic details of a way of life nonetheless far in the past by the time the sagas were written down, that is, in and around the thirteenth century. It is worth calling to mind here the mythological scholarship of Snorri Sturluson, who also wrote in the thirteenth century, separated from the pagan past by the same distance as the authors of the family sagas.

Not all sagas were family sagas. Snorri, as we have seen, was also the author of a vast biographical compilation, *Heimskringla*, a history of the medieval rulers of Norway, from the legendary past up to the historical near past of the twelfth century. Since in the Middle Ages it was largely kings and princes who took upon themselves the conversion of their peoples, Snorri recounts in fascinating detail some of the struggles these Norwegian rulers had in imposing Christianity on their pagan subjects. There were also heroic sagas, manifestly fictional adventure stories about legendary heroes, who lived in an imaginary Scandinavia before real historical time, and whose authors felt free to include episodes of gods – especially Odin – appearing in the world of human affairs, and human reactions to them.

These Icelandic prose narratives are full of information about the worship of Norse gods, but there is no way of determining how reliable any of this material is. Family sagas have a ring of authenticity, but this is actually an aspect of their literary style, and their authors were after all separated by several centuries from the societies – and practices – they describe. And like Snorri, their authors were Christian. Indeed, Snorri's *Heimskringla* narratives tend to be told from the point of view – naturally – of the Christianizing ruler, and there is a certain predictable triumphalism about the exposure of pagan worship as either reprehensible or just plain silly. And finally, the open fictionality of the heroic sagas undermines their use as serious sources for pagan practice.

The description of pagans' practice by contemporaries who did not share their religious beliefs is always likely to be undermined by bias. Thus the *Germania*, an account of the earliest Germanic tribes by Tacitus, the Roman historian of the first century AD, is full of information about Germanic gods, but for one thing, one of Tacitus's aims in writing the *Germania* was to shame his decadent fellow Romans, and for another, the Germanic tribes described may have little or no connection with the later pagan Scandinavians we are concerned with. In the eleventh century, a cleric called Adam of Bremen wrote an account of the bishops of Hamburg, which describes the missionary activities of Christian churchmen in Scandinavia; it contains some of the most sensationalist material on pagan practice we have – especially human sacrifice – but may have been written up with the express aim of stressing how vital the work of converting such active pagans was. And in Anglo-Saxon England, reference to the paganism of the early Anglo-Saxons themselves seems to have been very heavily censored by the Church, and stories of the work of missionaries, such as we find in the work of the Venerable Bede, show the pagans – without going into suggestive detail about their rituals – to be sadly misguided and deluded. Nevertheless, these are all very valuable sources, as we shall see.

Documentary evidence such as place names, personal names and runic inscriptions needs careful interpretation, but can tell us a surprising amount about the worship of pagan gods. And archaeology, which needs more careful and skilled interpretation than almost any other source, is perhaps the most informative of all, and what it can tell us about pagan conceptions of death and the otherworld is unrivalled.

The god Thor must have been the chief god of those first settlers of Iceland. He has been called 'the patron and guardian of the settlement itself'. More than a quarter of the names in the Icelandic account of the settlement – *Landnámabók* ('The Book of Land-Takings') – are prefixed by the element derived from his name: Thorolf, Thorgeir, Thorkel and many more; and women's names too, such as Thordis or Thorbjörg.

There are very many references to the settlers' devotion to the god Thor in the family sagas, but the saga about the people who settled in the area called Eyrr – *Eyrbyggja saga* – contains the most sustained detail. At the beginning of the saga, we hear of a Norwegian chieftain called Thorolf, who is considering his future prospects. He holds a sacrificial feast and asks his 'dear friend' Thor what to do; divine advice, the saga author tells us, tells him to go to Iceland. In preparation for emigration, Thorolf takes down his temple – apparently made of wood – so that it can be shipped over to his new home. Once in sight of the Icelandic coast, Thorolf throws overboard some pillars from the throne which had stood in his temple in Norway, one of which had an image of the god carved on it. The sacred pillars seem to make their own way ashore, and Thorolf believes that they are guided by Thor himself, and that the place where they are washed up will be a propitious place for settlement. This motif is repeated in a number of family sagas.

Settled in Iceland, Thorolf rebuilds his temple. The saga author describes it in detail: it is large, with a door in the sidewall; the sacred pillars (complete with their 'sacred nails') are inside, and the whole place is a sanctuary. There is a raised platform, like an altar, with a ring for swearing oaths on. The blood of sacrificial animals is held in a sacrificial bowl, and the priest can sprinkle it around with a sacrificial twig (which is just like a Christian priest's holy water brush, the saga author adds). Part of the temple is shaped like the choir in a Christian church, and idols of the gods stand in a circle there.

It is quite clear that this description is filtered through its author's knowledge of Christian church layouts and practices. It would be invaluable to have some archaeological record of such a building and its contents, but none exists. One of the great puzzles of early Scandinavian archaeology is that nothing has ever been found that can definitely be identified as a site of pagan worship. Scholarship directs us to Tacitus's account of the early Germanic tribes, who worshipped out of doors, in sacred groves. Common sense questions the practicality of open-air devotions in out-of-season Scandinavia. So far, the nearest we can get to the identification of a temple is the excavation of buildings which do not contain the sort of domestic refuse which would characterize a lived-in site.

Eyrbyggja saga also contains a reference to a site of human sacrifice. Where there used once to be an assembly site, the saga author tells us, one can still make out the circle where people were sentenced to be sacrificed, and within it, the stone of Thor, on which one can still see bloodstains. References to human sacrifice are extremely rare in saga literature, and one might note the slightly voyeuristic quality of this reference, as if the saga author were a tour guide inviting his audience to peer at the remains and imagine the horrors of an earlier age. Human sacrifice is conventionally attributed to pagan peoples by Christian writers – in much the same way as adventure novelists used to portray distant tribes as cannibals, a motif eagerly seized on by writers and film-makers everywhere.

In his biography of St Olaf, King of Norway, Snorri Sturluson describes an encounter between the king and his regrettably still pagan subjects. The spokesman for the pagans is a chieftain called Guthbrand, and he contrasts the invisible god of the Christians with the always evident pagan gods who are worshipped in the form of idols. A pagan hostage describes to the king their idol of Thor: 'He carries a hammer in his hand, and is very large, and hollow inside, and there is a sort of pedestal he stands on, when he is out of doors. He has any amount of gold and silver. Every day, four loaves of bread are brought to him, and meat.' The following day, the idol of Thor is brought out, and everyone bows down before it. Guthbrand proudly points out his terrifying gaze to Olaf – and we may remember that this is one of Thor's attributes in the mythology. In fact, anyone who has read thus far in this book could have produced such a description of an idol of Thor.

As the sun rises, Olaf dramatically gestures towards it, proclaiming the arrival of the Christian deity. As all turn to look, the king's henchman smashes the idol, and from it run fat mice and adders and snakes. Guthbrand's pagan faith is routed, and he is converted. There is a strong similarity between this story and the biblical account of the prophet Daniel and the idol of the Babylonian god Bel: in both, the idol's apparent receiving of food and drink is revealed as a sham (sacrifices to Bel were being eaten and drunk by the priests and their families). Evident too is the influence which such stories have had on later adventure novels and travel books.

A humorous gloss on the supposed abilities of idols is provided by an account in *Njáls saga*. A disreputable Icelander called Hrapp, on the run in Norway, finds in a temple an image of a female deity known as Thorgerd Hölgabrud. Next to her is a statue of the god Thor. Hrapp loots the shrine, dragging out the idols, and then burns down the temple. When the desecration is discovered, Guthbrand, co-owner of the temple, notes admiringly that the pagan gods have saved themselves from the fire. But his companion Earl Hakon, though himself a pagan, is less gullible: 'The gods had nothing to do with it,' he retorts. 'A real person must have set fire to the temple, and carried the gods out.' Nonetheless, his curse on the culprit is pious enough: 'May he never enter Valhalla'.

Runic inscriptions reinforce our conception of Thor as a protective deity: perhaps even a guardian of the dead. For instance, the runic inscription ÞUR VIKI ('may Thor hallow [this]'), carved on a memorial stone, is the simplest possible expression of it. Such inscriptions are often also accompanied by a carving of what is apparently the hammer Mjöllnir. Archaeological artefacts bear out this widespread dependence on the protection of Thor: dozens and dozens of amulets in the form of a hammer have been found in Scandinavian graves, sometimes with a little loop so that they could be worn, and therefore kept close always. In the saga about the Icelandic poet Hallfred, who converted to Christianity, it is said that he carried with him a little image of Thor carved in ivory, and a vivid bronze figurine of Thor has been found in northern Iceland.

Religious text pure and simple is very rare. We have nothing even approaching a stretch of pagan liturgy. There is, though, a quotation from a fragment of a pagan law code from Iceland in which the person giving evidence must make an oath which includes the words 'So help me Frey and Njörd and the all-powerful god [Thor?]' – just like 'So help me God' in a modern court. The classic form of text as worship is the hymn, and this is how the poems about Thor bashing giants have been interpreted: 'you killed this or that giant or giantess'. Such straight-forward praise for violence must have seemed very alien to the Christian missionaries. Yet there is evidence that Thor and Christ might be seen to form a complementary pair. Helgi the Lean was a settler who was brought up in Ireland, and we are told in *Landnámabók* that he was 'very mixed in his faith': he believed in Christ, but called on Thor during sea voyages, or in times of particular peril. He was also one of those who prayed for Thor's guidance in showing him the most propitious place for his new settlement in Iceland. The significance here is the implied comparability: that Christ and Thor are seen as the two representatives of the two rival religions. There's a nice commercial twist to this: a Viking-age mould has been unearthed in Denmark which would allow the craftsman to produce both a Thor's hammer and a Christian cross: depending, one supposes, on demand.

As one might expect from an agrarian community like Iceland – and perhaps particularly so given the vicissitudes of Icelandic farming – there are just as many – and as interesting – references to Frey: the god of sunshine and rain, as Snorri describes him.

There is an unremarkable – and for this reason, perhaps relatively reliable – mention of Frey worship among farmers in *Gisla saga*. A man called Thorgrim decides to hold a feast one autumn 'to welcome winter, and make a sacrifice to Frey'. He invites friends and neighbours, and we are being told this story because preparations for the feast lead to a row about borrowing some valuable tapestries to decorate the hall. This is a straightforward domestic affair. The final outcome is that the hero of the saga, Gisli, kills Thorgrim. A little later in the narrative, it is noted that one side of Thorgrim's burial mound never freezes, and 'people explained that this must be the case because he was especially favoured by the god Frey – because of all the sacrifices he made – and Frey didn't want frost to come between them'. Here we see classic supplication – make sacrifices, your land is productive – with a twist: the god will even look after the grass on your burial mound.

We can find an even more detailed account in the short saga about Hrafnkel: *Hrafnkels saga*. Its hero was a powerful chieftain in the east of Iceland. When he establishes a farmstead, he also has a large temple built, and makes great sacrifices. We are told that he loved no god more than Frey, and that he was called for this reason *Freysgoði* ('Frey's priest–chieftain'). Hrafnkel dedicates a stallion to the god Frey, and swears a solemn oath that he will kill anyone who rides the horse without permission. A shepherd who thinks he won't be found out rides the horse, and Hrafnkel duly kills him. Hrafnkel is such a powerful figure in the locality that he thinks that if he can buy off the shepherd's father with a generous offer of compensation, that will be the end of the matter, but unexpectedly, he is taken to court for the killing, and stripped of his farm and all his assets. The horse Freyfaxi is put to death: those who kill the horse (by driving it over a cliff) are reported as saying that it is fitting that 'the one who owns the horse should have him back' – clearly a reference to a form of sacrifice. Hrafnkel's temple is also burnt to the ground. At this, the (no doubt) Christian author has Hrafnkel see the light: 'It's pure stupidity to believe in gods,' he says, and never sacrifices again.

At this point, it is interesting to look at another account of a sacred horse, also by a Christian author, the Venerable Bede. In his eighth-century *History of the English Church*, he relates the circumstances of the conversion of King Edwin of Northumbria. Having heard the preaching of the Christian missionary Paulinus, Edwin's chief priest Coifi notes wryly that if his gods had had the power he placed in them, he would have got more rewards from the king than he has, since he has devoted his life to serving them. Another counsellor describes the shortcomings of the pagan worldview with an image which has become very celebrated: he compares the life of pagans to the flight of a sparrow through a royal hall in which the king's men are feasting around a great central fire. It is winter, and it is snowing and dark outside. The bird flies in, and for a heartbreakingly brief time it is safe from the storm; but a moment later it flies out of the hall, back into the terrifying and unknowable darkness from which it came. Only Christianity can offer a divine context for human existence.

The high priest Coifi volunteers to be the first to destroy the shrines of pagan idols, and desecrate the holy places. This he does by riding on a stallion – something, Bede tells us, forbidden to pagan priests – and by throwing a spear into them, which we now recognize as Odin's special weapon, though Bede does not tell us this. *Hrafnkels saga* and Bede's *History* are two very different sources, and each is unreliable in its own way, but nevertheless both attest to a connection between pagan worship and sacred horses. We can find more procedural detail in Snorri's biography of King Hakon the Good of Norway.

Hakon was the foster-son of the Anglo-Saxon king Æthelstan, and a Christian. Relations with his pagan subjects were always tricky. On one particular occasion, having failed to persuade them to convert, Hakon is invited to a sacrificial feast they are holding. He causes offence by making the sign of the cross over his drink when the rest of the company are toasting Odin, Thor and Frey. One of his most influential earls (himself an ardent pagan, but a close friend of the king's) covers for him by explaining that Hakon's gesture was rather to make the sign of Thor's hammer. But worse is to come. Horses have been sacrificed for the feast, and their meat boiled in great cauldrons. Hakon refuses to eat the meat, or even the broth in which it has been cooked. The earl suggests a tactful compromise: Hakon will breathe in the steam from the cauldron. Hakon submits to this, but like many compromises, it pleases neither side. The following year, tension between the king and his pagan subjects is even greater, and Hakon reluctantly manages to force down a little bit of horse liver. This only strengthens his resolve to force Christianity on his equally reluctant subjects.

The devotion to pagan gods such as Frey, and to the practices associated with him, like the eating of horsemeat, were evidently widespread in early Scandinavia. In *Íslendingabók* ('The Book of the Icelanders'), a short history of the setting up of the Icelandic state, it is recorded that the eating of horseflesh was one of the two pagan practices that were allowed to continue after the conversion (presumably to ease the transition from paganism to Christianity). The other was the exposure of new-born babies.

There is plenty of place-name evidence for a Frey cult throughout Iceland and Scandinavia, and it is especially significant, given Frey's role as a fertility deity, that fields were often named for Frey. And the pre-Christian chieftain Ingimund in *Vatnsdœla saga* carried around with him a little silver image of Frey. There are also, so far as the distinction can be made, philologically, Freyja place names, although there is no specific mention of cults associated with Freyja. But rituals involving a fertility goddess are described, as we have seen, in Tacitus's *Germania*: he describes how the goddess Nerthus (*id est Terra Mater*, 'that is, Mother Earth') is paraded around – though covered by a cloth – by a priest, and everywhere her chariot stops is blessed with happiness and peace. We can perhaps connect these travelling goddesses with Freyja given what Snorri says about her: that she had many names because she travelled far and wide looking for her husband Odr.

And so we come, finally, to Odin. There is little reference to Odin in family sagas, except for in *Egils saga*: the saga of the celebrated Viking poet Egill Skalla-Grímsson, perhaps written by Snorri himself. Verses, ostensibly by Egill himself, and quoted in the saga prose, testify to a perceived personal relationship between god and poet which is close and reciprocal, though little or nothing is said in verse or prose about any form of religious ritual. How much is this a portrait of a historical character, and how much a literary attempt to model a poet on the god of poetry himself, by an expert on Odin mythology, such as Snorri was?

In *Víga-Glúms saga* ('The Saga of Killer-Glumr'), there is evidence of fierce rivalry between Frey and Odin. The hero of the saga is an unattractive character. In Iceland, Glumr seems to be associated with the god Frey: he has a field called Vitazgjafi ('the certain yielder'). But he kills an enemy on the field – does he therefore desecrate a field dedicated to Frey with spilt blood? Certainly he seems to be out of favour with the god: one of his enemies sacrifices an ox to Frey, and towards the end of the saga, Glumr sees the god in a dream, surrounded by Glumr's dead kinsmen, who warn him that Frey is angry, and remembers the sacrifice. Glumr never quite fits into Icelandic society: he is obsessed by the knowledge that he has ancestral estates in Norway, and goes to Norway to visit his maternal grandfather, who gives him a present of a spear and cloak: these are plainly Odinic objects. He also, famously, speaks an ambiguous oath. He is invited to deny a killing, and swears as follows: '*at ek vark at þar, ok vák at þar*' ('that I was [not] there, and I killed [not] there'). In Old Norse – but especially characteristic of poetry – a negative particle can be suffixed to any verb. Thus in poetry, *vark-at þar* means 'I was not there'. But the preposition *þar*, 'there', can also be preceded by the particle *at*, so that *vark at þar* can equally mean 'I was [at] there'. Glumr is a classically Odinic figure here. But he gives away his totemic spear and cloak, and is eventually driven out of his home. Frey has prevailed.

The question of Odin worship in historical societies remains a conundrum. As Woden, he is as prominent as any pagan deity might be in Anglo-Saxon traditions which rigorously air-brushed mentions of paganism from the record. He is named in a number of royal genealogies as an ancestor, and there are many place names based on his name. Even the day of the week Wednesday – from the Old English *Wodenesdæg* – remembers him (not even in Iceland has this survived: Christian influences have substituted *miðvikudagur*, 'midweek day'). The tenth-century Anglo-Saxon chronicler Æthelweard has this to say about genealogy and worship: 'And above all Vortigern who was then king of all the Britons gave counsel, and the entire aristocracy yielded to him, and they decided to bring help from Germany. Two young men, Hengist and Horsa, had already been paid in advance. They were descendants of Woden, a king of the barbarians. And after his death the pagans, honouring him as a god with respect not fit to be mentioned [!], offer him a sacrifice in order to have victory or be courageous.' There's also an Anglo-Saxon charm, the so-called 'Nine herbs charm': 'A snake came crawling; it killed nothing. For Woden took nine glory twigs; he struck the adder then so that it flew into nine parts.' Is this a charm against snake poison? It has been suggested that glory twigs are runes, and that the nine runes are the initial letters of healing herbs. Nine is, of course, the Odinic number: we may remember *Hávamál*, in which Odin learnt 'nine mighty spells', and in which eighteen charms are enumerated. The Anglo-Saxon Woden seems to have exactly the same job description as Odin: responsibility for war, royalty, magic, perhaps poetry (if a charm is poetry, or at least, powerful discourse).

We certainly wouldn't expect details of religious practice in Anglo-Saxon writings (Bede mentions no pagan god by name, except once, Woden, as an element in a royal genealogy). But such details are not very prominent in Old Norse sources either. Sometimes Odin is mentioned as part of a triumvirate (as in the toast in the story of King Hakon: the pagans drink first 'to Odin for victory and power to the king'). But there's a major contrast with his prominence in the mythology (perhaps because of the poets). There are, for example, no Odin place names in Iceland.

Frey has been associated with animal sacrifice, as we have seen both here and earlier. But of course, Odin is more sensationally associated with human sacrifice, and we have already seen how in *Hávamál*, Odin is weirdly sacrificed to himself, and in *Gautreks saga*, he intervenes in what is intended as a mock sacrifice to make it real. In both accounts, he is both hanged and pierced. This has been seen as a disturbing analogue to Christ's torment on the cross, but is it not rather a distinctively Odinic ritual? The difficulty is, however, that any mention of death at the hands of Scandinavians becomes temptingly likely to be interpreted by medieval commentators as Odinic sacrifice. So was it what the Vikings did to poor King Edmund of East Anglia? His biographer, the tenth-century Anglo-Saxon monk Ælfric, substitutes the way St Sebastian was martyred, as if he could not bring himself to detail an Odinic ritual, but still reports that Edmund was both pierced and tied to a tree. In fact, some scholars have argued that Edmund was subject to an even more horrible fate: that the Vikings 'carved a blood-eagle' on his back. This has been understood as the practice of opening up the ribcage and drawing out the lungs from a dead or dying warrior – in effect, turning the human body into the form of an eagle – in order to dedicate a slaughtered enemy to the god: 'they made you warm wings for your shoulders,' as the poet Seamus Heaney puts it. The authenticity of this practice has been called into question: it may be simply a medieval mis-reading of a typically cryptic poetic allusion to an eagle clawing the back of a dead warrior on the battlefield. But the more shadowy, oblique or obscure the Odinic reference, the more convincing it may be held to be, in view of the Christian practice of suppressing mention of, or forgetting, such rituals.

There are further literary allusions to Odinic sacrifice. Was it what the vicious old Swede Ongentheow threatened to do to the Geats, a neighbouring tribe he was at war with, in the Anglo-Saxon poem *Beowulf* – that 'he in the morning / with the edges of a sword / would destroy / some on the gallowstree / to please the birds of prey'? Or perhaps, in an Old Norse Eddaic poem, it was what the brutal King Ermanaric (mentioned in *Beowulf*) did to his son Randver, whom he suspected (or was led to suspect) had slept with his new young wife, like the story of Tristan and Isolde, and the jealous King Mark: Randver was 'wounded on the gallows, the bait of birds of prey'. All of these accounts maintain the central motif of hanging as well as piercing.

Whether such rituals actually happened, or were just literary motifs, is a difficult question. Two notably detailed accounts of human sacrifice which purport to describe 'what happened' remain to be considered. The first is by Adam of Bremen, an eleventh-century German chronicler who wrote a history of the bishops of Hamburg, which includes an extra-ordinary description of a pagan temple at Uppsala, in Sweden, which was converted to Christianity rather later than the rest of Scandinavia. Adam reports that in the temple, people worship statues of three gods: Thor, Wodan and Fricco (probably Frey). Wodan is said to govern war, and make warriors brave – he is clearly Odin. Every nine years, a great sacrificial festival is held in a sacred grove: both animals and humans are sacrificed, and in great numbers. The Odinic number nine is prominent:

as well as taking place every nine years, the festival itself lasts nine days, and nine male dogs and horses are sacrificed, and their bodies hung from trees. On each of the nine days, a man is also sacrificed. Two other details echo what we already know from the mythology. Firstly, next to the temple there is a great tree, with a well, and sometimes men are sacrificed in the well, so that the people's prayers may be answered. This is strongly reminiscent of what the mythology tells us about the World Tree, Yggdrasill, and especially about Mimir's well beneath the tree, into which Odin placed his eye in exchange for the wisdom it contained. And secondly, Adam provides a tantalizing allusion to the actual forms of pagan worship: he tells us that songs are sung to accompany the sacrifices, and that they are 'manifold and disgraceful, and therefore it is better to be silent about them'. Adam's description may well be accurate, but his Christian purpose must be taken into account: he may have been writing this to impress upon his Christian audience the urgent need to send missionaries to such depraved savages. Some of his details seem to echo biblical sources. And it is clear from his chronicle that he was not an eye-witness to any of it; some was told to him by another Christian, some may be little more than unfounded hearsay.

The second account of human sacrifice is even more sensational. A tenth-century Arab merchant, Ibn Fadlan, describes a lavish ship funeral he witnessed in Russia. At this time, a Swedish tribe known as the Rus (from which the name Russia is derived) were living on the banks of the Volga, and Ibn Fadlan watched their funerary rituals. Much of what Ibn Fadlan recounts concerns the meticulous preparation and dressing of the body for its deposition in a ship, but a shocking aspect of these pre-parations is the selection of one of the dead man's female slaves to be sacrificed, her body to accompany her master's in the ship. She is made to drink intoxicating liquor, and to have sex with the other men, and finally an old woman of the tribe (somewhat histrionically referred to as the Angel of Death) kills her. Her murder takes a familiar form: she is strangled with a rope, and at the same time, repeatedly stabbed with a blade. Then the bodies of her and her master and two horses, together with various treasures and food and drink, are burnt in the ship.

There are several reasons to be sceptical about Ibn Fadlan's account of this Scandinavian ship funeral, not least that although he writes as an eye-witness, much of the explanation of what was happening was filtered to him through an interpreter. But there are many details which echo what we already know of pagan ritual – especially the Odinic murder of the slave girl. And as we shall see in the next chapter, many of the details of the ship funeral are confirmed by archaeology.

It is, as I have said, only to be expected that later, Christian, writers would not recount in detail the actuality of pagan worship. We are left with a patchy and often contradictory record. Tacitus, for example, is clear in his *Germania* that the Germanic tribes worshipped in sacred groves, and records the pagans' proud claim that their gods would not tolerate being confined within four walls. Archaeology, as if to confirm this, can provide no certain remains of pagan temples. And yet family saga authors routinely speak of temples, and the idols within them are vividly described, especially when they are smashed or destroyed. We must always be on the alert for Christian bias – either in sensationalizing the wicked practices of pagans, or in portraying them from the perspective of Christians who automatically thought of churches, and altars, and priests. Nonetheless, there is clear evidence of all the expected forms of religious action: offerings, sacrifice, temples, idols, even hymns of praise, charms, amulets and, perhaps conclusively, a mythology.

If we make direct comparison between this picture of the pagan religion – flawed as it is – and the mythology, the literary representation of the gods, some striking inconsistencies emerge. Thor is the pre-eminent deity in Iceland: there is no sign of familiarity, let alone the ridicule expressed in the literature. Odin is prominent (as far as any pagan deity is) in Anglo-Saxon tradition, but oddly shadowy in Scandinavian sources, apart from the questionable descriptions of Odinic sacrifice. But he is extremely prominent in the mythological literature. Frey worship is very widely attested, in all sorts of forms and contexts, but there are few extended narratives about him or his sister Freyja. And there is no evidence that Loki, who plays such a very large role in the mythology, was ever worshipped at all, anywhere in Europe. In the next chapter, we can make similar comparisons between actual beliefs about death and the afterlife, and the most famous of all Norse myths, the story of Ragnarök, the end of the world and of the gods themselves.

CHAPTER 4

Aferlife and
Apocalypse

I n the absence of contemporary writings by Scandinavian pagans
themselves, the best source of information about their views about
the possibility of an afterlife – and the form it might take – is the
archaeology of funeral practices. But of course archaeology takes a lot of
careful interpreting, and sometimes material remains are just not enough
to provide even the most imaginative scholars with a picture of the
afterworld view underlying them. For instance, in prehistoric Europe, the
major change in funeral rites was the shift from inhumation – burying
the body – to cremation: burning it to ashes. But we have no idea about
the revolution in beliefs about the afterlife which might have caused this
change. Similarly, it is not even always possible to distinguish a pagan
grave from a Christian one in the Viking age, even though the beliefs of
all concerned with the funeral were so very different. And finally, it is
sometimes not always possible even to tell from a burial place what
actually happened to the body: whether the ashes have disappeared, or
the skeleton has dissolved. Nevertheless, it is archaeology which has
given us our most vivid images of how pagans imagined life after death,
especially in the case of the great ship-burials of Norway, Sweden and
Anglo-Saxon England.

Archaeologists have found graves in the shape of ships – the outline
of a boat picked out in large stones to form a frame for a grave – from
the beginning of the Iron Age (about 500 BC) in Scandinavia. But the
remains of burnt and buried ships are found in Scandinavia from about

the seventh century AD – that is, from just before the Viking age – culminating in the magnificent finds such as the ships from Gokstad and Oseberg in Norway, which contained bodies, and treasure. These ships were preserved by the clay in which they were buried. In Anglo-Saxon England, the most famous ship-burial was excavated at Sutton Hoo, in East Anglia. The ship itself had decayed away, leaving a perfectly clear impression in the earth of its timbers and rivets. It was full of treasure, and evidently a royal burial. But there was no trace of a body (although the soil is acidic, and it may have dissolved). At Sutton Hoo, there is evidence not only of ship-burial, but also of human sacrifice; the remains of hanged men naturally recall what we know from elsewhere of Odinic sacrifice. Sutton Hoo was a royal burial place, and such sacrifice would match what we know about Odin worship and its apparent links with the aristocracy. The excavation has suggested to archaeologists an almost fanatical paganism which had strong links with Sweden, where, as we have seen, place-name evidence of Odin worship is strongest, and the whole cemetery complex at Sutton Hoo matches in many respects what Adam of Bremen wrote about the pagan sacrifices at Uppsala. But a word of caution is needed: some of the remains of hanged men are not from the pagan period, but date from much later, when Anglo-Saxon England had been Christian for centuries. These are perhaps the remains of criminals who had been publicly executed. One might legitimately ask, though, what precisely was – and indeed is – the distinction between death by sacrifice, to appease the gods, and public execution?

Were the dead in ship-burials imagined as making a journey in the boat? Or was it rather just that the boat makes an appropriate sarcophagus for a Viking-age ruler who, as we know from Icelandic praise poetry, was likely to have been celebrated as the victorious leader of a fleet? There is an interesting reference to a ship-burial in an Icelandic family saga – *Gisla saga* – in which a man called Thorgrim is buried in a boat, and a mound is raised over the boat *eptir fornum sið* ('according to the old custom'). Does this brief aside betray a bit of fake antiquarianism, as if the thirteenth-century saga author knew about royal funerals in Scandinavia and Anglo-Saxon England, and wanted to show his Icelandic ancestors getting the same treatment? Interestingly, a boulder is put in the boat, to anchor it down, and the great Oseberg ship in Norway was also anchored with a stone – as if the ship-sarcophagus would otherwise sail off into the otherworld.

69

Thorgrim had been killed in revenge for a killing he himself committed, and when that victim was buried, the saga author has Thorgrim say, 'It is a custom to tie Hel-shoes onto someone so that they can be used to walk to Valhalla'. Again, the over-explicit aside 'it is a custom' betrays a degree of artificiality – if this really were a custom, Thorgrim would hardly need to explain it to his friends and neighbours. But it raises the important issue of whether the dead were imagined as living, in some sense, beyond the grave, and needing practical grave goods to be buried with them. The remains of foodstuffs are very often found in Viking-age graves, for instance. But the archaeology has to be very precisely interpreted: are animal bones evidence that food has been provided for the journey to the otherworld, or are they part of a sacrifice, or a pet even, like the sad, arthritic old dogs sometimes found in Anglo-Saxon graves? Horses – or parts of them – are also commonly found in graves; were they the proper accoutrements of royal princes, sacrifices, a means of transport for the final journey, or just food?

Literary accounts of ship funerals show the journey to the otherworld dramatically enacted: the funeral ship is sent out to sea, burning. Perhaps the most celebrated example is the ship of the Danish king Scyld Scefing in the Anglo-Saxon poem *Beowulf*. There is a remarkably similar Norse account in Snorri's *Ynglinga saga*:

> King Haki was so badly wounded that he realised that his life was almost at an end. So he had a warship loaded with dead warriors and weapons, and had it launched out to sea … and a funeral pyre built on the ship, and set alight. The wind blew from the land. Haki was by then nearly dead, or actually dead, and he was laid on the pyre. Then the ship sailed out to sea, burning, and this was celebrated for a long time after.

Scyld Scefing is also said to organize his own ship funeral. Of course, literary references are all we have to rely on here, since such a funeral could leave no trace for archaeologists to find!

Turning then to literary evidence, we find that the mythology of death, like its archaeology, is also high status, whether it concerns gods or princes. The dominant image is of course Valhalla, the hall of the slain, a place of endless feasting and perhaps (according to one source) fighting. Most of the information about Valhalla comes from the mythological poems we have already looked at: *Vafþrúðnismál*, and *Grímnismál*. They portray a magnificent hall, with many doors, with spear shafts as rafters and roofed with golden shields. According to the High One, the chief speaker in Snorri's *Gylfaginning*, all of the warriors who have fallen in battle in the whole history of time are gathered in Valhalla. Valhalla can cater for a potentially infinite number of such warriors, because they feed on the meat of a boar called Sæhrimnir which reconstitutes itself every evening. And these warriors do not drink water – the High One acidly points out that they will have got a very bad return for an agonizing death in battle if they only get water to drink. Instead, they have an endless supply of mead from the udder of a goat called Heidrun. Wine, though, is both meat and drink to Odin; he gives the food on his plate to his two wolves, Geri and Freki. His two ravens, Hugin and Munin (Thought and Memory), fly out every morning to gather news, and perch on his shoulders at evening, whispering into his ears. Valhalla even has its own version of the World Tree Yggdrasill, which provides leaves for the goat to graze on.

Food and drink are served by Odin's valkyries. The word 'valkyrie' means 'chooser of the slain'. These handmaidens of Odin are very variously portrayed in poetic sources: sometimes they are bloodthirsty women riding horses, delighting in slaughter, the battlefield their natural environment. But in *Hákonarmál*, a tenth-century memorial poem for the Norwegian king Hakon the Good, who had such trouble with the sacrificial horsemeat, we have a very different picture. Hakon died fighting Eirik Bloodaxe, a pagan who later became the fierce ruler of the Kingdom of York. *Hákonarmál* is a dignified, sad poem, and shows Hakon being delivered up to Odin after his last battle. The poem's opening sums up, succinctly and quite explicitly, the role of Valhalla in the aristocratic afterlife:

> Göndul and Skögul
> were sent by Odin
> to choose which of the kings,
> which of the line of Yngvi
> was to go with Odin
> and live in Valhalla.

These grave valkyries come to Hakon on horseback, elegantly leaning on spears, and very graciously announce that Hakon has been summoned 'home' by the gods. This is the paradox at the heart of Valhalla mentioned earlier: if Odin chooses the finest warriors, then they cannot be the defeated side. But this poet neatly gets around this: Hakon has won victory, say the valkyries, but has been killed nevertheless. The valkyries make preparations for Hakon to be given a hero's welcome, but he is nervous – as a Christian might naturally be. The valkyries reassure him: the *einherjar*, Odin's company of dead warriors, will not be hostile; he can accept the ale of the Æsir without worry. But Hakon nevertheless keeps hold of his weapons and armour. The poet concludes with a paean of praise for Hakon, the Christian king who nevertheless respected the pagan temples and their gods. The wolf Fenrir will break its fetters, he says, before a king as good as Hakon will be seen. This is a reference to the chaotic events of Ragnarök, the final apocalypse. And as we shall see, when Ragnarök comes, there will be no Valhalla any more, and no Odin.

Does this poem reflect a general belief in an aristocratic afterlife for warriors, or is it rather an elegant literary construct, a way to flatter the memory of a king whose religious affiliations were awkward for his successors, the pagan earls of Hladir, by imagining his reception by Odin? Perhaps his grieving subjects really did believe in Valhalla: after all, Hakon, we are told by the historians, was buried as a pagan, and 'they spoke over his grave according to the custom of heathen people, and in this way he was directed to Valhalla'. But this is all still high-status afterlife. What about the non-warriors? How was an afterlife for ordinary people imagined?

In the mythological cosmos, as we saw in the chapter about creation and cosmos, there is an otherworld, or underworld, which is imagined as a place beneath the earth: Niflheim, or the dark realms of Hel. But the conception is confused, even within Snorri's work. Hel is on the one hand a place for wicked people – clearly a sort of Hell. But on the other hand, Hel is the name of a goddess who rules over Niflheim, 'and those who die of sickness or old age go to her', according to Snorri. And then there's a relatively elaborate picture of Hel as a hall in an otherworld for the gods, reached by a perilous journey of nine nights through deep dark valleys, and then across the river Gjöll over the Gjallar Bridge, which is guarded by a strange female creature called Modgud. Even then, the hall is protected by great gates.

In family sagas, to which we might turn to look for more naturalistic accounts of religious practice, there is a completely different picture of non-aristocratic afterlives. Insofar as an afterlife is envisaged at all, it seems to involve the dead living on in their burial mounds – like Gunnar, in *Njáls saga*, who is seen by his son looking radiantly joyful, sitting up in his burial mound, surrounded by light. This image is picked up by Seamus Heaney in 'Funeral Rites', from his collection *North*, in which the vision of Gunnar in his mound is (ironically) used as an image of the possibility that the dead – even those dead by violence – are at peace. But (as Seamus Heaney certainly knew very well) Gunnar is exultant because he knows he's going to be avenged. Linked to these visions of the dead living on within their mounds are the many stories in Old Norse sagas, especially the legendary sagas, about more malevolent mound dwellers – as, for instance, in *Grettis saga*, in which the hero Grettir descends into a mound to get treasure, and finds down there the occupant of the mound, sitting in a chair. Grettir fights with him, and manages to cut off his head.

The idea of the dead coming back to haunt the living is also prevalent in the family sagas, although the dead here are not wraithlike phantoms, but big, strong, physically threatening creatures – *draugar* – like the dead shepherd Glamr, whom Grettir also fights, in an episode which is a celebrated analogue to the monster fights in *Beowulf*. There are two ways of silencing the unquiet dead: burning, or decapitation. But are we talking here about genuine and coherent religious beliefs about the afterlife, or about folk beliefs, superstitions? Did the *draugar* fit into a pagan view of the afterlife any more neatly than a Christian's belief in ghosts? Indeed, contemporary Christian conceptions of the afterlife are notably uncertain. The Roman Catholic doctrine of purgatory was a medieval invention, and in this twenty-first century, the Church is about to abandon the idea of the *limbus infantium* – limbo for infants who have died unbaptized. Popular, rather than orthodox, conceptions are even more various. Who has not heard of St Peter's 'pearly gates'? And different Christian sects have very different visions of the day of judgement. We must be careful, by the same token, not to assume that Germanic paganism was a single, homogeneous belief structure. Bede's account of the conversion of King Edwin vividly attributed to Anglo-Saxon pagans a gaping ignorance of any context for human life, before or after: was this simply Christian propaganda, designed to expose the weaknesses of pagan belief, or does it reflect actuality as Bede knew it, or at least understood it, to be?

For all these reasons, it is extremely difficult to be sure how actual pagans viewed an afterlife, and how that might relate to the very various literary representations of it, or the archaeological evidence. By contrast, literary representations of the end of the world – Ragnarök – are vivid and clear.

The most striking aspect of the treatment of death and the afterlife in Norse mythology is that the gods themselves are doomed to die. Accounts of Old Norse mythology, both in the poem *Völuspá* and in Snorri's prose work *Gylfaginning*, climax in a final, cataclysmic battle between gods and giants, a battle which proves fatal for both sides. And in both sources, this Nordic Armageddon is presaged by a single, tragic event: the premature death of the most beautiful and beloved of the gods, Odin's son Baldr.

THE DEATH OF BALDR

Baldr is first introduced by Snorri in *Gylfaginning* as the best of all gods: the most beautiful (so radiant that he glows) and the wisest. He is also the most merciful (perhaps a trace of Christian influence here) and, somewhat unexpectedly, he has the most beautiful speech. But none of the decisions he makes is ever effective. It is perhaps in keeping with this serene passivity that the only narrative we have about him is the story of his death.

Snorri's story – framed as a dialogue between the High One and Gangleri – begins when Baldr has bad dreams about his impending death. The Æsir set about devising a plan to ensure protection for him: his mother Frigg exacts oaths from all things (fire and water, iron and all other metals, stones, the earth, trees, illnesses, animals, birds, poisons and snakes) that nothing will harm him. The other Æsir then amuse themselves by throwing things at Baldr, and the evil spirit Loki determines to find out why, annoyingly, nothing hurts him. In the guise of a woman, Loki goes to visit Frigg, who asks for news of the Æsir (clearly the assembly is an all-male gathering; the goddesses have stayed at home). Loki tells her about the way Baldr is being used as target practice, and Frigg explains the oath she has exacted from everything – except, as she confides to Loki, the mistletoe, a plant she thought too young to bother getting a promise from. This is crucial information for Loki. He at once goes to find himself some mistletoe, and returns to where the Æsir are throwing things – all of the Æsir except one, the blind god, Hödr. Loki urges him to join in, offering the mistletoe as a weapon, and to guide his unseeing aim. Hödr shoots, and Baldr is killed. The gods are devastated, so paralysed by their grief that they can neither speak nor even pick Baldr up. Odin, we are told, is the most distressed, because he sees most clearly what a terrible loss the death of Baldr will be to the gods.

The essence of this story is alluded to in the poem *Völuspá*, in which we hear how mistletoe formed the fatal missile which killed Baldr, and how its shooter was Hödr. But we also hear there that Baldr – Odin's child – was destined to be a sacrifice. And there is no mention of Hödr or Loki, of Frigg's exclusion oath or the target practice. It is tempting to infer that Baldr was indeed sacrificed, by Odin, in the hope or expectation of his resurrection, symbolized by the mistletoe, a sacred plant in both Germanic and Celtic mythology. We might recall the account of Starkad's mock sacrifice of Vikar, in which a hopelessly ineffective weapon – a floppy reed, almost as unpromising a missile as the mistletoe, which has no proper stem because it winds itself around the trunks of other trees – is unexpectedly transformed into a lethal one. Snorri makes no mention of sacrifice (which leaves his gods playing a childish game of target practice), perhaps because he did not know the story – though he had certainly read a version of *Völuspá* – or perhaps because it was too disturbing an analogue to Christianity for him. It may even be the case that Snorri recognized in earlier versions of the story, such as *Völuspá*, a myth which had been radically influenced by a Christian motif, and was not authentic. It has also been noticed that the aspects of the story in Snorri which do not echo what is said in *Völuspá* – the blind man firing a fatal shot, the exclusion oath, the target practice – have striking analogues in, for instance, early commentaries on the Bible (derived from ancient Jewish scholarship), or saints' lives, which by Snorri's time had become standard Christian works of reference. The surprising conclusion to be drawn from all this, then, is that the pivotal event in Old Norse myth may be a strange amalgam of pagan, Christian and even Jewish traditions.

Once the Æsir recover some semblance of composure, they decide to send one of their number, Hermod, on the road to Hel, to try to bring Baldr back. Meanwhile, they organize Baldr's funeral: he is to be laid in a ship which will be set alight and pushed out to sea. Many details echo what other literary sources tell us about ship funerals: we are even told that his wife Nanna joins him on the pyre, though Snorri tactfully says that she died first of a broken heart, and was only then cremated with him. But many of the details are quite bizarre, and surprisingly undignified. The funeral ship sticks on its rollers, and cannot be launched, so the gods send to Giantland for a powerful giantess to give it a push; she launches the boat with such force that sparks fly from its keel, and Thor has to be restrained from striking her with his hammer. Thor kicks a dwarf called Litr into the funeral pyre. And as well as Baldr's Æsir family (Odin with his ravens and valkyries, Frigg, Frey with his boar-drawn chariot, Freyja with her cats, and even Heimdall, of whom we shall hear more at Ragnarök), more distant relatives come to the funeral: all the frost-giants and mountain giants. It seems likely that for some of these details Snorri was drawing on poems which have been lost to us.

Once in Hel, Hermod finds Baldr in a seat of honour in a fine hall, though as we have seen, his earthly body has gone up in flames already. The goddess Hel makes a bargain with Hermod: if all things in the world will weep for Baldr's death, then she will release him. After a polite exchange of gifts (Baldr's ring Draupnir, burnt with him on the funeral pyre, to be sent back to Odin; a nice linen dress from his wife Nanna to her mother-in-law Frigg) Hermod rides back to Asgard to report the news. The Æsir at once set about encouraging everything to weep. Snorri makes clear the mythic significance of this: 'everything wept just as anybody can see things weep when they move from freezing temperatures to warmth'. Baldr symbolizes the spring, the thaw, new life after the sterility of winter. But an old giantess in a cave refuses to weep. People suppose that she is Loki in disguise. And so Baldr remains in, or with, Hel.

The gods take vengeance on Loki, of course. He flees, and then periodically turns himself into the form of a salmon, so that he may evade capture by plunging into a river. This series of events becomes the context for a series of stories about how certain things came into being – like Rudyard Kipling's *Just So Stories*. The gods track him down, and Thor catches tight hold of the Loki-salmon, which explains 'why the salmon's body tapers towards its tail'. Most mystifyingly, Loki sits in his house and ponders how the gods might devise a contraption for catching a salmon. He invents the first net, but when he sees the gods approaching, he tosses his invention in the fire. However, it leaves its imprint in the fire's ashes, and the gods recreate the net, and eventually catch Loki with it. Finally, they bind Loki to three flat stones, using the intestines of one of the wolfish sons of Loki himself as the fetters, and fix a poisonous snake above him to drip poison on his face. Loki's loyal wife Sigyn collects the drips in a bowl, but when she turns away, some drips catch his face, and he struggles against his bonds. This, Snorri has the High

One explain, is what causes what we call an earthquake. But the High One's final piece of information is more significant. Loki, we are told, will lie bound like this until Ragnarök. At once Gangleri, to whom this story is being told, pricks up his ears: he hasn't heard of Ragnarök. What does it mean? In this way, almost incidentally, Snorri begins his account of the doom of the gods.

RAGNARÖK

According to the High One, the coming of Ragnarök will be presaged by a monstrous winter, *fimbulvetr*, three times the length of a normal winter with no intervening summers. It will be ferociously cold and snowy, and the sun will have no force at all. This savage weather will be matched by moral chaos: Snorri quotes at this point a stanza from the poem *Völuspá* which sums this up:

Brothers will fight
And kill each other,
sisters' children
will defile kinship.
It is harsh in the world,
whoredom rife
– an axe age, a sword age
– shields are riven –
a wind age, a wolf age –
before the world goes headlong.
No man will have
mercy on another.

This familiar apocalyptic imagery is overtaken by bizarre spectacles: wolves will swallow the sun and the moon; the stars will disappear from the sky. A great earthquake – Loki's final convulsion? – will shake the earth, trees will be uprooted and mountains will collapse. In sum, all fetters will break apart: moral, social and topographical certainties are thrown into confusion. It is significant to note at this point that the gods are referred to in Old Norse sources by words which mean fetters or bonds: divinity itself used to hold things together. As the poet W.B. Yeats – conceivably influenced by this account – put it:

> Things fall apart; the centre cannot hold;
> Mere anarchy is loosed upon the world...

The giants and monsters, which the gods have striven to control, now break loose: it is time for the wolf Fenrir to free himself, and he strides forward, his jaws gaping from heaven to earth, flames burning from his eyes and nostrils. The World Serpent slithers up on to the land, thrashing around in mounting fury, spouting poison everywhere. The giant Hrym steers the ship Naglfar. The sky splits apart, and the sons of Muspell advance, among them the fire-giant Surtr, surrounded by flame. They all ride over Bifröst, the quivering bridge – perhaps the rainbow which links Asgard and Midgard. But it shatters under their weight. On the field called Vigrid, the enemies of the gods prepare for a pitched battle.

Back in Asgard, the gods respond. As *Völuspá* has it,

> Loud blows Heimdall
> – the horn points to the sky –
> Odin talks
> with Mimir's head.
> Yggdrasill shivers,
> the ash as it stands.
> The old tree groans,
> and the giant slips free.

Heimdall, who has remained a shadowy and mysterious figure in the extant mythology, plays an important role here: he is the watchman of the gods, and like the angel Gabriel, summons the gods with his trumpet.

The final battle is described in terms of individual combats. Odin takes on the wolf Fenrir; Thor fights the World Serpent; and Heimdall takes on Loki. The god Tyr pits himself against the monstrous dog Garmr, who was until now chained up, perhaps by Hel's gates. Tyr is another god who is little mentioned in the myths, but he was clearly of great importance: he has not only given his name to Tuesday, but also the rune T, which is frequently found inscribed on weapons. Tyr has a long history with the wolf Fenrir, for of all the gods, only Tyr was brave enough to feed him. The gods twice attempted to chain this creature, as he grew bigger and bigger, and more and more terrifying, and at length commissioned from the dwarves a magic fetter made from the most intangible things imaginable: the sound of cat's footstep, the beard of a woman, the roots of a mountain, the sinews of a bear, the breath of a fish and the spit of a bird. But this fetter proves to be unexpectedly strong, and the wolf is suspicious of it. He tells the gods that he will suffer it to be put on him, but only if, as a gesture of good faith, one of them places a hand between his jaws. Tyr complies, the magic fetter successfully binds Fenrir, and Tyr loses his hand. Now, at Ragnarök, Fenrir is, like all other hostile forces, unbound. The gods and their enemies do battle, and both sides in each encounter are killed. Finally, the fire-giant Surtr burns up the whole world; according to *Völuspá*:

> The sun starts to blacken,
> land sinks into the sea,
> the radiant stars
> recoil from the sky.
> Fume rages against fire,
> fosterer of life,
> the heat soars high
> against heaven itself.

It seems likely that the idea of Ragnarök was a familiar one, and not just a dramatic literary motif. Snorri several times mentions certain folk beliefs that involve the idea of Ragnarök as something very far distant in time, but gradually nearing. So, for instance, he notes that the ship Naglfar is made from the parings of corpses' nails, and will thus be a long time building; humans can put that eventuality off still further if they take care to trim the nails of their dead, and so deprive the otherworld forces of them. Similarly, when the wolf Fenrir devours Odin, the god's son Vidar will destroy the wolf by ripping its jaws apart. To do this, he must place one foot on the wolf's lower jaw, and so he will need a strong shoe. Mankind can help with the provision of this shoe: it will be made out of the little bits of leather which people can helpfully cut away when they shape heels and toes.

Ragnarök, then, is the end of heaven and earth and the whole world, of the gods and the *einherjar* and all mankind. The cataclysm is complete. But like a medieval Christian, Gangleri is not satisfied: what happens next?

Snorri continues his account with a description of realms of torment which are strongly reminiscent of Christian otherworld visions such as the Italian medieval poet Dante described in his *Inferno*. There are good places, but also horrifying ones – especially 'corpse beaches', where a hall made out of poisonous snakes stands, or the dreadful Hvergelmir, where a creature called Nidhögg ('Malice-Striker') sucks the corpses of dead men. But it is significant that the references to these places of torment come much earlier on in the poem *Völuspá*; it is Snorri who places them after Ragnarök as if they are a vision of an afterlife. The sibyl in the poem itself moves suddenly on to an idyllic vision which resembles nothing so much as the new heaven and earth of the biblical Book of Revelation:

> She sees come up
> a second time
> earth out of ocean
> once again green.
> The waterfalls flow,
> an eagle flies over,
> in the hills
> hunting fish.

> Æsir meet
> on Edying Plain
> and discourse on the mighty
> enmesher of earth,
> and call to mind there
> the momentous judgements
> and the Gigantine God's
> ancient runes.

> There will once more
> the miraculous
> golden chequers
> be found, in the grass,
> those that in the old days
> they had owned.

> Without sowing
> cornfields will grow –
> all harm will be healed,
> Baldr will come.

One manuscript – a later one – includes a stanza which introduces a discordant element into this moving aftermath. It announces that a powerful one will come at the time of great judgement, a strong one from above, one who governs all things. This stanza has been interpreted by Norse scholars as being a straightforwardly Christian reference to doomsday, inserted by a later writer, and not at all in keeping with the drift of the poem's narrative, since the conflagration which equates to doomsday has already taken place. How ironic, then, that it was this stanza which was to be taken as an ancient Germanic prophecy of the coming of a messianic dictator, and that a German translation of one line, the *Starke von Oben* ('strong one from above'), became a key phrase in Nazi ideology.

PART TWO

THE RECEPTION
OF NORSE MYTH

CHAPTER 5

The Viking Legacy

T he story of how Old Norse myth came to have such a major impact on Western culture – an impact which continues to the present day – falls into two distinct parts. The first, smaller, part concerns the direct influence of Scandinavians and their traditions on the culture, art and literature of the earliest period of English history, when, somewhat contrary to popular belief, Anglo-Saxons and Scandinavians not only lived side by side, but also intermarried, so that in due course a new and distinct Anglo-Scandinavian culture developed. The precise nature of Scandinavian influence is rather hard to determine, though, because ultimately the Anglo-Saxons and the Norse already shared, at least to some degree, a common language, and perhaps a common world-view – or even mythology. But whether similarities are due to this common heritage, as Germanic peoples, or whether they arose because of the new waves of Scandinavian immigration into what had been Anglo-Saxon England, there are recognizably Norse elements to be found in early English literature – especially the Anglo-Saxon poem *Beowulf* – and we can trace this influence – dwindling and faint though it may be – even as far as the works of Shakespeare. However, it was not until the dramatic rediscovery of Norse literature in the seventeenth century, a discovery which quickly swept throughout Western Europe, that we can see again the impression of Old Norse mythology on European culture.

The Vikings have come down to us in popular history as savage alien raiders, wreaking havoc on Western Europe in general, and the British Isles in particular, notorious for sudden murderous attacks on a peaceful population. According to the *Anglo-Saxon Chronicle* – actually several series of monastic annals recording the most notable events to happen each year – Scandinavians raiders first came to England in the year 789 AD. In the words of the chronicler, in this year, near Dorchester in Dorset, 'there came for the first time three ships of Northmen from Hordaland; and the reeve rode there, and wanted to make them go to the king's town because he did not know who they were; and then they killed him. And these were the first ships of the Danish men which sought out the land of the English.' The chronicler, like his colleagues who composed the very many other entries in this vast compilation, is evidently uncertain about the identity of these 'Northmen', for Hordaland is in western Norway, though he confidently calls them Danes. But the unfortunate official – the king's reeve – was left in no doubt as to whether his visitors were merchants or raiders.

The most notorious Viking raid was the so-called 'sack of Lindisfarne' – Vikings attacked the monastery on Lindisfarne, an island on the northeast coast of England, in the year 793, and caused great destruction and terror there. The Anglo-Saxon scholar Alcuin, who was at the time based at the court of the Emperor Charlemagne in France, sent back to England a letter of sympathy about the raid to the king of Northumbria, a letter which set the tone for the reporting of Viking raids by Christian clerics:

> Lo, it is nearly 350 years that we and our fathers have inhabited this most lovely land, and never before has such terror appeared in Britain as we have now suffered from a pagan race, nor was it thought that such an inroad from the sea could be made. Behold the church of St Cuthbert spattered with the blood of the priests of God, despoiled of all its ornaments: a place more venerable than all in Britain is given as a prey to pagan peoples...

Christian clerics understandably penned the fiercest denunciations of the Scandinavian invaders: they were, in their richly stocked but often isolated monasteries, prime targets for the raiders. Alcuin's letter, with its vivid expression not only of outrage, but also of shock and surprise, is often quoted by historians. Less often quoted, though, is the rest of the letter. Alcuin invites King Ethelred to examine whether or not his subjects have in some way brought this terrible tribulation upon themselves. Have they been behaving badly in the usual old ways: 'fornications, adulteries... incest'? Or has the punishment perhaps fitted very particularly the crime?

'Consider,' writes Alcuin, 'the dress, the way of wearing the hair, the luxurious habits of the princes and people. Look at your trimming of beard and hair, in which you have wished to resemble the pagans. Are you not menaced by terror of them whose fashion you wished to follow?' The Anglo-Saxons may well have been taken aback by the ferocity of the raids, but Scandinavians were plainly neither new nor – at least in terms of style – undesirable aliens. The reeve at Dorchester, for instance, took the men from Hordaland to be merchants. And in fact, there is some archaeological evidence to suggest that Scandinavians had been happily settled for some time in the north of the British Isles. But what has passed into the historical record are accounts of these first violent, sporadic and destructive incursions.

What stands out from all the clerical accounts is that the Vikings were above all else pagans, and this is true not only of Anglo-Saxon records, but of those written by Irish or Frankish monks – indeed, those written by any of the Vikings' victims. What does this tell us about how much was known of their beliefs? Did the invaders perhaps invoke Odin, the god of war, in their attacks? Or even sacrifice their victims? In 869 we have an event which rapidly achieved almost mythic status in English Christian folklore: the horrible martyrdom of King Edmund of East Anglia by the appalling Ivar the Boneless, who according to some traditions brought a great Viking army to England in pursuit of revenge for the killing of his father, the semi-legendary Ragnar Lothbrok, executed by the king of Northumbria. The description of how the Vikings killed Edmund is bloodthirsty even by the gory standards of martyrdoms in saints' lives, 'his ribs laid bare by numberless gashes, as if he had…been torn by savage claws'. Could this be a reference to the notorious 'blood-eagle' rite, a form of sacrifice to Odin so gruesome that many modern scholars have felt unable to accept the possibility that the Vikings practised it, and have argued that it was the result of a medieval misunderstanding of earlier texts?

Whether or not the Anglo-Saxons could have learnt anything of Scandinavian beliefs from the brief and bloody encounters they had with these early raiding parties, there is no doubt that the relatively peaceful co-existence of English and Norse following the extensive settlement of Scandinavians in the British Isles from the ninth century onward could naturally have led to the exchange of ideas, beliefs and stories: the basis of mythology. And there is plenty of evidence that pagan themes were highly influential in Anglo-Scandinavian England: as we shall see shortly, Viking-age sculpture, even of Christian subject matter, uses pagan imagery, as do coins from the Viking kingdom of York, something unparalleled elsewhere in Europe. And although it seems that the Scandinavians in England – like the Norse who settled in Normandy – soon took to the language and faith of their new homeland, it is worth remembering that in Scandinavia itself there was longer resistance to conversion to Christianity than anywhere else in Europe. The Vikings' gods, or at least the stories about them, were very powerful.

There has been much debate about the actual extent of the Scandinavian settlement in England: essentially, whether smallish but powerful groups of invaders dominated large parts of northern and eastern England, or whether great waves of immigrants simply poured into the area. What is not in doubt is that much of England – from Yorkshire as far south as Kent, and westwards to include Derby, Leicester and Buckingham – operated according to Scandinavian legal custom, and was not under the control of the English crown. This area was known as the Danelaw, and as its name suggests, far from being a wasteland of anarchy and pagan savagery, it was run according to the impressively civilized tenets of Scandinavian legal institutions – including, for instance, the twelve-man jury system which still forms the basis of present-day British and American justice. The English language – as yet the language of the Anglo-Saxons – was flooded with Scandinavian loanwords, and indeed some linguists have argued that the influence of Norse speakers created a new language altogether, an Anglo-Scandinavian creole. The Norse inclined towards urban life, and, as was even more evident from their settlements in Ireland, founded and expanded the trading and manufacturing centres which developed into the towns and cities of present-day Britain and Ireland: York, Lincoln, Peterborough, Cambridge, London; Wexford, Waterford, Dublin and Cork. All in all, the influence of these settlers has been summed up as a 'thorough enrichment' of the Anglo-Saxon community. We must now turn to the specific issue of whether their pagan mythology was an element in this enrichment.

One matter which remains to be resolved – or at least taken into account – is the degree to which Anglo-Saxon culture already resembled its Scandinavian counterpart. The Anglo-Saxons and the Norse were both Germanic peoples – that is, both had their origins in continental Europe, and spoke different, but related, versions of a language derived from a common ancestral language, early Germanic. Recent attempts to chart the genetic heritage of Viking invaders in the present-day population of Britain have foundered precisely because it is not possible to tell apart the genetic profiles of the descendants of Anglo-Saxon and Viking populations. The situation is similar with regard to language. Many common English words – for instance, 'husband', 'window', 'sister', or verbs such as 'to take', or even the pronouns 'they', 'them' and 'their', the very core of the English language – were borrowed from Old Norse (and one should not forget the word 'law' itself). But it is not always easy, or even possible, to distinguish Norse borrowings from similar words which already existed in Anglo-Saxon, because of the similarities in the two languages. For example, whether the word 'call' in English derives from the Anglo-Saxon verb 'ceallian' or from the Norse 'kalla' is unresolved. The word 'die' in English has been identified as a Norse loanword (from the verb *deyja*) because no-one has found an example of an Anglo-Saxon verb similar in form to 'die' – but this may be more because there are so many euphemisms and poeticisms for dying in Anglo-Saxon literature that the bare verb 'to die' has simply not been recorded.

I have dealt in some detail with the linguistic and genetic similarities between the Anglo-Saxons and the Norse because they mirror the situation with regard to mythology and religion. The very first Anglo-Saxons in England were pagans, but only a century or so later, from the time of the first Christian mission to Kent, in 597, they began, at various times in the several Anglo-Saxons kingdoms, and with many false starts, to turn towards Christianity, and away from the gods of their ancestors. As we have seen, in due course Anglo-Saxon monks wrote up a history of the period which proved, naturally, so hostile to the Scandinavian invaders. By the same token, with their clerical monopoly on books and literacy, very little account of Anglo-Saxon paganism has survived. As Sir Frank Stenton, the celebrated Anglo-Saxon historian, has wearily pointed out, 'the heathen background of Old English history is impenetrably vague'. There are some tantalizing hints. Anglo-Saxon kings traced their genealogies back to Woden, whose name identifies him as the Anglo-Saxon counterpart of Odin, and both the middle day of the week – Wednesday – and a considerable number of English place names are named after him: he must have been as important to the Anglo-Saxons as Odin was to the Norse. But how similar was this divinity to the figure we know so well from Norse traditions? Other days of the week also owe their names to gods we recognize from the Norse pantheon: Tyr and Tuesday, Frigg and Friday. But we know little else. The upshot of all this is that apparent echoes of Norse myth in Anglo-Saxon writings are tricky to source. Are they survivals of the pre-Christian traditions of the earliest Anglo-Saxons, rubbed smooth enough to have escaped the highly effective censor of Anglo-Saxon Christianity? Or are they freshly borrowed ideas from the new immigrant population of the Danelaw? At this point we must turn to *Beowulf*, the greatest of all the poems of the Anglo-Saxons, a celebration of the deeds and noble values of the hero Beowulf, who fought against terrifying monsters, and was victorious until his last encounter with a mighty fire-breathing dragon.

Although *Beowulf* is an Anglo-Saxon poem, no-one knows where or when in Anglo-Saxon England it was written. The poem survives in a manuscript which can be dated to the very beginning of the eleventh century – that is, fifty years or so before the Norman Conquest, an event which is usually taken to mark the end of the Anglo-Saxon period. It may have been composed much earlier – almost as early as the beginnings of Anglo-Saxon England itself. But it is set in sixth-century Scandinavia, none of its characters is Anglo-Saxon, and none of its action takes place in the British Isles. In fact, its very first editor, an Icelander called Thorkelin, judged it to be not an Anglo-Saxon poem at all, but a Danish work which had been translated into Old English. It tells the story of a young Swedish hero, Beowulf, who hears of the terrible trials suffered by Hrothgar, the elderly ruler of the Danish kingdom. Hrothgar's hall, Heorot, is being ravaged by a monster: 'Grendel was the name / of this grim demon / haunting the marches / marauding round the heath / and the desolate fens.' The monster's origin is a chilling one: he is one of 'the banished monsters / Cain's clan / whom the creator had outlawed / and condemned as outcasts'. Beowulf successfully rids Heorot of Grendel, and even takes on Grendel's vengeful mother, earning Hrothgar's gratitude and respect. He returns to his own people, the Geats, in southern Sweden, and is welcomed home in triumph. Eventually he becomes king, but towards the end of his life, his own kingdom comes under threat from the dragon. Beowulf overcomes this mighty foe, but dies in the process. The poem ends with the laments of his people, and their dread at what the future holds in store for a small and now leaderless nation.

Beowulf is about more than just monsters. It is a heroic poem – that is, it celebrates warlike deeds and virtues such as courage, loyalty and the desire for fame. But it also raises wider and more humane issues: what it means to live in a world dominated by political instability and conflict; what the role of a leader should be; how to live with the knowledge that even the greatest glory passes into history, to become little more than the half-remembered subject matter of a poem like *Beowulf* itself. Beowulf's success against the monsters reflects the age-old archetype of the battle between good and evil. But these encounters are set against a kaleidoscopic background of human affairs, with the poet offering innumerable allusions to historical and legendary conflicts, to good and bad kings, to feuds and reconciliations, to the apparently inevitable and endless cycles of hostility and violence.

The audience of *Beowulf*, faced with such a multifaceted text, finds itself questioning the whole basis of heroic behaviour: how exactly does it relate to squalid, everyday violence, the staple of human history? Does *Beowulf* celebrate or undermine a heroic ideal? The poet of *Beowulf* was certainly a Christian, and probably a monk. This raises a fundamental question about the poem: how might a pious Anglo-Saxon Christian represent his pagan ancestors (for it seems likely that the Anglo-Saxons recognized their shared Germanic heritage with the Scandinavians in the poem)? Certainly the poet could not hold up their paganism for admiration, and yet it would be a dreary and one-dimensional poem which simply portrayed them as misguided sinners. And – depending on whether the poem was written early or late in the Anglo-Saxon period – the poet may have known less about the beliefs and practices of actual pre-Christian Scandinavians than we do.

Equally, it would be ridiculous to present his characters as Christians like himself and his audience. The poet of *Beowulf* has faced this challenge with remarkable poise and grace. He neither condemns nor commends paganism, because the characters in the poem are portrayed as occupying a sort of religious no-man's-land. The world of Beowulf and Hrothgar is a wholly secular one. Their virtues – whether the warlike qualities traditionally celebrated by heroic literature, or their wisdom, humanity and ethical standards – are not specifically Christian ones. They are not shown engaging in specifically pagan practices (only once the poet tells us that in despair about Grendel's attacks, the Danes resort to begging for help from heathen idols – as if, significantly, this were not their usual practice), and though many scholars have searched, none has been able to point to any authentically pagan element in the rites associated with Beowulf's burial at the end of the poem. So out of either ignorance or piety, the poet of *Beowulf* does not portray pre-Christian Scandinavia as a pagan society, and we can learn little or nothing of Germanic paganism from the way his characters are portrayed in the poem. It is rather in the array of allusions to and episodes of conflict that we might expect to find echoes of Norse myths.

We could not, in an Anglo-Saxon poem by a Christian, expect direct re-tellings of mythical episodes. The question of whether any remaining traces of Norse myth are the remnants of centuries-old story patterns which date right back to pre-Anglo-Saxon times, or are versions of material which later Anglo-Saxons learnt from their new neighbours, the Scandinavian settlers in England, is a complex one which requires more space and scope than I have here. It is, however, likely that on at least four occasions, the poet, whether consciously or not, is presenting a trans-formation of originally mythical material.

Beowulf opens with an account of the legendary founder of the Danish royal house, Scyld Scefing. His name might be translated as 'Shield Sheaf's-son', and it combines the two most important functions of kingship: defence of the realm, and its fruitfulness. Scef plays no part in any Scandinavian source; he seems to have a wholly Anglo-Saxon identity. But Scyld figures in Scandinavian sources as a king so illustrious that the Danes were named after him: Scyldings, as they are called in *Beowulf*. In the poem, we are told that Scyld 'flourished' and that he had a son called Beow, whose name means 'barley'. Beow too was a successful ruler, and his fame spread widely. But the word used for 'fame' is *blæd*, which is itself related to the word 'blade', as in a blade of grass. These early Scyldings are surely fertility deities of some kind, transformed by time and/or the poet of *Beowulf* into kings. Did the poet of *Beowulf* learn about the progenitors of the Danes from Scandinavian contacts, and skilfully connect the Danish Scyld with a figure from an Anglo-Saxon fertility myth, thus creating a united myth of origin for both nations?

Later on in the poem, Beowulf is rewarded by Hrothgar with magnifi-cent gifts, including a neck-ring so fine that the poet is moved to compare it with a legendary treasure, the *Brosinga mene* or 'necklace of the Brosings'. This treasure, the poet tells us, was stolen by Hama, when he escaped from the notoriously wicked Emperor of the Goths, Ermanaric. This sounds very like a distant echo of the Old Norse story of the *Brísingamen*, the necklace which Freyja bought from the dwarves –

perhaps the Brisings – in exchange for her sexual favours. In the Norse poem *Húsdrápa*, we hear how Heimdall (the first part of whose name corresponds to the Anglo-Saxon Hama) fought with Loki for possession of a precious thing, which may well have been the necklace. Just as with the peculiarly vegetative early Danish kings, the poet, or his source, whatever it might have been, has shifted myth into the real, or at least legendary, human world. A more detailed example concerns a family tragedy which befell the royal house of the Geats, Beowulf's people.

Beowulf's grandfather, Hrethel, King of the Geats, had three sons, one of whom, Hygelac, was Beowulf's uncle and patron. The other two sons were Herebeald and Hæthcyn. One day Hæthcyn, toying with a bow and arrow, accidently shot dead his brother Herebeald. No vengeance can be taken for Herebeald's death, and Hrethel, though grief-stricken, is quite powerless. There is nothing to be done to mitigate this dreadful calamity. This episode bears a striking resemblance to the Norse myth of the death of the god Baldr. The name of the Geatish prince Here*beald* is plainly related to Baldr, who was shot by his brother Hodr, who did not mean to kill him. In its original form, this name, *Höðr*, echoes the Old English name of the inadvertent killer, *Hæðcyn*. Hrethel's titles in the poem recall some of the poetic synonyms for Odin himself. The gods, like poor Hrethel, are paralysed with grief. But here the resemblance ends. For Odin goes unhesitatingly for vengeance: he has no living son to take on the duty, so he begets another especially for the purpose, a child who reaches maturity in the space of a day, created for the sole purpose of carrying out the sacred duty of revenge. Hrethel's response could not be more different. He 'chose God's light', dying of grief. This story of Geatish tragedy has been doubly transformed: its protagonists are turned into historical, not mythic, figures, and the Odinic response is pointedly passed over in favour of a quasi-Christian resolution. Nevertheless, the Norse myth is still evident beneath the new surface.

If we stay with the transformation from divine to (legendary) human characters, we can discern some fundamental parallels between Beowulf's encounters with monsters and the basis of Norse myth: the struggle between the gods and the giants, figured as monsters at Ragnarök. It might be argued that the archetypal battle of good versus evil lies behind these and many other such episodes. But there are obvious parallels between Beowulf's last encounter, with the dragon, and Thor's final fatal fight with the World Serpent; especially striking is the mutual death of the protagonists in both cases. But we should look also at the larger context of the fight. As we have seen, the Geats, left leaderless, fear invasion and annihilation at the hands of their long-term enemies, the Swedes. The death of Beowulf is the end of a world, the end of a brief phase of peace and prosperity for the Geats, whom Beowulf as their king had ably defended and wisely ruled. It was the same for the Danes: though the poet does not record it, the Danish royal house descended, after Hrothgar, into internecine warfare, killings and betrayals notorious throughout the Scandinavian world. And so it is at Ragnarök: the bright but flawed world of Asgard is wiped out in a mighty conflagration, preceded by a series of cosmic encounters between gods and monsters. For the Danes and the Geats, though, life in fact went on, as history both proves and demands. And after Ragnarök, as Norse myth makes clear, there will be a new world, freshly risen from the wilderness of the old one. This is of course an idea so archetypal that it also figures in Christian teachings: the apocalypse of the Book of Revelation entails the coming of a new heaven and a new earth.

The poet of *Beowulf* is relatively restrained about making Norse mythic elements serve Christian doctrine. But other Anglo-Saxon poets could re-use Norse myth in the service of explicitly Christian dogma. The author of the poem known as *The Dream of the Rood* (the vision of the cross on which Christ was crucified) presents Christ as a heroic warrior, complete with retainers, bravely stepping into battle by ascending the cross. But the poet makes a sly, but telling, distinction between Baldr and Christ, both young gods sacrificed in the hope of resurrection. We may recall Snorri's account of how the gods sought to reclaim Baldr from Hel by persuading everything to weep, and how a giantess in a cave refused. At Christ's death, though, the poet triumphantly affirms, *Weop eal gesceaft* ('All creation wept'). It is significant that parts of this poem are carved in runes on a great stone cross which stands at Ruthwell, in Dumfriesshire. As we shall see, the influence of Norse myth on Viking-age Christian sculpture in the British Isles was dramatic and far-reaching.

Sculpture in stone was not a feature of Viking-age Scandinavian culture. The Scandinavians who settled in the British Isles did not bring with them any such artistic tradition. By contrast, highly decorated stone crosses had been a feature of Anglo-Saxon Christianity, and were distinctive features of monastic settlements. Many Viking-age stone monuments in Britain – largely crosses, and the so-called 'hogback stones', great lumps of ornamented stone in the shape of little houses – are decorated with patterns which art historians have demonstrated as coming from Scandinavian models. But more striking for our purposes are the many depictions of what seem to be scenes from Norse myth and legend. There are for instance a number of scenes showing the hero Sigurd, who killed the dragon Fafnir and roasted its heart. Though many have worn faint, it is usually possible to distinguish one of two dramatic moments: either when Sigurd drove his sword through the dragon's belly, or when, having roasted its heart, he sucked his burnt thumb, and learnt the language of the birds, who warned him of treachery.

The so-called Gosforth Stone, in Cumbria, depicts quite plainly Thor's expedition to fish for the World Serpent. We can see Thor, armed with his hammer, in a fishing boat with his companion, the giant Hymir, and the fishing line, with its clumsy bait of an ox's head, dangling over the side. Around the boat are the fragmentary coils of the World Serpent. This flat stone may have originally formed part of a frieze, a series of scenes which recalls the saga account of the poem *Húsdrápa*, which described the scenes carved on wall panelling in an Icelandic hall. The Gosforth Cross is an even more dramatic monument. The panels in characteristically Scandinavian patterning of elaborate plaits and knotwork suddenly end in the gaping jaws of ravenous monsters, precariously held at bay by diminutive human figures. One of these figures is unquestionably Odin's son Vidar, who is shown with one foot wedged against the monster's lower jaw, just as Snorri describes it. Another panel on the cross shows Loki, bound until Ragnarök beneath the poison-spewing snake; his loyal wife Sigyn, with her bowl to catch the poison, is perfectly clear.

It is on the face of it remarkable that such iconic scenes from Old Norse myth have not only been associated with the Anglo-Saxon Christian tradition of monumental sculpture in general, but have also been incorporated into actual Christian monuments, many of which still stand in their original positions in churchyards, and presumably still served their original Christian function. But there is even more to it than this. In very many instances, the mythic scene is actually carved alongside an orthodox Christian motif. The Gosforth Cross, for instance, includes a moving crucifixion scene, blood gushing from Christ's side. Thor's fishing expedition on the stone is topped by a carving of the traditional Christian motif of the hart and the snake, a conventional representation of good versus evil. It has been suggested, therefore, that the sculptors – or rather, those who commissioned the art – were actually making a doctrinal point about relationships between the two belief systems, paganism and Christianity. The Norse hero Sigurd fought against a dragon, just like St George, or like the angel who fought against a serpent, which signified the devil in the Book of Revelation. Thor took on the World Serpent just as, in the Old Testament, God took on Leviathan, 'that crooked serpent'. The Christian apocalypse in the Book of Revelation – the end of an old world and the coming of a new one – is a parallel to Ragnarök.

This sort of pairing seems surprising on the face of it, but it may have had a long and widespread history wherever Germanic peoples were converted to Christianity. In such cases, it is the Christians who are the newcomers, not the immigrant pagans. Two very celebrated and striking instances are the eighth-century (that is to say, pre-Viking) Northumbrian Franks Casket, a highly decorated little box made out of ivory, inscribed with runes and depicting scenes from both biblical and mythical traditions, and the Ruthwell Cross, from around the same date, which has lines from the Christian poem *The Dream of the Rood* carved on it in runes. Such syncretism (the bringing together of two religious systems) is also evident from later continental Scandinavian art. A Swedish rock carving of the Sigurd story, dated to about the year 1000 AD, has a runic inscription (which follows the line of the dragon's body as it encircles the whole scene) which explains that a woman has had a bridge built for the salvation of a male relative's soul. This is plainly a Christian context; even plainer is the context of the Sigurd carvings at Hylestad in Norway: they are actually on the pillars of a medieval church. It is not always clear where the parallels between myth and Christian story lay. On the Franks Casket, a scene showing the coming of the Magi at Christ's nativity is juxtaposed with a carving of the Norse smith Völund – known as Weland in Anglo-Saxon sources, and Wayland in English folklore. In the Eddaic poem *Völundarkviða* (Völund's Poem), he was taken captive and hamstrung by King Nidud, but having raped the king's daughter and murdered his two small sons, he escaped by means of a magical feather coat, and flew away. Unlikely as it may seem, some Christian parallel must have been perceived, for episodes from the Wayland story are also found on Viking-age sculpture in England (often with wonderfully inventive representations of his feathered flying machine). It is interesting that early medieval commentators on the Bible regularly proposed ingenious parallels between the events and characters of the Old Testament and those of the New, and tempting to think that this way of giving validity to the Old Testament for Christians provided a model for recuperating the old faith and its attendant mythology.

There is little doubt, then, that Norse mythology left its mark on the visual arts in Viking-age England. But nobody knows for certain how long Scandinavian-speaking communities survived in mainland Britain, and might thus preserve and pass on to their neighbours stories from Norse myth. In Orkney and Shetland, a Scandinavian language – Norn – was still spoken until the end of the eighteenth century. As we shall see in the next chapter, the novelist Sir Walter Scott, on a tour of these northern islands, claimed he was told that the islanders recognized an Old Norse poem about valkyries which had just become all the rage among the fashionable literati in London – having been translated into England from Old Norse via Latin, as part of the revival of Norse culture in eighteenth-century Europe. But there is little evidence of such happenings further south. Only one example gives a tantalizing glimpse of the continuance of an active Norse culture in England.

The story concerns an Anglo-Scandinavian earl called Waltheof, who was the son of one of the Danish earls who came to England with King Knútr – Canute – at the beginning of the eleventh century, that is, a few decades before the Norman Conquest. In spite of his clear Scandinavian connections, Waltheof kept his high office under the new rule of William the Conqueror, but not for long: he became involved in a rebellion of northerners against William's rule, and was executed by William in 1076. His demise is recounted in two very different sources: a history of the Normans by a twelfth-century monk, Orderic Vitalis, and a thirteenth-century Icelandic history, *Fagrskinna* (its name – 'fair-skin' – referred not to its contents, but to its cover). The author of *Fagrskinna* presents Waltheof's death as martyrdom, rather than as an execution: Waltheof, like St Martin, gives away his cloak before he dies, and his shed blood has miraculous healing powers. Orderic Vitalis has an even more sensational end for Waltheof. He begs his Norman executioners to allow him to say the Lord's Prayer before he dies. But his emotion was so great that he could not get further than 'Lead us not into temptation' because of his tears, and the executioner, becoming impatient, drew his sword and cut off his head. And then, as the story goes, everyone heard how the head, in a clear voice, finished off the prayer: 'But deliver us from evil'.

Waltheof was well placed to be honoured as saint by all those who opposed Norman rule in England. But his cult did not seem to take off, and there is little further to be heard of Waltheof for at least two centuries.

However, *Fagrskinna* provides some interesting material about the immediate aftermath of Waltheof's death. We are told that Waltheof, though born and based in England, had employed an Icelandic poet to compose verses in Old Norse – just as the great earls and kings of Norway did – and that this poet fulfilled the traditional role of the Old Norse court poet by composing a flattering memorial lay after his master's death. Some of this verse has been preserved in Norse sources. It is quite indistinguishable from similar poetry from Scandinavia, and in the cryptic diction typical of skaldic praise poetry, it celebrates Waltheof in a kenning based on the name of the god Odin: as a brave warrior he can be called 'Yggr of battle'. Wolves are called the mounts or steeds of giantesses, and one phrase, about how William betrayed Waltheof, echoes very precisely a formula from a Viking-age runic inscription. It is perhaps not all that surprising that a man like Waltheof, conscious and proud of his second-generation Scandinavian identity, might grandly seek to identify with the aristocracy of his homeland. But there is a more difficult question here: after Waltheof's execution, what audience might there be for such a thoroughly Scandinavian poem – in its language, ethos, sympathy and mythological reference? Who might have commissioned the poem? (Not Waltheof's wife, as it happens, since she was actually William's own niece, and played a part in revealing Waltheof's rebellion to her uncle.) The possibility emerges that even after the Norman Conquest, when the reign of the Danish king Canute was long past, there were aristocratic courts in England who appreciated Norse culture and understood Norse mythological references. But for how long might this have continued? A curious aftermath to this story may offer an answer.

While he was alive, Waltheof had been a benefactor of the East Anglian abbey of Crowland, and after his execution, the monks of Crowland took his body back there. Many years later, at the beginning of the thirteenth century, the abbey was suffering economically, and the enterprising abbot of the day evidently embarked on a fund-raising project which involved raising the profiles of saints with which the abbey was associated, including Waltheof. And it is to this period that we can date a Latin life of Waltheof, the *Vita Waldevi*. For our purposes, the significance of the *Vita* lies not in its account of Waltheof's life or death, nor in the miracles associated with him, but in a preface to it, an account of the life of Waltheof's father Siward, the Danish earl who came to England with King Canute.

The story of Siward is full of Norse mythological references. Siward himself is said to be the son of one Beorn Bear's Son, and his ancestry was evident to all because of his furry ears. Siward himself fought a dragon on Orkney, and on his way back to Northumberland, he comes across an old man, sitting on a mound, who advises him about his future. This is of course a classic example of a warrior meeting with the god Odin, and being given a gift, for the old man, Odin, gives Siward a banner called *Ravenlandeye*, which the author explains as meaning 'Raven, land-terror'. This is the kind of banner mentioned in the *Anglo-Saxon Chronicle* as carried by the pagan Scandinavian armies; the raven, it will be remembered, is Odin's bird, and later English sources claim that the special property of a raven banner was that if it fluttered in the wind, such that the raven seemed to flap its wings, it predicted victory, while if it dipped, defeat was near. According to Norse sources, King Haraldr harðráði carried a banner called *Landeyðan* ('land-waster') when he fought at Stamford Bridge in 1066. An account of Siward at the court of King Edward, and of a dramatic encounter with Tosti, the Danish earl of Huntingdon, is very similar in tone and quality to the historical sagas written in Iceland. And finally, Siward finds himself on his deathbed, horrified at the prospect of not dying in battle. The author describes how he is then dressed in his mail coat, and lifted upright, so that he can die like a warrior – and, presumably, secure his passage to Valhalla.

This story, with its distinctively Scandinavian features, is one of the very few pieces of evidence we have that a literary culture influenced by Norse mythology continued in England beyond the Viking age. As the centuries pass, possible traces of Norse myth become fainter and fainter, and more and more indirect. Given that Chaucer's *Canterbury Tales* is an anthology of various stories from very various sources, we might look here for an echo of Norse mythology. And indeed some scholars have proposed some connections. The notorious Wife of Bath, for instance, with her five husbands and mercenary attitude towards sex, fell for her final husband on rather unusual grounds: 'me thoughte he hadde a paire / of legges and of feet so clene and faire'. Does this recall the Norse story of the giantess Skadi, invited by the gods to choose a husband from among them, but granted sight only of their feet? (You will remember she assumed that the most beautiful feet must belong to Baldr, but they were Njörd's.) The word *scathe*, meaning something harmful, is used twice in relation to the Wife; one might think its similarity to the Old Norse form of the giantess's name, *Skaði*, is a coincidence, but the word is used by Chaucer nowhere else. The Old Man in Chaucer's *Pardoner's Tale* is a mysterious wanderer who knows how to find both treasure and death: could he be modelled on Odin? And then finally there is the eagle which transports the narrator to the House of Fame in Chaucer's poem of that name; the House of Fame is a place where discourse of all kinds ends up. Could there be a connection with the eagle in the Old Norse myth of poetry – actually, the god Odin, in shape-shifted form – who transports poetry from the dwarves to the world of the gods, for re-distribution to mankind?

In all these cases, though the similarities may be suggestive, the absence of any evidence for direct influence – how Chaucer might have got to know of Norse myth – weakens the case for a connection. It is just as likely that attractive legs, mysterious old men and poetic eagles existed elsewhere, independently, in medieval storytelling, and that the similarities are either coincidences, or analogous – that is, that both Chaucer and the Old Norse sources tapped into an age-old tradition and re-told a story with a similar theme or pattern. Indirect influence, though, is worth pursuing, and there are at least two intriguing instances of how Norse stories found their way into Shakespeare's plays.

The first concerns the Danish earl Siward, whose father had furry ears and an encounter with Odin. He was earl of Huntingdon, and as such, features in the work of a twelfth-century English historian, Henry of Huntingdon. Henry's account is largely based on that of Orderic Vitalis, but he adds a heroic flourish at the end of Siward's life. Told that his son has been killed fighting against the Scots, Siward anxiously enquires whether his wounds were in front or behind. He is triumphant that his son has died from wounds to his front, for of course that means that he was not cut down in flight from the battle, but while still bravely advancing on his enemies. This story finds its way into one of Shakespeare's sources, Holinshed's *Chronicle*, and Siward duly finds his way into Shakespeare's play *Macbeth*, again rejoicing about his son's death. What is striking is that this heroic ethic, as expressed by Siward's joy, rather than grief, about his son's glorious end, is baffling to the other characters in the play, who simply cannot understand why Siward is so pleased, and refuses to mourn. It looks very much as if the Norse warrior ideal of a glorious afterlife with Odin in Valhalla lies at the root of this harsh scene at the end of the play.

The second example concerns one of Shakespeare's most celebrated heroes, the Danish prince Hamlet. *Hamlet* is a story of revenge set in the Danish court; its Scandinavian connections are fundamental. One of Shakespeare's sources for the subject matter of his play was possibly a sixteenth-century French author called Belleforest. This Belleforest took his material from a work by the early medieval historian Saxo Grammaticus, whose *History of the Danes* was first printed in France at the beginning of the sixteenth century, though it had been composed more than three centuries earlier. And Saxo names among his own sources Icelandic prose and poetry. The connection is certainly indirect, but it is neatly documented.

The beginning of Saxo's life of Hamlet (or Amleth, as Saxo calls him) is instantly recognizable as the same story as *Hamlet*. Here we have the uncle marrying the mother, and Amleth pretending to be witless in order to escape his uncle's clutches. There is even an eavesdropper behind the arras. What we lack, though, is a version of the story in an Old Norse form. However, there is a striking reference to the whole affair in a cryptic piece of Old Norse poetry. In his list of kennings for the sea, Snorri Sturluson, in his *Skáldskaparmál*, quotes a verse attributed to a poet called Snæbjörn (the only reference to this poet in the whole of Old Norse, and the only surviving fragment of his poetry). The verse seems to allude to the sea as 'the ale of Amlóði's meal'. Ale here stands for any kind of liquid; in the context of the kenning, it is a liquid which is especially associated with 'Amlóði's meal'. At this point, Saxo can enlighten us: he tells us about Amleth (whose name seems to be related to Scandinavian words for 'fool') pretending to idiocy, and agreeing with his courtiers who tell him that sand dunes are piles of flour, or meal. Thus 'Amlóði's meal' is sand, and the kenning falls into place – sea is the liquid associated with sand.

Snorri himself has understood the kenning differently – he reads 'Amlóði's flour mill' which churns out seawater: our Hamlet-figure is thus not a pretend madman, but an obscure sea-deity. Whatever the explanation, this poetic allusion to someone called Amlóði who con- nected sand and flour must have been recognized and understood by an Icelandic audience, whether Saxo's story is the original explanation, lying behind the kenning, or a story invented later. What remains from this welter of uncertainty is a surprising and very compelling link between Old Norse myth and legend, and the feigned madness of a Shakespearian hero.

But from this point on, any influence of Old Norse traditions has become too faint or confused to trace with any confidence or conviction. The story of Hamlet marks not the end point of the legacy of connections between the British Isles and Scandinavian settlers and raiders, but the precocious beginning of a new relationship: Norse material transmitted by Scandinavian antiquarians and historians. Saxo and Belleforest are special cases, though. We must wait another couple of hundred years for the real re-emergence of Norse lore, and its impact on European thought and literature.

CHAPTER 6

Romantic
Revolutions

I t is something of a puzzle to literary historians that in Iceland, in the second half of the thirteenth century, the state of the Icelandic nation on the one hand, and the quality and quantity of its literary output on the other, seemed so completely at odds. It was during this time, the so-called 'classical period' of Icelandic saga writing, that many of the great family sagas were being committed to vellum. Snorri had completed his huge compendium of biographies of the Scandinavian kings and earls; and also his remarkable treatise on Norse mythology and poetry, the *Prose Edda*. Sometime before 1270, an anthology of mythological and heroic poems, the *Poetic Edda*, had been carefully made, and was re-copied around that year. *Völsunga saga*, a prose re-telling of the heroic poems in the *Edda*, is usually dated to this period, too. Many texts now celebrated remained to be composed – or at least set down in writing: *Grettis saga*, which has been called 'the last of the great Icelandic sagas', is thought to have been written around 1350. But in the thirteenth century, literary production was in full swing.

Politically, things were very different. The old political system of power-sharing among a large number of independent farmers, all with more or less equal access to the annual parliament, the Althing, and its legislative processes, was breaking down. Power had become concentrated in the hands of a few great landowning families, and there were murderous conflicts between them as they jostled for dominance, a dominance which entailed establishing liaison with and support from the Norwegian royal house. In 1262, Iceland formally ceded its independence to Norway, and this date marks the end of the Icelandic commonwealth, whose political egalitarianism has been overstated, but which was nonetheless, in both political and literary terms, an extraordinarily precocious nation state.

There is a certain amount of debate as to whether this loss of independence had as great an actual impact on Iceland at the time as its symbolic impact for later generations of Icelanders. For instance, the Norwegian crown tried to impose a new law code in Iceland, but it was not popular, and a few years afterwards a second law code – this time including a greater proportion of the old Icelandic legislation than its predecessor – was substituted for it; clearly Iceland retained a fair measure of autonomy. But the year 1262 at least marks a turning point in Icelandic history: in the later Middle Ages, Iceland went into a slow but steady decline, economically and culturally.

During the centuries from settlement in 870 AD to the end of the commonwealth in 1262, Icelanders must have felt themselves to be at the geographical centre of a North Sea kingdom. To the east lay Norway, the 'old country' for many in Iceland, and the rest of continental Scandinavia. To the south and west were the British Isles, with their many Norse colonies and kingdoms. The reason why the most northerly region in Scotland is now called Sutherland ('the southerly country') is because it was the most southerly part of the independent earldom of the Orkneys. And stretching due westwards, the Icelanders knew not only Greenland, with its Icelandic settlers there, but also the eastern seaboard of North America, as far as Vinland itself.

But once it became a colony of the Norwegian crown, Iceland's central position shifted dramatically. At the beginning of the fourteenth century, a new king of Norway moved his royal seat from Bergen eastwards to Oslo. At the end of the century, Norway came under Danish rule, and from a Danish point of view, Iceland seemed a very long way distant from Copenhagen. The Danes eventually lost all interest in Orkney and Shetland, and pawned them to the Scottish crown (they never redeemed them). And as the climate gradually worsened in the late Middle Ages, the Greenlanders were simply abandoned when the long and dangerous journey by boat became more difficult and finally unfeasible. The last recorded sailing from Greenland, from a much weakened community, took place in the fifteenth century, although archaeologists have since found burials of bodies dressed in late fifteenth-century clothes. Two hundred years later, though, in 1605, a Danish expedition out there found no sign of Norse life, only the melancholy remains of a Norse settlement, now occupied by Inuit people.

The geographical marginalization of Iceland was matched by a decline in literary output. Saga writing never actually stopped, but there was nothing to match the family sagas, in either quality or ambition. From about the middle of the fifteenth century, Icelanders even stopped compiling the annals which had run throughout the Middle Ages. And as a direct result of this geographical and cultural isolation, the language itself fell out of step with the Norwegian language, which was, unlike Icelandic, continually changing, due to the influence of its continental neighbours, and by the sixteenth century we have no Old Norse – a medieval language common to Norway and Iceland – but two separate languages, Icelandic and Norwegian.

The odd combination of dominion and neglect which characterized the Danish attitude to Iceland is vividly illustrated by accounts of the Icelandic Reformation in the sixteenth century. The king of Denmark, Christian III, declared from faraway Copenhagen the institution of a reformed Protestant Church in Iceland. This, so far as we can tell, was either simply ignored or coolly rejected in Iceland – much as, incidentally, Roman rules about the celibacy of Catholic priests had always been quietly disregarded. The issue became one not of religious affiliation, but of the authority – or not! – of the Danish king. But what could he do? Sending an invading army to Iceland to assert his authority was hardly feasible. A small group of Danes, apparently intending to occupy the bishop's see at Skálholt, the southern diocese, was ambushed by local farmers. Some years later, the bishop of the northern diocese in Iceland, Jón Arason, arranged for a staunch supporter of Catholicism to be elected bishop there, and Jón's sons captured and imprisoned the Danish nominee. By 1550, Bishop Jón found himself the last remaining Catholic bishop in Scandinavia. Something had to be done with him, and the Danish king organized the execution of Jón and his two sons. (There were reprisals – said to have been led and organized by the bishop's daughters.)

Now even the traditional independence of the Icelandic Church (as evidenced by those sons and daughters) was gone; the Church's traditional freedom to dispense justice and punishment, and its control over schools and education, was replaced by central authority from Copenhagen. Added to all this, worsening climatic conditions, volcanic eruptions, and even plague, saw Iceland's living standards plummet, and economic conditions hit rock-bottom.

How then, from this depressing story of isolation, cultural decline and poverty, do we reach the point at which the mythology written down in Iceland again became a force in Europe? Two consequences of geographical remoteness and Danish neglect had unexpectedly positive results.

The sixteenth century was a time of adventure and exploration in Europe. Travel writing – as exotic and sensational as possible – became popular all over Europe. Iceland was the last known point before the mysterious North-West Passage, and its isolation lent an obvious glamour to stories about it. And it was of course the perfect subject for travel writing, with its glaciers and geysers, its volcanoes and lava fields, its black sands and hot springs. The volcano Hekla was imagined to be the mouth of Hell itself. In fact, writers went overboard about the awesome wonders of Iceland, and included its savage inhabitants as part of the picture. Icelanders were described as frightening barbarians, who washed in urine, gorged themselves on candle-wax whenever they had the chance, and lived lives of unspeakable brutishness. Towards the end of the century, the Icelander Arngrímur Jónsson wrote a passionate defence of his native country, published in 1593 in Copenhagen. Much more influential, however, was the work he followed it up with: the *Crymogæa* (Greek for 'Ice-land'), published in Germany a few years later. The *Crymogæa* has been called 'the manifesto of Icelandic patriotism'. But its significance from our point of view is that it contained an account of the Norse gods, and therefore introduced Norse mythology to anyone who could read Latin – that is, to the educated reader in Europe. Arngrímur's accounts of Iceland's medieval literary culture were of very special importance and significance for continental Scandinavians, as we shall see. There is one other important piece of the jigsaw to fit in here: as a Danish colony, Iceland had special privileges to have its students educated at the University of Copenhagen. These close scholarly links between Iceland and Denmark explain how Arngrímur – and his successors – came to be writing and publishing books about Norse history and culture in Copenhagen.

The survival, little changed, of the Icelandic language was a second major consequence of Icelandic isolation. The will of Icelanders to maintain Icelandic as the language of the new Church was not opposed by Denmark, and this language – in essence, the very same medieval language in which the sagas, myths and histories were originally composed – was enshrined for ever in this one official, written capacity. So when the continental Scandinavians, themselves interested for nationalistic reasons in the earliest histories of their own nations, began to realize that Old Icelandic texts contained just the material they needed, another realization soon followed: that Icelanders themselves could read and understand these texts, and could be their guides.

Medieval texts were a gift to Scandinavian historians and politicians, and the Icelanders who could interpret them were eagerly competed for. Scandinavia felt very keenly the disdain of other European nations for its supposed cultural backwardness. Arngrímur was quickly taken on by the Danes to write an early history of Denmark from Icelandic medieval sources. The Icelander Þormóðr Torfason (usually referred to by the Latin form of his name, Torfaeus) was appointed Royal Historian in Norway. But it was the Swedes who fought hardest for intellectual recognition in seventeenth-century Europe.

During the seventeenth century, Sweden established itself as an impressive military power. But it was still regarded as a cultural backwater. However, in 1554 the historian Johannes Magnus produced one of the most significant books in the whole history of Sweden: significant not because of its historical scholarship – which was extremely dubious – but because of its ideological power. Johannes's chronicle, the *Historia de omnibus Gothorum Sveonumque regibus* ('A History of All the Kings of the Goths and the Swedes'), laid the foundations of 'Gothicism', a remarkable theory which held that the Swedes – that is, the descendants of the Goths – were the oldest people in the whole world. According to Johannes Magnus's elaboration of this fanciful idea (which was not a new one), Sweden had been founded by Noah's grandson, Magog (the son of Noah's oldest son Japheth), in distant Uppsala, and had therefore not been involved in the building of the Tower of Babel, thus managing to avoid the great confusion of languages that was God's punishment for those who had. Swedish was for this reason the oldest language in the world: mankind's original language, and indeed the language in which God had first spoken to mankind. These Goths did everything worth doing in the ancient world; they had taught philosophy to Plato, produced the mighty Amazons and the Argonauts, and conquered imperial Rome. And they were, naturally, the authors of a magnificent literary tradition, now surviving only in the form of a few runic inscriptions in stone around Scandinavia. Thus the Swedes set the pace for Scandinavian claims to a glorious national past. The twelfth-century Danish history of Saxo Grammaticus, which had been published in Paris in 1514, with its proclamation of Danish antiquity, was no match for this.

As might be expected, Johannes Magnus's theories, influential as they were both inside and outside Sweden, did not remain unchallenged. But it was on the back of Gothicism, and the pride thus conferred on the Swedish nation, that during the seventeenth century scholarship was sponsored and supported in Sweden. And part of this scholarly output, stimulated by the competitive nationalist interest throughout Scandinavia in the origins and early history of the Scandinavian countries, was the translation and publishing – with the help of Icelanders – of Old Icelandic texts. (There was one extraordinary hiccup. 'Gothicism' reared its head again in the form of a claim that Sweden was the home of Plato's great lost civilization of Atlantis, the source of all European culture. Olaus Rudbeck's massive four-volume treatise *Atlantica* [1679] uses the Old Icelandic texts which were just at this time coming to light to back up his theories. Oddly enough, Rudbeck was a professor of medicine at the University of Uppsala, and a very distinguished scholar: he discovered the lymphatic system.)

The seventeenth century saw the publication of seminal texts of and about Old Icelandic literature. The Swedes were particularly interested in the so-called *fornaldarsögur* (legendary sagas), since the setting was so often Sweden. But in 1665 the Danish scholar Peder Resen published an edition, with a Latin translation, of Snorri's *Prose Edda*, as well as texts of the chief mythological poems *Völuspá* and *Hávamál*. Resen's scholarship was hugely important in making Norse mythology known outside Scandinavia. Just as influential were two treatises on Norse traditions by Danish antiquarians. The first was Ole Worm's *Runer, seu Danica Literatura Antiquissima* ('Runes, or the Most Ancient Danish Literature'). Worm's big idea was that ancient Scandinavian literature was all originally written in the runic alphabet, itself derived from Hebrew script (the short title of his book is actually printed in runic letters on the title page). But even more influential than this mistaken idea was the appendix to *Runer*, which included (transliterated into runic script, of course) a selection of actual Old Norse poems, together with Latin translations. Thomas Bartholin's *Antiquitatum Danicarum de Causis Contemptæ a Danis adhuc Gentilibus Mortis* ('Danish Antiquities Concerning the Reasons for the Pagan Danes' Disdain for Death'), published in 1689, established almost single-handedly the stereotype of the brave Northern hero, proudly laughing in the face of certain death.

This interest in national history was not, of course, confined to Scandinavia. In the seventeenth century in England, antiquarians were delving into the history of Britain and the origins of its people. William Camden had produced his study of the British Isles, *Britannia*, in 1586, though it was not translated (from Latin) until 1610. Camden writes about the old Saxon gods, but does not connect the Saxon 'Woodan' (Woden) with the Odin he learnt about from Scandinavian sources such as Saxo (though he does make the first modern reference to the Vikings in English, calling them 'Wiccinga'). In 1605, Richard Verstegan published an investigation into the Saxon ancestry of the English with a wonderfully eloquent title: *A Restitution of Decayed Intelligence in Antiquities, concerning the … English Nation*. As the century went on, contact between Scandinavian and English scholars continued. Diplomats, emissaries and official visitors to Scandinavia were often men of letters (the poet Andrew Marvell visited Queen Christina, and flatteringly compared her to Elizabeth I in elegant verse). The diplomat Sir William Temple wrote two essays, *Of Heroic Virtue* and *Of Poetry*, under the influence of the then very recent scholarship of Bartholin. Sir Henry Spelman corresponded with Ole Worm, who sent him a copy of his *Literatura Runica*. It was Spelman who correctly suggested that the word 'rune' might be related to the Anglo-Saxon word for a secret or hidden thing, and it was through Spelman that knowledge of runes came first to England. In 1670, Robert Sheringham is already quoting from Peder Resen's edition of the *Edda*, published only five years before; Sheringham highlighted the link between Odin and the runes – Odin as the inventor of runes and god of poetry – which was to prove so influential in English thought. Valhalla also comes to notice, but there is no explanation of Ragnarök yet. This had to wait for Thomas Hickes, whose highly scholarly *Thesaurus* of old Northern languages (1703–5) included an Old Icelandic grammar and much useful information on the poetry, as well as a poem which he called 'The Waking of Angantyr' – the first ever translation of a whole Old Icelandic poem into a modern language.

English writers also produced a share of silliness, as myths of origin are inclined to provoke. Aylett Sammes put a lot of good scholarship to poor use in his attempt to demonstrate that the English were descended from the Phoenicians – although he wrote sensibly on the link between

Odin and runes. But all this Gothic knowledge, impressive as it now seems, remained the preserve of fusty antiquarians – 'Gothic lumber', as a sarcastic contemporary playwright called it. Perhaps the most memorable put-down of the antiquarian fashion for old northern things comes from William Congreve's play *The Way of the World*, dating from 1700. His heroine Millamant, elegant and metropolitan, is being clumsily courted by a country aristocrat, Sir Wilfull Witwoud; in an urbane aside to the audience, she mocks his unwelcome advances: 'Ah, rustic – ruder than Gothic!' But half a century later literary opinion was to swing dramatically in favour of Norse mythology, when the poet Thomas Gray caught the mood of the times with his versions of two Old Norse mythological poems, his *Norse Odes*.

Mrs Millamant, in Congreve's play, with her cool wit, her contempt for the country, and fastidious good taste, was a heroine very much of her time. English literature of the Augustan age measured itself by classical standards, shunning anything felt to be wild or extravagant, and heavily influenced by classical literary forms and subjects, including mythology. It was no wonder that in the first half of the eighteenth century, old northern learning was regarded as an eccentric, rather than fashionable, pursuit. But everything changed with the work of three quite different writers – a historian, a translator and a poet – who, each in their own way, promoted the kind of literature which came to dominate the latter part of the century: the Romantic sublime.

The first was Paul-Henri Mallet, a Swiss scholar who had been commissioned by the king of Denmark to write an account of the early history and culture of Denmark – another attempt to counter the still prevalent view of Scandinavia as a cultural backwater. Mallet produced two volumes in 1755 and 1756; in 1763 they were revised and combined with the title *Introduction à l'histoire de Dannemarc*, the subtitle proposing a treatment of early Denmark's religion, laws, manners and customs. Of course, Mallet's *Introduction* contained a great deal of information about Norse religion and mythology; what had originally been the second volume included a translation of Snorri's mythological treatise *Gylfaginning*, an account of *Völuspá* and sections of *Hávamál*. Mallet had based his work on the familiar seventeenth-century Scandinavian scholars like Bartholin and Worm.

Thomas Percy, Bishop of Dromore, translated Mallet's work into English as *Northern Antiquities* in 1770, and as such it became the standard reference work on Norse mythology in Britain. (Mallet – in common with a good many scholars of the period – muddled Celtic and Germanic, so that the Norse poetry and mythology described in his work is described as Celtic; fortunately Percy was clear on the distinction, and corrects Mallet – very frequently – in his translation.) Although Mallet's work did not of itself create any great movement towards Old Norse literature (such 'Runic mythology' as Mallet included in the second volume was dismissed by an influential contemporary reviewer as mere 'childish fancies', too silly to quote), with its learned discussions and selections of actual Old Norse material, it was the single most influential authority on Old Norse mythology for other scholars and writers, if not for more fashionable readers.

Percy himself published, in 1763, English translations of five Old Norse poems. He translated not directly from the Old Norse, but from the Latin versions of the poems produced by Scandinavian scholars in the previous century: Worm, Bartholin, Verelius and Peringskjöld. However, Percy did print the Icelandic originals in full at the back of the volume. In fact, *Five Pieces of Runic Poetry* is more a scholarly than a literary work, and many reviewers were disappointed with Percy's carefully literal translations – especially in comparison with what has been called the literary sensation of the time: the publication only a little earlier of James Macpherson's *Fragments of Ancient Poetry*, verses he claimed to have collected in the Highlands of Scotland, and then translated from the 'Galic or Erse language' of their mysterious poet, Ossian. This was what the British reading public expected of ancient poetry, not Percy's flat paraphrases. As it happened, Macpherson's Ossianic poems did themselves help to direct popular taste towards Norse antiquities: his Celtic heroes (and heroines) were pitted against savage Scandinavians so vividly depicted that it has been suggested that Macpherson too had dipped into Mallet. What is certain is that it was the publication of Macpherson's *Fragments* which drove Percy to produce his translations from the Norse. Percy explains this himself in the preface to *Five Pieces*, and is confidently challenging about Macpherson's purported originals: 'Till the translator of these poems thinks it proper to produce his originals, it is impossible to say whether they do not owe their superiority, *if not their whole existence*, entirely to himself' (my emphasis). And it was against this background of scholarly work on Old Norse from Percy and Mallet, and the sweeping craze for ancient poetry kindled by Macpherson, that Old

Norse mythology enjoyed its own phase of fashionability, thanks very largely to the poetry of Thomas Gray.

Thomas Gray is perhaps best known as the author of *Elegy Written in a Country Churchyard*, a melancholy and meditative poem about unrecognized talent and the uncertainty of fame and poetic reputation. In both form and subject matter it is plainly an Augustan poem, with little or nothing of the quality of the coming Romantic movement – especially not the 'Romantic sublime'. But Gray was already writing prose descriptions of wild and awe-inspiring landscapes, and had read widely in early Norse scholarship (including even Arngrímur Jónsson's *Crymogæa*); his interest in northern antiquities was a long-standing one. He began work on his *Norse Odes* – the very use of the word 'ode' betrays the classical taste he was rooted in – before Percy had published either his *Five Pieces* or his translation of Mallet. Gray attributes the source of *The Fatal Sisters* directly to Torfaeus's *Orcades* – a selection of Norse material about the Orkney islands – and to Thomas Bartholin; and *The Descent of Odin* to Bartholin. It seems that he first began work on translating these Norse poems as part of a major project: a history of English verse, which would include not only Norse material, but also translations from Welsh and Gaelic. Gray had been greatly taken by Macpherson's Ossianic *Fragments*, though he hedged his bets about their authenticity. If they were indeed authentic translations, then according to Gray, Macpherson had 'lighted on a treasure hid for ages'. But their literary quality was unaffected even if they were forgeries, for if they were the work of Macpherson himself then 'this man is the very Demon of poetry'. Gray never completed his grand history, but through him, Norse poetry – at least in the shape of these two poems – found a place in the canon of English literature nevertheless.

The poem which Gray called *The Fatal Sisters* is found in *Njáls saga*, a thirteenth-century Icelandic family saga about the families which settled in the south of Iceland in the period just preceding and just following its conversion to Christianity. The saga reads as if the author is telling us, simply, and without comment, 'what happened'; and what happens in the saga is the slow struggle of the settlers to replace a society steeped in violence and the fierce ethics of revenge with a new order based on respect for the law, and rational negotiation as a means of settling feuds. The climax of the saga – which is also its lowest and most hopeless point, when attempts at negotiated settlement have failed – is the murder of the peaceable lawyer Njáll, together with his family, when they are burnt alive in their farmhouse by his enemies. After this dreadful act, society in Njáll's part of Iceland breaks up. There is chaos. The burners flee the country, and some end up in Ireland, in another cataclysmic conflict: the Battle of Clontarf, in 1014. This battle has long figured in popular Irish history as the moment when the country was at last rid of its Scandinavian invaders, although in fact King Brian Boru himself was killed, and Clontarf was actually a victory for the combined forces of Norsemen and Brian Boru's Irish enemies.

In both Irish and Norse sources, the encounter was said to have been presaged by all manner of startling omens. Gray's own preface to *The Fatal Sisters* sets the scene in dramatic prose:

> In the eleventh century *Sigurd*, Earl of the Orkney-islands, went with a fleet of ships & a considerable body of troops into Ireland to the assistance of *Sictryg with the silken beard*, who was then making war on his Father-in-Law Brian, King of Dublin: the Earl & all his forces were cut to pieces, & *Sictryg* was in danger of a total defeat, but the enemy had a greater loss by the death of *Brian*, their King, who fell in the action. on Christmas-day (the day of the battle) a Native of *Caithness* in Scotland saw at a distance a number of Persons on horseback riding at full speed towards a hill, & seeming to enter into it. curiosity led him to follow them, till looking thro' an opening in the rocks he saw twelve gigantic figures resembling Women: they were all employ'd about a loom; & as they wove, they sung the following dreadful song, wch when they had finish'd, they tore the web into twelve pieces, & (each taking her portion) gallop'd six to the north & as many to the south.

The saga is a little more restrained in its introduction: the women are not 'gigantic' and their song is not 'dreadful'. But the verse itself, the 'song' of these women, is horrifically unrestrained: they are valkyries, delighting in the prospect of blood and slaughter at Clontarf, and as the saga prose explains, before the poem is quoted, the women's loom 'has men's heads in place of weights, their intestines forming the weft and warp; what served for a beater was a sword, and their shuttle was an arrow'. In Gray's version of the poem, the women exult in their work:

See the grisly texture grow,
('Tis of human entrails made,)
And the weights that play below,
Each a gasping warrior's head.

Gray adds a footnote to explain what valkyries are (and according to the *Oxford English Dictionary*, this is the first occurrence of the word in English): 'The *Valkyriur* were female Divinities, servants of *Odin* (or *Woden*) in the Gothic mythology. Their name signifies *Chusers of the slain*. They were mounted on swift horses, with drawn swords in their hands; and in the throng of battle selected such as were destined to slaughter, and conducted them to *Valkalla*, the hall of *Odin*, or paradise of the brave; where they attended the banquet, and served the departed Heroes with horns of mead and ale.' The misprint of *Valkalla* for *Valhalla* (one of Gray's editors misread his handwriting) shows how unfamiliar the word still was, and again, the *Oxford English Dictionary* cites this footnote of Gray's as the first English mention of the term. Gray's definition of the valkyrie in Old Norse tradition could hardly be bettered – and certainly not corrected – by modern scholars, and in spite of the general scholarly view that Gray did not know any Old Norse – he does seem to have produced his 'imitations' by working on the Latin versions in his sources – it is striking that the term *Valkyriur* is the grammatically correct Norse plural, unlike Bartholin's Latinized term 'Valkyriae'.

The original Norse poem, now known as *Darraðarljóð* ('The Song of Dörruðr' – according to the saga prose, the man who saw and heard the valkyries, but more likely the song of the pennant, or spear), is a surprising and anomalous inclusion in the otherwise largely sober and naturalistic *Njáls saga*. The valkyries' prophecy about the course of the battle does not even square with what we are told in the saga prose. But what really distinguishes the poem from its context in the saga prose is what must have attracted Gray to it in the first place: its 'wild spirit', as Gray approvingly puts it, and the 'frightful images' and 'dreadful horrors' that contemporary critics noted with some relish. The valkyries are triumphantly 'weaving many a soldier's doom' as they produce their gory textile, and long for the battle itself, when they will be 'wading through the ensanguined field'. Although there is no attempt to echo the original metre or diction of *Darraðarljóð* (unsurprisingly given Gray's apparent dependence on Latin paraphrases of the poem), the incantatory repetition of the Norse poem is dramatically conveyed as the women repeat their mantra: 'Weave the crimson web of war'. Gray's freedom with his (Latin) original allows him some thrilling effects; at the end of their weaving, the women have amply demonstrated their terrifying power, and draw back, sated:

> Horror covers all the heath,
> Clouds of carnage blot the sun.
> Sisters, weave the web of death;
> Sisters, cease. The work is done.

Gray's valkyries, like their counterparts in the original, carry drawn swords as they ride away from – or, as Gray more poetically puts it, towards – the battle: 'Sisters, hence with spurs of speed / Each her thundering faulchion wield / Each bestride her sable steed'. And Gray's most effective and sinister innovation is his presentation of the valkyries as 'sisters' (the poem did at one stage have the provisional title 'The Song of the Weird Sisters', with obvious reference to the witches in Shakespeare's *Macbeth*). Nowhere in either the Latin or the Old Norse poem are these bloodthirsty apparitions called sisters, but the word was used invariably of mythological female creatures, and especially the three Fates of classical tradition. *The Fatal Sisters* – an ode – invokes traditional classical forms, but its content was shockingly novel.

The ode which Gray called *The Descent of Odin* is derived from a Norse original usually called *Baldrs draumar* ('The Dreams of Baldr'); Bartholin called it *Vegtamskviða* ('The Poem of Way-Tamed', the name Odin gave himself when travelling incognito). Baldr is having bad dreams, and his father Odin travels down to the underworld to question a *völva* – a sibyl, as in the poem *Völuspá* – about what is in store for Baldr. In Old Norse mythological poetry, a hostile exchange between an enquirer – in this case, Odin – and a wisdom figure – a giant, or as here, a prophetess – provides a dramatic structure for setting out central facts about Old Norse mythology. In *Baldrs draumar*, Odin urgently questions the prophetess: 'Tell me what is happening in Hel. For whom is the funeral feast being prepared?' When the prophetess – angry at being raised from the dead, and exhausted by her journey from Hel – tells him tersely that Baldr is expected, Odin asks more questions: 'Who will kill him? And who will take vengeance for this killing?' The prophetess, anxious to return to her underworld, and be rid of these tiresome questions, tells

Odin briefly the extraordinary story of Baldr's avenger: he will be a son of Odin, miraculously come to maturity in the space of one day. Odin, perhaps despairing because the prophetess has confirmed what he already knows – that Baldr will die, sacrificed by Odin himself in the expectation of his resurrection, a disturbing analogue to the Christian story – suddenly drops his guard and lashes out wildly, provocatively asking the prophetess a question that he alone can answer: a traditional riddle based on the image of waves being like women throwing their headdresses in the air. With a brief but vicious exchange of insults, the prophetess disappears. Her last word is of Ragnarök, her own trump card – the final end of all the gods.

It is clear even from this summary that *Baldrs draumar* is at least as packed with sensational incident as *Darraðarljóð*, and Gray's imitation, *The Descent of Odin*, does full justice to it. Odin is called 'The king of men' in the first line, and his 'descent' is spectacular:

> Down the yawning steep he rode,
> That leads to Hela's drear abode.

His first encounter down there is with a fierce hell-hound which figures only briefly in the original, but which Gray presents as a terrifying 'dog of darkness' whose

> …shaggy throat he opened wide,
> While from his jaws, with carnage filled,
> Foam and human gore distilled:
> Hoarse he bays with hideous din,
> Eyes that glow and fangs that grin;
> And long pursues with fruitless yell
> The father of the powerful spell.

Gray borrows many of these 'Gothic' details from other English poets: Pope, Spenser and Dryden are all echoed in these few lines, and allusions to Milton and Shakespeare figure prominently in both Norse odes. In this way, Gray is trying pull his examples of Old Norse/Icelandic poetry into the great tradition of English poetry – just as he would have done, in fact, had he completed his proposed history of English poetry, with examples included from Old Norse and Welsh.

One obvious difference between Gray's *The Descent of Odin* and the Old Norse original is that nowhere in the Norse poem is there depicted any architectural feature or aspect of the landscape. Gray, in common with the great Romantic poets, sought to move his audience with awe-inspiring descriptions of mysterious evocative ruins and dramatic natural scenery. Gray's Odin reins in his horse (Gray prefers the classical 'coal-black steed' to the Norse naming of Sleipnir, Odin's grotesquely eight-legged horse) before 'the portals nine of hell' which tower above him, and sitting on a 'moss-green pile' he begins to wake the dead prophetess with the ever-popular 'runic rhyme'. Always watchful to avoid bathos, Gray has the magically begotten avenger never 'comb his raven-hair / Nor wash his visage in the stream' before completing his vengeance, whereas the Norse less picturesquely has him failing to wash his hands.

Interestingly, neither Gray nor his first editor understood the verse in which Odin gives away his identity to the prophetess, though Gray elaborated the Latin beautifully:

> What virgins these, in speechless woe,
> That bend to earth their solemn brow,
> That their flaxen tresses tear,
> And snowy veils, that float in air.
> Tell me whence their sorrows rose:
> Then I leave thee to repose.

The original Norse is simpler, but more obscure:

> Who are those maidens
> who weep for their pleasure,
> and fling to the sky
> the scarves on their necks?

Elsewhere in Old Norse, this is presented as one of a set of riddles, to which the answer is the waves. But the notes to *The Descent of Odin* suggest 'These were probably the Nornir or Parcæ', and that, being 'invisible to mortals', Odin in speaking of them 'betrays himself to be a god'. It is remarkable – and evidence of how sympathetic Gray was to these strange poems, so unlike anything else in English or classical tradition – that even without knowledge of the solution to the riddle, he can convey the mystery and beauty of the lines.

It is perhaps worth noting here that these two poems are very far from central even to Old Norse literary tradition. *Darraðarljóð* is found nowhere but in *Njáls saga*, in which it sits extremely oddly, and *Baldrs draumar* was not included with the other Eddaic mythological poems in the great *Codex Regius* manuscript: it too is an outsider, an oddball text. Neither poem was included in Percy's *Five Pieces of Runic Poetry*, and neither became one of the eighteenth-century 'canon' of familiar Old Norse poems to be translated, with varying success, into English.

Gray's conclusion to the poem, his rendering of the prophetess's malicious allusion to Ragnarök, describes the doom of the gods in masterly terms: she will not return to be interrogated,

> Never, till substantial Night
> Has reassumed her ancient right;
> Till wrapped in flames, in ruin hurled,
> Sinks the fabric of the world.

Gray's imitations – as he called them himself – of Old Norse poems (the only two he attempted) had an enormous impact on the English literary world. During the next few decades, dozens of (mostly very inferior) imitations were produced. There was, simply, a craze for poetry and plays on Old Norse themes. The most popular subjects – by a long way – were Odin and Valhalla, because it was here that the literary taste for horror, blood, battle and awesome incident could be satisfied. But no-one produced anything nearly as good as Gray's *Odes*, and many seem positively comic today. Horace Walpole – who wrote what is regarded as the first Gothic novel, *The Castle of Otranto*, which is full of horror and fantastic incident, though not specifically northern horror – was a great admirer of Gray's poetic talent. However, in a letter to a friend he was less than complimentary about the *Norse Odes*, noting dismissively: 'they are not interesting'. Warming to his theme, Walpole went on: 'Who can care through what horrors a Runic savage arrived at all the joys and glories they could conceive, the supreme felicity of boozing ale out of the skull of an enemy in Odin's hall?' Walpole was not much taken by Mallet's work, either, commenting dismissively, 'I cannot say he has the art of making a very tiresome subject agreeable'. And although as is clear from letters and journals, celebrated English Romantic poets like Wordsworth and Coleridge were well aware of the old northern craze, there is little evidence of it in their work. Robert Southey, who was to become Poet Laureate in 1813, immersed himself in Norse literature, and passed on to his friend Coleridge a new translation of the *Poetic Edda* by Amos Cottle. Cottle's translation was not a distinguished one.

The first scholar to offer English translations of Norse poetry not from a Latin version, but directly from the original language, William Herbert, was scathing about it. If Cottle had tried to claim the translation as his own work, Herbert mocked, 'he could scarce have been accused of plagiarism'. Coleridge in turn gave Cottle's collection to Wordsworth, who responded fairly politely, while pointing out its 'many inaccuracies'. Norse influence on the work of either poet is minimal.

Norse themes may not have been eagerly taken up by mainstream Romantic poets, but the strange, visionary poems of William Blake were heavily indebted to Norse myth. In his long poems, Blake created epic mythic systems, and it has been argued that the very form of such poems as *Jerusalem*, *Milton* and *Vala, or the Four Zoas*, peopled by mysterious divinities and exploring themes of conflict, revolution, and death and apocalypse, was influenced by the busy sweep of Old Norse mythology. There can be no doubt but that Blake would have shared in the literary craze for Old Norse poetry. And he evidently took seriously the culture which had given rise to these myths: in an irritated annotation to the work of a contemporary theologian who was claiming that before Christianity ancient peoples had no moral or intellectual sense, Blake wrote: 'Read the Edda of Iceland!' Blake himself probably read the *Edda* – either Snorri's prose, or the poems themselves – in *Northern Antiquities*, Percy's translation of Mallet. But he had a very particular knowledge of two Old Norse mythic poems – at least in an English version – because he was commissioned, in 1797, to illustrate a new edition of Gray's poems which contained the *Norse Odes*, and he used disbound pages from an earlier edition as the basis for his plates. Blake is one of the clearest examples we have of the close links between the sublime Romantic visions shared by poets and artists; and he himself was both.

Blake produced ten illustrations for *The Fatal Sisters* and another ten for *The Descent of Odin*. His sisters are invariably three in number (only in one illustration is there a possible suggestion of more women as the drawing shades off into the background) in spite of Gray's clear indication (actually reproduced in the text of the fourth plate) that there were twelve of them. Blake invested his depiction of these dreadful women with enormous power and drama – not only as they engage in the weaving which Gray's poem so vividly describes, or even as, galloping across the battlefield, they trample despairing warriors underfoot, but also in their inscrutable and yet challenging stares, their gaze fixed implacably and directly at the viewer. In *Northern Antiquities*, the valkyries' role in Valhalla is as heroic waitresses, biddable servants of Odin's warriors: 'there are...a great many virgins who officiate in Valhall, pouring out BEER and ALE for the heroes, and taking care of the cups, and whatever belongs to the table'. But Blake clearly envisaged them as controlling destinies. It may be that Gray's title *The Fatal Sisters* suggested the three Fates to Blake; it is interesting that both in Gray's poem, and in the original Norse, the sisters are determining the fates of the warriors, not just choosing from among those slain, and conducting them back to Valhalla. There were also three female Fates in Old Norse tradition – 'Happened', 'Is Happening' and 'Will Happen' – and these three figures were often conflated with valkyries by later readers.

In his illustrations for *The Descent of Odin*, Blake sometimes picks out Gray's own distinctly sublime additions to the original poem: Odin's precipitous ride down into the underworld, and his encounter with the hell-hound. But other illustrations are disappointing. Hel's hall, described in the Norse poem as all set up for Baldr's funeral, is bleak and empty, apparently unfinished (but there is a grotesque skull to drink out of. This mistaken element of Old Norse myth was so enticing that it became extremely long-standing: warriors drinking out of their enemies' skulls. The misunderstanding goes right back to Ole Worm and his *Literatura Runica*; a Latin translation of an Old Norse kenning for drinking horns – the curved branches of the skull – became 'the skulls of slaughtered opponents'. Even the [much] later corrections of Norse scholars failed to shift this irresistible image.).

The illustration of the great avenger, Vali, depicts an undistinguished sea or river scene, and a rather characterless young man, naked, and about to comb his hair. Odin himself is a stiff, small and oddly prim figure in blank armour. He is in stark contrast to the dynamic, muscular, naked figures of Odin drawn by the Swiss artist (and friend of Blake) Henri Fuseli, who also produced illustrations for Gray's work. Fuseli's Odin, armed only with a dagger strapped to his waist, struggles mightily to control his rearing horse on the edge of a yawning abyss – but the work owes much to classical sculpture in Rome. A later engraving shows a very classical-looking seated Odin, with a patriarchal beard, massive thighs, and sandals, gesturing gravely towards three female figures in diaphanous draperies who illustrate the three maidens in the riddle at the end of the original poem. But on the right-hand edge of the illustration is a wildly sinister horse, eyes bulging and mane flying: the shocking creature from Fuseli's most famous work, *The Nightmare*.

Much of the visual art inspired by Old Norse myth around this period reflects a great gulf between the formal restraint of classicism and the romantic reaction to it. A good example is the work of the seventeenth-century Scandinavian artist Peter Cramer, whose piece *The Death of Balder* depicts daintily horrified goddesses with elaborate, fashionable coiffures clustered around Baldr, who is wearing what looks like a Roman centurion's helmet. Cramer's contemporary Johannes Wiedewelt produced a more innovative drawing of Thor driving his chariot, but it is significant that when Wiedewelt was writing about how to depict the Norse gods in suitably classical form, he recommends the following compromise: 'I would conceive that the figures be Greek and the names Gothic'. In Scandinavia, dramatic scenes from Norse myth, still popular as a response to romantic nationalism, continued to be classicized in the visual arts. Eckersberg's *The Death of Baldr* (1817) shows colourful but stiffly posed gods with stern faces staring accusingly at a vividly blind Höðr, while Loki, hiding his face in his cloak, skulks in the shadows at the edge of the composition. Baldr lies dead in the foreground, the shaft piercing his shiny breastplate just as improbably as, in Snorri's account, the mistletoe arrow was supposed to have pierced Baldr.

No-one could accuse Fuseli of stiffness, or lack of drama. His *Thor Battering the Midgard Serpent* is full of imaginative life: Thor, boldly naked, a figure owing much to Michelangelo, hauls up the World Serpent by a great chain, while the giant Hymir cowers almost comically in the boat, and Odin, a tiny, spectral figure crouched in the top left-hand corner of the frame, looks on. The background is tellingly unspecific, a swirl of waves and spray. Though they could not be more different in execution, we might compare this with Blake's depiction of the World Serpent to illustrate the first page of *The Descent of Odin*: the serpent stands alone in the plate, its great gaping, shark-like jaws dominating the whole. In both, the artist's imagination has had free rein, and the fantastic is uncontrolled. As Fuseli himself maintained, 'Genius, inspired by invention, rends the veil that separates existence from possibility; peeps into the dark, and catches a shape, a feature, or a colour, in the reflected ray'.

Blake could have learned of the immense intellectual power and authority of the Old Norse sibyl from Mallet's summary of the Old Norse poem *Völuspá*:

> The prophetess having imposed silence…declares, that she is going to reveal the decrees of the Father of Nature, the actions and operations of the Gods which no person ever knew before herself. She then begins with a description of the chaos; and proceeds to the formation of the world, and that of its various species of inhabitants…she then explains…the functions of the Gods, their most remarkable adventures…At last, she concludes with a long description of the final state of the universe, its desolation and conflagration; the battle of the inferior deities and the Evil beings: the restoration of the world…

This is wisdom unparalleled in its range and profundity. The sibyl has absolute command of the totality of human and – significantly – divine knowledge. Blake's illustration of the first appearance of the sibyl shows a stern and sorrowful mature woman, face heavily lined and lips parted, about to speak. She is a stark contrast to his Fatal Sisters.

Not unexpectedly, the powerful female voices from Gray's odes, both sibyl and valkyrie, find their way into Blake's poetry. Several of Blake's poems feature sinister female weavers, 'covered with Human gore', singing over their task, weaving 'the black Woof of Death', or even, in a bizarre variation on the textile in Gray's *The Fatal Sisters*, which is 'of human entrails made', creating a web 'in soft silk drawn from their own bowels'. His long prophetic poem *Vala, or the Four Zoas* announces its debt to the sibyl in its title, for 'Vala' was the standard anglicization of the Norse form of the word for sibyl, and several translators entitle their version of *Völuspá* 'The Song of Vala'. Most notably, Gray himself, who listed Old Norse texts in his Commonplace Book, called this poem 'The Oracles of Vala'.

Vala, or the Four Zoas is a story of Creation and Apocalypse, like *Völuspá*, and its final section, 'Night the Ninth, being the last Judgement', opens with two deities, Los and Enitharmon, weeping over the body of Christ crucified, just as the Old Norse gods weep at the death of Baldr. This final section of the poem concludes with an apocalyptic vision, followed by a new world order, which is closely similar to the accounts in *Northern Antiquities*. Even though much of the imagery in the Norse is also familiar from the biblical Book of Revelation (a point which Bishop Percy himself draws attention to), the verbal echoes between Blake's poetry and Percy's translation are very striking.

In both literature and the visual arts, the fashion for Norse subjects in the late eighteenth century invigorated and was invigorated by parallel developments – revolutions, one might say – in aesthetic taste and sensibility. The thrill of the weird and the warlike, for terrors of the imagination and awesome shocks to the senses, made for an extravagant reaction to classical restraint, and Norse themes were the perfect vehicle. But the Gothic in England moved on, in art and literature, and left behind its early northern subject matter, just as the Romantic poets following Gray and his imitators failed to take up Norse subjects. The impact of Norse myth followed from now on quite different paths, both of which had been laid down at earlier stages.

Firstly, there was a historical, or antiquarian, interest in the culture of those who settled the British Isles. Secondly, there was a continuing interest in the early Scandinavians as founders of political liberty, which combined, oddly, with a darker element, derived ultimately from Bartholin: the Norse as superhumanly brave warriors, laughing in the face of death, with Odin as the powerful leader of an early Germanic empire which conquered all before it and despised all things southern and decadent.

Like the early English antiquarians, William Blake had evolved his own version of a historical myth of the origins of Britain. For him, Britain had been – like Sweden, for the Swedes – the cradle of humanity: as he put it in *Jerusalem*, 'All things begin and end in Albions ancient Druid rocky shore'. According to this scheme of things, the Norse gods represented the barbarous enemy –

Woden and Thor and Friga wholly consume my Saxons:
On their enormous Altars built in the terrible North

– as, indeed, in the presently accepted version of British history. A more orthodox, but broadly similar, response to the history of the British Isles was that of Sir Walter Scott, who was very widely read in Norse material (his library was a fine collection of all the best Norse books of the time, both editions of texts and learned textbooks). He was approaching Old Norse traditions from another perspective altogether – not the mystery of myth, or the bloody horror of battle, but the historical significance of the Norse who settled in England and Scotland. His poetry and prose – especially novels such as *The Pirate*, and poems such as *Rokeby* – used his considerable learning in Old Norse to provide local colour for the communities and landscapes Scott saw as having been determined by Scandinavian settlement. *The Pirate* is set in Orkney and Shetland, where a form of Old Norse was actually spoken almost until Scott's own time, the early nineteenth century. The novel's characters are shown acting out the Norse traditions which Scott had read about from authorities such as Bartholin – not the military ones, but the prophesying of a sibyl (the oddly named Norna of the Fitful Head) and the recitation of the skaldic verse which Bartholin had quoted in his influential book. In a striking footnote to *The Pirate*, Scott claims that on a visit he himself had paid to the islands, he had been told how the inhabitants had immediately recognized Gray's *Fatal Sisters* as a version of a poem they themselves knew in the original Norse.

Rokeby, a poem about the English Civil War, is set in the area of northern England around the River Tees, where Danes and more particularly Norwegians settled, and left their mark in local place names. Evoking this past in the opening of *Rokeby*, Scott produces many stock Norse elements which have already been mentioned here: Odin, father of the slain, with his raven banner; Baldr and Thor; 'runic' place names. However, Scott is not interested in myth for its own sake, but only as an identifying feature of actual Norse culture (as he supposed it to be from his reading, and perhaps rightly).

Very important was the somewhat unexpected idea that the ancestors of the earliest Scandinavians – often identified as the Goths, as the sixteenth- and seventeenth-century Scandinavians had done – were characterized by their strong attachment to political liberty and the democratic rights of the individual. This notion goes back a long way in Britain. English writers identified their Saxon ancestors as one branch of the great Gothic nation; Sir William Temple had written of them as one of those 'Gothic nations...swarming out of the northern hive', an allusion to the sixth-century Gothic historian Jordanes, who described the Gothic tribes as 'bursting forth like a swarm of bees' and colonizing Europe, and whose work was influential in England. The Roman historian Tacitus, writing just after the birth of Christ, was cited in his praise of the virtues and democratic ideals of the Germanic tribes, that is, the

Goths; according to Tacitus, the authority of kings was very limited among these tribes, and this was a feature which particularly recommended itself to parliamentarians in England. The rosy English view of the ancient Goths was that they had evolved, by democratic means, their own laws, and that these laws had survived until the present day – ironically, uninterrupted by the Norse invaders (who, as we have seen, in fact introduced many of the legal institutions, such as the jury system, which are still a fundamental feature of British and American systems). In the seventeenth century, therefore, parliamentarians in England used the term 'Gothic' to distinguish the freedoms they upheld against the tyranny of absolute monarchy. And just as the Germanic tribes – the Goths – had toppled the Roman Empire, notorious for its political and moral decadence, so the Reformation had constituted a second toppling of a decadent hierarchy, in favour of a fresh, reformed and energetic order: the Protestant Church, which had triumphantly proved the equal of a Roman Catholic monarchy.

It was generally believed that these early Germanic peoples had established something like a parliamentary constitution, whose chief principle was the freedom of the individual, and that the coldness of the northern climate had contributed to their hardy love of liberty and vigorous opposition to political oppression. Mallet had reinforced this idea in his work, and Percy eloquently transmitted it in *Northern Antiquities*: Norse society was regulated by 'a religion simple and martial as themselves, a form of government dictated by good sense and liberty, a restless unconquered spirit, apt to take fire at the very mention of subjection and constraint'. A chilly climate had the effect of rooting out decadence because it dampened the passions, as the French political philosopher Montesquieu had already claimed. The North was the ancient home of political liberty, and southern nations did not enjoy the benefits of this healthful rigour.

The connection between this political mythology and actual Norse mythology is twofold. Firstly, there is the link between ancient Norse culture and the new world order which will come into being after the actual revolutions in France and America. America appears in *Northern Antiquities* as a New Scandinavia; Europe used to be an uncivilized, barbarous place, but once the forests are cleared (Blake's symbolism of forests of ignorance is dramatically appropriate here) and the hunter-gatherers formed towns and cities, liberty and industry flourished; so it will be with North America (but not South America, of course, because of its climate). Secondly, there is the connection with Odin. According to Snorri Sturluson, in both his mythological work, *Gylfaginning*, and his political history, *Heimskringla*, the origins of the Scandinavian people lay in Asia, and the emigration northwards was led by Odin. The theory of this movement out of Asia was not a new one; it has been traced back to the earliest historical chronicles – from the seventh century AD – of the Franks, a Germanic people who came to rule what we now call France. But Snorri gives us a detailed account of how their leader was a powerful general called Odin, who was such a successful and charismatic leader that his people came to worship him as a god.

This combination of the powerful leader and the superior race – in spite of its connection with popular liberty – was to prove lethal. Even as early as Robert Southey, we can see the strange results. His poem *The Death of Odin* opens with an excitable invocation by Odin:

SOUL of my much-lov'd FREYA! Yes, I come!

Odin is determined not to succumb to 'pale disease's slow-consuming power' – he will rush to Valhalla by joyfully killing himself. (Freya, of course, was not Odin's wife; that was Frigg.) Another poem, *The Race of Odin*, praises the valour and military success of 'the race of Odin', and celebrates the fall of Rome. The whole verse is worth quoting here:

I shall quaff the foaming bowl
With my forefathers in yon azure skies;
Methinks I see my foeman's skull
With the mantling beverage full;
I hear the shield roof'd hall resound
To martial music's echoing sound;
I see the virgins, valour's meed, –
Death is bliss – I rush to bleed.

We can see the familiar paraphernalia of Norse Valhalla myths – the 'shield roof'd' hall, the valkyries, classicized as virgins, the old misconception of warriors drinking out of their enemies' skulls – but the final line of the stanza is of course not only an embarrassing anticlimax, but also deeply disturbing. The view that Norse warriors, freedom-loving and scorning luxury – unlike the Romans – were descended from standard-bearers of liberty who had toppled the Roman Empire and established the democratic political institutions preserved by Northern Europe was a powerful one in the nineteenth century in England and America, when contemporary imperialists were apt to be compared with Vikings. But Southey and others had taken the image of brave warriors welcoming death in battle – which goes right back to seventeenth-century scholarship, primarily Thomas Bartholin – a chilling step further. The old 'death before dishonour' adage had been elevated to a celebration of suicide, an implicit denigration of the value of ordinary human life, and this too became a destructively influential political ideal.

CHAPTER 7

The Rise of Racism

A t the beginning of the nineteenth century, as the literary craze for
Old Norse mythological themes died down in Britain, involve-
ment with the Old Norse and their literature took new directions.
Norse literature was of course not confined to mythic material: as we
have seen, one of the reasons why the Scandinavian nations took such a
keen interest in these early texts was the historical information about early
times which many of them contained – even if the definition of 'historical'
might include material now regarded as totally – and evidently – fictional,
not to say mythical. The British, aware that Britain and Ireland had been
heavily, and sometimes permanently, settled by Scandinavian immigrants,
also wanted to know more about these early Scandinavians.

The very strangeness of Old Norse mythology had been a key part
of its attraction in Europe in the late eighteenth century, with its wild
incidents and supernatural creatures; mythology after all tends to be the
most surreal manifestation of any culture. But now, as interest in the
mythology of both Snorri's *Edda*, and the poems of the *Edda*, was waning,
interest in 'actual' Vikings grew. English translations of saga prose began
to be produced, not just of soberly historical texts – such as Snorri
Sturluson's *Heimskringla* – but also of the family sagas, naturalistic but
(as scholars now believe) fictionalized accounts of the first Icelandic
settlers, and of the fully fictional *fornaldarsögur*, or legendary sagas. In
fact, the very first complete saga to be published in an English translation
was *Fridthiofs saga* by George Stephens, in 1839, a highly romantic

fornaldarsaga, or 'legendary saga'. Its hero, Fridthiof himself, conformed to the nineteenth-century stereotype of the Viking: not only brave, fearless in the face of death, and dashingly romantic, but also fiercely independent, in awe of neither the old pagan gods nor, significantly, the hereditary monarchy of his native Norway.

Fridthiof's attitude to pagan worship – he burns down a temple dedicated to Baldr – is especially interesting. References to the Norse gods, and the myths associated with them, naturally continued to figure as part of the presentation of heroic Vikings, but there was some lingering unease about their historical situation as pagans. Nevertheless, a new Viking myth was developing in Britain. It had its roots in eighteenth-century notions of the old north as a place of political liberty (fostered, it will be remembered, by the bracingly cold climate, and distinguished, somewhat oddly, by its high regard for strong leadership), and of cool, peerless bravery. Vikings came to be figured as bold conquerors, intrepid explorers, pioneers, innovators, all-round fitting antecedents for Victorian imperialists and industrialists. In the words of George Webbe Dasent, one of the most celebrated saga translators of the Victorian period, 'they were like England in the nineteenth century: fifty years before the rest of the world in her manufactories, and firms – and five-and-twenty years before them with her railways. They were foremost in the race of civilisation and progress; well started before the rest had thought of running. No wonder, then, that both won.'

And there was more: the Vikings were not exotic strangers, even if they had an outlandish mythology and bizarre beliefs. They had come from a country which was, as the last great early nineteenth-century translator of Eddaic verse, William Herbert, put it in the dedicatory preface to his work, 'intimately allied to England in ancient blood and language'. These perceived blood ties between modern nations and their historical counterparts were to become highly significant, nowhere more so than in Germany.

Questions of racial origin, ethnic identity, and nationality dominated political and academic discourse all over Europe. The term 'race' itself, though it was, and still is, very widely used, is a curiously elusive concept. In fact, it has no scientific basis at all. It is simply an ideological construct which enables certain groups to define themselves against others on the basis of inherited physical appearance. Although nowadays, racial discrimination is generally assumed to be negative – discrimination *against* a particular group – its equal and opposite tendency is the doctrine of racial supremacy, that is, the privileging of one's own perceived group as superior. It is not actually possible to elevate (or indeed reduce) the infinite variations of human physical difference to any scientific level of classification in order to mark out separate races, though there have been many notorious attempts to do so. Nevertheless, and perhaps because of its ideological usefulness, people have always seen racial difference as self-evident. Roman historians such as Tacitus characterized the Germanic tribes as physically distinct from themselves – as tall, blonde and blue-eyed, in fact – and extolled these features. Arthur de Gobineau, who has been called the father of European racism, following his influential *Essay on the Inequality of the Human Races*, published in 1855, also disting-uished people with these physical characteristics; he called them Nordic Europeans, as opposed to 'Alpine' and 'Mediterranean' people. (That not all Germans, or English, or even Scandinavians, conformed to this physical type led Gobineau to conclude that interbreeding had already taken place to such an extent that the European peoples were fatally damaged, and doomed to degeneration and ultimate extinction.) These 'Nordic' people were held to be inherently superior to the other 'racial' groups in terms of culture and physique (old ideas about the cold climate often surface here). At the same time, the academic study of language had defined roughly the same group in a different way: they were the original speakers of Germanic languages. Descended in common from a single prehistoric language – Indo-European – many of the languages of Northern Europe, including English, German and the Scandinavian languages, were seen to be predictably similar in grammar and vocabulary, and were evidently closely related.

There was as yet no unified German state, and this very lack led to the growth of Romantic nationalism – the idea that racial, cultural and linguistic ties, common origins and aspirations, naturally bind people together into a nation. One of the key elements of Romantic nationalism throughout Europe was the revival of the common historical roots of the nation, and this very often entailed the celebration of medieval culture. In this sense, Romantic nationalists looked back to a glorious, unified past. But the same theories of race and language which fostered Romantic nationalism enabled German nationalists to call up a grand vision of a much wider Germanic identity, which, crucially for our purposes, included the modern nations of Scandinavia, with their ancient, supposedly common, culture and hence, of course, the mythology: the surviving and intimate expression of what came to be known as the race-soul. The collective identity offered by this pan-Germanism was prestigious, time-honoured and potentially immensely extensive geographically, if not, by its own definitions, ethnically. Norse mythology was adopted as its cultural heart.

Britain was in a very different position, for many reasons. Britain was far less concerned with gathering itself together than with furthering the imperial project: spreading its culture, language and political traditions throughout the world. Imperialism was to be in many ways the very opposite of Romantic nationalism, and it certainly involved looking forwards, to ever-increasing trade and industry, not back to a pre-modern golden age. The British Isles, unlike Germany, had unarguable geographical borders. And as a United Kingdom of Great Britain and Ireland, the emphasis had to be on political rather than organic, racial unity. Some Victorian English liked to think of themselves as descended, at least in part, from the Vikings, and that this went some way towards explaining the success of the nation as a whole, but ancestry was mixed: there were also the Anglo-Saxons, with, as it was believed, their admirable tradition of legal and political freedoms, and the Normans as well. The Scots, as we shall see, remained bitterly divided in their allegiance to either a Celtic or Norse racial origin, and the native Welsh and the Irish were plainly Celts. And Britain was understandably not always keen to be seen as a far-flung outpost of a wider Germanic realm. George Stephens, the translator of *Fridthiofs saga*, believed that Britain's cultural and linguistic roots were Anglo-Scandinavian rather than Germanic. In linguistic terms, his literal translation of the saga, with its lexical and syntactic archaism, reinforces his vision of a 'mighty and noble and thoroly Scandinavian NORTH ENGLISH...the birth-tung of England'. In terms of racial origins, Stephens belligerently maintained (in flat contradiction of William Herbert) that 'our nearest homeland is Denmark; our furthest kin-land is Germany', and he fiercely opposed what he called (with chilling future echoes) the 'annexing' of the English language on the one hand, and Old Norse mythology on the other, by German scholars.

James Joyce's Jewish hero in *Ulysses*, Leopold Bloom, offers a minimal definition of a nation which is plainly derived from Romantic nationalism: 'A nation is the same people living in the same place'. But his tentative addition, a mild attempt to allow for the Jews themselves, completely blows open his own formulation: 'Or also in different places...' Today, with Romantic nationalism a thing of the past – not to mention its discredited offspring, apartheid and ethnic cleansing – one might add, further, 'Or different people living in the same place'. German nationalists were not wholly misguided in recognizing some sameness among those included in the nation: undeniable physical similarities among long-established population groups do develop, and the close relationship and common origin of the Germanic languages is easily demonstrable, and still a staple of the academic study of comparative philology. But Romantic nationalism in Germany eventually realized its inherent potential to humiliate, exclude and eventually attempt to eradicate those outside its own self-definition, even though, paradoxically, the ideals of pan-Germanism sought to enlarge dramatically the group which might be included within it. Everyone knows where European racism led, cata-strophically bolstered and sharpened by scientific theories in areas such as genetics, evolution, and medicine. But for the moment, what is important is an understanding of the relationship between German Romantic nationalism, pan-Germanism and Norse myth. It is the key to why Norse mythology was taken up by Germans as the historical heart of their national culture, so that when Richard Wagner embarked on his great new poem, the complete libretto of the *Ring* cycle – 'it contains the world's beginning, and its end' – he naturally turned to the mythology preserved in Icelandic texts.

Wagner's operatic cycle *Der Ring des Nibelungen* ('The Ring of the Nibelungs'), first performed in its entirety in 1876, was begun decades earlier, in 1848. It is based almost entirely on Old Norse sources, though this has not always been recognized, partly because of its title: *Nibelung* is the German form of the family name of the legendary Burgundian heroes Gunnar and Högni, familiar from the title of a medieval German poem about them, the *Niebelungenlied*, though they are also celebrated in Old Norse prose and poetry as Niflungs. This naturally tends to foreground the German poem as Wagner's primary source. Moreover, the Nibelung after whom the *Ring* cycle is named is a dwarf called Alberich, and although this figure is a little like a dwarf called Andvari in the Norse sources, he is clearly based on the dwarf Albrich in the *Niebelungenlied*; indeed the whole idea of Nibelungs being the name of dwarves (and not legendary heroes) is taken from another German source Wagner used. In addition, the celebrated Rhinemaidens, who guard the treasure so coveted by the malign dwarf Alberich, and with whose joyful singing the

132

whole cycle opens, have no counterpart in either Old Norse or German sources. So first acquaintance with the *Ring* cycle – either from its title, or its opening scene – gives a misleading impression of Wagner's dependence on Norse mythology. But Wagner did not begin at the beginning. In fact, he began at the end, with the opera now called *Götterdämmerung* – 'The Twilight of the Gods', a literal translation of *Ragnarøkkr*, the old form of Ragnarök, the doom of the gods, a concept found only in Old Norse. The opening scene is completely atypical: the *Ring* cycle owes almost everything to Old Norse myth.

Wagner's subject – 'the world's beginning and its end' – sounds exactly like the grand sweep of *Völuspá* itself, and his project encompasses nothing less than the whole of Norse mythology – and not only the gods and the giants, but also dwarves and valkyries, and the most celebrated heroes and heroines of the Old Norse legendary past. Wagner welds all this widely disparate material into a single coherent (if complex) narrative. He weaves in all manner of echoes and motifs from other Old Norse sources. He presents this voluminous synthesis in a metre and poetic language which insistently recalls (but does not simply imitate) the Old Norse originals. And finally, he sets the whole to music, transforming poetic narrative into operatic drama. I want to look at each of these literary transformations in turn; the music must speak for itself.

In 1848, Wagner completed a preliminary prose summary of his subject, which he called *Der Nibelungen-mythus* ('The Nibelung Myth'). He was intending to compose an opera based on the final stages of this material, which he was going to call *Siegfrieds Tod* ('The Death of Siegfried'). The *Nibelungen-mythus* would explain everything about the great hero Siegfried: his relationship with the gods, the origins of the great treasure hoard he wins, his love for Brünnhilde, and his – and the gods' – dramatic end. This first outline of the whole *Ring* cycle is a virtuoso transformation of the source material in itself.

The *Nibelungen-mythus* begins with the Nibelungs, a race of dwarfish smiths living beneath the earth in Nibelheim; this is a German version of the name of the mysterious Norse underworld Niflheim; its first element means 'mist', or 'darkness'. In the Norse, the connection between the Niflung heroes – perhaps named for their dark colouring – and the underworld is coincidental, and even confusing, but Wagner has drawn together the underworld and the sinister dwarves who inhabit it – 'like worms in a dead body', as the *Nibelungen-mythus* vividly has it, a direct borrowing from Snorri Sturluson's account of the dwarves in the Old Norse mythological cosmos. Alberich establishes himself as the tyrannical leader of the Nibelungs when he seizes a treasure hoard called the Rhinegold, and fashions from it a ring which secures his control over them. With the ring and the Tarnhelm, a helmet which confers on its wearer both invisibility and the ability to shape-shift at will, Alberich can rule the world. The giants are the rivals of the dwarves, and so enter into a bargain with the gods: they will build a great hall for them, in exchange for the Nibelung treasure, which the gods then have to steal from Alberich. Alberich curses the hoard, and the giants, too stupid to put it to any use, have a monstrous dragon guard it for all time.

This is cosmic stalemate. Gods, giants and dwarves are all powerless. What is needed is a hero: one of mankind, acting of his own free will. And impressive humans already exist, fathered by the gods, the most heroic of them returned, at their deaths in battle, to the gods in Walhall – Valhalla – by the Walküren – Odin's valkyries. This stretch of narrative forms the basis of what was to become the first (though last composed) libretto of the *Ring* cycle: *Das Rheingold* – 'The Rhinegold'.

Wagner developed this basic outline – part Norse, part medieval German – into a final libretto by adding a host of details from Old Norse. Although the Rhinemaidens are his own invention, the mysterious gold they guard is clearly influenced by Old Norse literary tradition. In skaldic verse, there is a strange affinity between gold and water: kennings used to denote gold describe it as the fire, gleam or ember of the wave, sea or river; sometimes, specifically, the River Rhine itself, as in 'the red metal of the Rhine' or 'the sun of the Rhine'. One explanation derives from the treasure hoard itself; that it was deposited in the river by the Niflungs in order to prevent the Hunnish king Atli (Attila the Hun) from getting his hands on it. It has been proposed that the glittering sands of the Rhine suggested to medieval observers that its bed was of gold. On a mythic level, there is the story in Snorri's *Edda* about the sea-deity Ægir, whose hall is said to be lit and warmed by gold instead of fire. More inventively, the vision of the sun setting on the ocean's horizon might have given rise to the idea that the depths received sunlight as gold – almost alchemically transformed into 'the fire of the ocean'. What is significant about Wagner's presentation of the Rhinegold is that, like the gold of the kennings, it is not a physical but a metaphysical entity. It is not actual metal, though the ring can, by a magic spell, be made from it. It is instead a thrilling apparition, which suddenly appears to the Rhinemaidens, to their delight. It is at first a glow, which intensifies, a 'brightly beaming gleam of gold', a stream of 'magical golden light', ethereal and dazzling. It rises like the sun.

The gods are easily recognizable from their Old Norse counterparts in Snorri's *Edda*: Wotan is Odin, the father of all the gods and mankind; Fricka, his wife, is Frigg. Donner (Thor) threatens the giants with his hammer. But from the many and sometimes contradictory references to the gods in Old Norse sources, Wagner creates complex characters, especially in his portrayal of Wotan, autocratic and troubled, which far exceeds the sources. The malevolent half-god Loki is also introduced as the cunning and untrustworthy Loge, whose alter ego is wildfire; this recalls Snorri's story about Loki's undignified eating contest with a character called Logi, whose name means 'wildfire' in Old Norse, and whose ability to devour not only the food but also its serving dish means that Loki is easily defeated.

The plot of *Das Rheingold* is more complicated than the *Nibelungen-mythus*, but it is still a carefully streamlined synthesis of Norse myth. The giants have built a great fortress for the gods – Walhall – and according to their agreement with Wotan, as directed by Loge, they are to be paid with the goddess Freia. This derives from the so-called 'master-builder story' in Snorri's *Edda*, in which a giant offers to secure Valhalla with a mighty defensive wall; the gods, supposing that the giant will not be able to finish the task within the stipulated time, offer Freyja as a reward – again, on Loki's advice. In Snorri's version, the story is comically ribald: the builder is being helped to finish the wall by a powerful stallion, and Loki, shape-shifted into a mare, distracts the stallion and slows the work. The giant is furious, Thor smashes his hammer against his skull, and the gods, in folk-tale style, are off the hook. Wagner's version is more menacing. The giants, having built Walhall, come to carry off Freia. This is a catastrophe for the gods, because, according to Wagner's neat conflation of this account with the Norse story of the goddess Idunn, guardian of the apples which confer eternal life, Freia's absence means that the gods will grow old and die. Wotan is bound by oath to give up Freia, and Donner's threat of violence is useless bluster. But Loge saves them, by tempting the giants with talk of the Rhinegold. He and Wotan descend into Nibelheim to steal the treasure.

Alberich, as the *Nibelungen-mythus* relates, curses the treasure when it is stolen from him. But Wotan uses it to pay the giants, and Wagner produces another masterly conflation of Old Norse myths. In Snorri's *Edda*, the gods make the mistake of killing an otter which turns out to be the shape-shifted son, Ottar, of a mysterious magician called Hreidmar. As compensation, Hreidmar demands as much gold as will completely cover the skin of the dead otter. Loki steals a treasure hoard from a dwarf, Andvari (a counterpart of Alberich, who also curses the gold, and tries to keep a ring from it), and the gods proceed to cover the otter skin. But one whisker shows through, and only the dwarf's ring, which the gods have kept back, will cover it. In *Das Rheingold*, the giants demand total coverage of Freia – so that, touchingly, they will be spared the sight of what they have given up so reluctantly. This time, there are two chinks in the gold, and the Tarnhelm and the ring must be included in the hoard to complete the covering. Walhall, and eternal life, are within the gods' reach, but Wotan is unwilling to part with the ring and the helmet. In a dramatic addition to the *Nibelungen-mythus*, Wagner introduces one of the most effective figures in the *Ring* cycle: Erda, who establishes her identity as the all-knowing sibyl, or Vala, of the Old Norse poem *Völuspá*:

> How all things were, I know;
> How all things are,
> How all things will be,
> I see as well;
> The endless earth's
> primeval Vala.

She predicts 'a day of darkness' for the gods. Wotan, like Odin, urgently wants to know more, but Erda departs. The giants fight over the ring, and the curse is fulfilled; Fasolt is killed by Fafner. The gods enter Walhall, but the Rhinemaidens lament their loss.

Wagner's use of Norse sources, even in this part of the *Ring* cycle, which contains more than usual non-Norse material, is easily demonstrable. But Norse influence is constantly evident in all sorts of details. Loge claims he has the skill 'to turn an enemy's grudge to advantage' – the proud boast of the Viking poet Egill Skalla-Grímsson as related in the Icelandic saga about him. Freia, in her distress at being taken away by the giants, calls on her brothers, Donner and Froh, for help, echoing the traditional family loyalties of Old Norse heroines. And the giants themselves, Fasolt and Fafner, in their half-repulsive, half-comic desire for the goddess Freia, their stupidity and their violence, are immediately reminiscent of the two Swedish berserks in the Old Norse *Eyrbyggja saga*, who hope to marry the daughter of their master but are given a building task to complete, and are eventually outwitted and killed. It may be that the author of the saga transformed some mythic source he himself knew – a version of the master-builder story, with the woman as reward – just as Wagner himself did, centuries later. Wagner's achievement is to synthesize his sources so seamlessly and cogently that his version seems to be the original one. As one of his contemporaries put it, 'it is simply as though the *Ring* were an original text which was no longer available to the Edda poets and partial comprehension of which can therefore be traced only here and there in their poems; so much does everything in the drama seem to be restored to its original unity and to be newly created and brought to life'. This ability is evident not only in *Das Rheingold*, but throughout the four operas which make up the whole cycle.

The next section of the *Nibelungen-mythus* tells the story of Brünnhilde, and of the ancestors of the hero Siegfried; it forms the basis of the second *Ring* opera, *Die Walküre* ('The Valkyrie'). With the introduction of human characters, we move from the scattered poetic references and prose re-tellings of Norse myth to the heroic Eddaic poems about the Volsungs, a race of legendary heroes, and *Völsunga saga*, the Norse source which brings them together in a continuous narrative. It has been argued that Wagner wrote the *Nibelungen-mythus* before he read *Völsunga saga*, but there are so many elements which closely parallel events in the saga that this is very hard to believe. Certainly Wagner re-read *Völsunga saga* before he completed his libretti. The author of the saga based much of it on the heroic poems about the Volsung dynasty found in the *Poetic Edda*, but the saga begins at a much earlier point than the Eddaic poems, and Wagner's *Nibelungen-mythus* relates and considerably simplifies the early history of the Volsungs.

In his re-telling of the material, Wagner cuts out the immediate ancestors of the Volsungs, and the story of Sigi, who is said to be the human son of Odin. According to the saga, Sigi's son, Rerir, and his wife have no children, but Odin sends them an apple, and through the eating of the apple, the hero Volsung, father of Sigmundr, is born. Wagner picks up this motif but in the *Nibelungen-mythus* the result of the bizarre

Odin/apple impregnation is a pair of twins: Siegmund and Sieglinde. In *Die Walküre*, Wagner drops the whole preamble: the opera opens in medias res with Siegmund the Wälsung (the name of the dynasty is the German version of the Old Norse *Völsung*; there are no Wälsungs in medieval German literature) taking refuge in the home of Sieglinde. She is married to a man called Hunding (this name is borrowed from Eddaic poetry, in which Hunding is an enemy of Sigmund's ancestors). That evening, Siegmund tells the story of his life: a missing twin sister, who turns out of course to be Sieglinde, and a brutal enemy, whom Hunding recognizes as himself. Hunding is unwilling to flout the traditional laws of hospitality, and both that, and a strong disapproval of murder under the cover of darkness, are familiar features in Old Norse texts. Hunding puts off his revenge until morning, and during the night, Siegmund and Sieglinde, brother and sister, fall in love. As they talk, Sieglinde also recalls past events – including an account of how, when she married Hunding, a mysterious old man came uninvited to their wedding feast, and thrust a sword into the trunk of the tree which grows in their hall. Whoever can draw the sword, he declares, shall keep it as a gift. This account is very closely based on *Völsunga saga*; the old man, hat pulled down low over one eye, is of course Odin/Wotan.

The incestuous union of Siegmund and Sieglinde features in all versions of this material. In *Völsunga saga*, the Sieglinde figure – Signy – is married to King Siggeir, and she sends her two sons to help her brother Sigmund who is living as an outlaw in the forest. Signy has persuaded her husband not to kill him outright, but to torture him by tethering him, and his other brothers, in the forest. A she-wolf comes each night to devour them, until finally only Sigmund is left alive. Signy arranges for him to be smeared with honey, and the wolf licks him, and puts her tongue in his mouth. Sigmund bites off her tongue, and in doing so kills her and frees himself. The story of what happens to the children is equally brutal and grotesque. They are sent to Sigmund, who sets them the apparently innocuous task of baking a loaf of bread. But both boys in turn fail to make the bread because they are squeamish about something wriggling in the sack of flour. On Signy's advice, Sigmund kills them both, and Signy's final recourse is to sleep with Sigmund and so produce a child who is of pure Volsung blood: this is the hero Sinfjötli, who joins his uncle/father in his forest exile, and both hunt at night in the shape of wolves. It was, it will be remembered, a poisonous snake in the flour sack, but Sinfjötli paid it no heed, and kneaded it into the dough.

Wagner evidently knew this werewolf story from *Völsunga saga*, though it does not figure in the *Nibelungen-mythus*, in which the incest is also presented as a deliberate attempt to produce a Volsung hero. But the reason given in Wagner's version is that brother and sister have no children by their respective spouses, so there is no association of pedigree with courage; there are also none of the bizarre wolfish elements. In *Die Walküre*, Siegmund, hiding his identity from Hunding, calls his father 'Wolfe' and speaks of exile in a forest, but makes no mention of any of the bizarre events in *Völsunga saga*. These fantastic adventures with wolves were clearly not the invention of the saga author: the author of the Anglo-Saxon poem *Beowulf* alludes to Sigmund and his 'nephew' Sinfjötli, and a fragment of Viking-age sculpture in England seems to show Sigmund biting off the she-wolf's tongue. And Wagner does not explicitly celebrate the sibling incest as a means of ensuring dynastic purity: in *Die Walküre*, the passionate union of brother and sister expresses rather the trans-cendence of true love. Later in the opera, Fricka demands that Siegmund be punished for scorning marriage, while Wotan argues that she cares only for outdated custom, and not for love. She wins the argument, however, and Wotan instructs his valkyrie Brünnhilde to favour Hunding when he and Siegmund meet in combat.

The concept of the valkyrie is peculiar to Old Norse. Valkyries are rather variously portrayed in Old Norse literature, but as servants of Odin they perform two linked roles: to choose which warriors on a battlefield should be taken to join Odin in Valhalla, and to serve those warriors in Valhalla. Brynhild is sometimes identified as a valkyrie in the *Poetic Edda*; sometimes, as in *Völsunga saga*, she is given a human identity as a princess, the sister of Attila the Hun. Her relationship with Odin is uncertain. Wagner identifies her simply and clearly as Wotan's daughter (later he reveals that Brünnhilde's mother is the all-knowing sibyl, Erda). When Wotan sends her to Siegmund to announce his imminent death and reception in Valhalla, the scene in *Die Walküre* – one of the most celebrated and moving in the opera – has clear echoes of the tenth-century semi-skaldic Old Norse poem *Hákonarmál*, in which two valkyries gravely approach King Hakon after a battle, and tell him that they have chosen him, and not his enemies, to be received in Valhalla. Hakon demurs – he fears that his Christian past will not please Odin – but he has no option. Siegmund too demurs, on the grounds that his beloved Sieglinde will not be there. Brünnhilde relents, thus disobeying Wotan's command, but although she attempts to protect Siegmund, Wotan himself intervenes and shatters the spear which was his gift to Siegmund. In the Edda, the disobedience motif is attached to another valkyrie who stubbornly favours the wrong hero, but this and Siegmund's shattered spear come straight from *Völsunga saga*. Brünnhilde's punishment is to be incarcerated on a mountain top, where, like the Sleeping Beauty of fairy tale, she is destined to wed whoever comes along and wakes her. She begs for mercy, or at least to be surrounded by flames, so that this man will have to be the greatest of all heroes, and Wotan, caught between moving affection for his favourite daughter, and the duty to establish his authority, relents in turn and agrees. The flames are produced by Loge – fire – himself. Wagner's libretto provides an emotional climax to *Die Walküre*. In *Völsunga saga*, there is no real sense of any relationship, loving or otherwise, between Odin and Brynhild.

In spite of basing character and event so closely on the Old Norse *Völsunga saga*, Wagner transformed his source, on the one hand by streamlining its rather repetitive and complex narrative, and on the other through the high emotional charge he gave to the sympathetic relationship between Wotan and his headstrong daughter Brünnhilde. We can see exactly the same process operating with Wagner's third opera, *Siegfried*, which tells the story of the greatest of all heroes. But Wagner's development of Siegfried's character, from Sigurd the dragon-slayer in the Norse sources, and the same hero in other German texts, is much less sympathetic, and even repellent to modern audiences.

The story of Siegfried – in Norse, Sigurd the dragon-slayer – is a celebrated one, and Wagner's re-telling of it, in the *Nibelungen-mythus* and the third opera, *Siegfried*, follows the sources closely. In the prose summary, Sieglinde gives birth to her brother's child, the pure-bred Volsung, but dies in childbirth. The boy is brought up by a foster-father, whom Wagner presents as Alberich's brother, who happened to witness the birth. In the Old Norse, Sigurd's foster father is Reginn, the third son of the magician Hreidmar. In the *Nibelungen-mythus*, Wagner retained the Norse name, but for his libretto he borrowed for Sigurd's foster-father the name Mime (Old Norse Mimir) from the wise Norse giant whose decapitated head becomes an oracle for Odin to consult. In *Völsunga saga*, Reginn's brother, Fafnir, has taken over the treasure hoard, and in his complacent greed has rather magnificently turned into the conventional mythic guardian of great treasures, a dragon. In Wagner's work, the same transformation has happened; Fafner the dragon is the shape-shifted brother of Fasolt; he killed his brother and stole the gold. Both Reginn and Mime are smiths, and the forging of a great sword is an important element in the dragon-slaying. The Eddaic poem *Fafnismál* ('The Words of Fafnir') dramatizes the dragon's dying words, and Wagner borrows closely from it. Having killed the dragon, Sigurd roasts its heart, and in the process licks his burned finger. At once, birdsong becomes intelligible to him, and the birds inform him of Reginn's proposed treachery. Wagner leaves out the cooking, but Fafner's blood similarly burns Siegfried's hand, and when Siegfried licks it, he understands the birds' speech. The birds warn the hero about the foster-father's treachery, and also direct him to Brynhild/Brünnhilde on the mountain top. Wagner introduces a wonderfully effective elaboration of Siegfried's enhanced understanding when Siegfried, and the opera's audience, hear not the words Mime thinks he is speaking, but a translation of them into his underlying treacherous and hate-filled thoughts. Finally, the hero kills his foster-father. None of the underlying narrative is found in the *Niebelungenlied*; it all originates in Norse sources, although some aspects of the story are also treated in other nineteenth-century versions of the Sigurd story which Wagner read.

As well as reproducing the story of Sigurd from *Völsunga saga*, Wagner incorporates two scenes featuring Wotan which are closely modelled on other Old Norse texts. Before the dragon-slaying, disguised (as so often in Old Norse myth) as the Wanderer, Wotan visits Mime, and engages him in a question-and-answer contest of wisdom which is clearly based on the mythic Eddaic poem *Vafþrúðnismál*. In the *Edda*, Odin is ostensibly trying to find out how much the giant Vafthrudnir knows; in literary terms, the poem is a vehicle for transmitting mythic knowledge. In *Siegfried*, Wagner uses the contest as a fine dramatic device for recapping what has happened in the previous operas. Wotan's second appearance in *Siegfried* occurs after the dragon-slaying. Here, he summons the sibyl, Erda, just as Odin calls up the sibyl, or *völva*, in the Eddaic-style poem *Baldrs draumar*: the sibyl is unwilling to rise from her interminable sleep, and their exchange ends in mutual recrimination. The scene is familiar from Thomas Gray's eighteenth-century reworking of it as *The Descent of Odin*. Wagner's version has the added emotional tension of Erda's lofty disapproval when she learns how Wotan punished Brünnhilde – her daughter, too – and of Wotan's own uncertainty, regret and resignation to his, and the gods', eventual demise.

Wagner's careful re-arrangement of relationships in the Sigurd story leaves intact, and even intensifies, the emotional tensions between the main characters. Brothers – whether the giants Fasolt and Fafnir, or the Nibelungs, Alberich and Mime – compete for the cursed treasure. And Siegfried, like Sigurd, is being manipulated by his foster-father in order to kill the dragon and recover the hoard, and there is evident hostility between them. But the character of Siegfried is not attractive. It may be true that the qualities of a hero are not in any case greatly admired today. Siegfried (like his prototype Sigurd) is originally 'one who knows no fear' (Wagner developed a German folk-tale from the Brothers Grimm to tell the story of how Siegfried learnt to know fear, but the central motif – 'he was never afraid' – comes directly from *Völsunga saga*), and his killing of the dragon is an admirable act, but this does not result in a character who is very sympathetic or humane. Siegfried's harsh masculinity is no longer very appealing. But much worse is his hateful treatment of his foster-father, Mime. Siegfried teases, bullies, insults and terrorizes Mime. He treats him with complete contempt, and Wagner gives full rein to Siegfried's loathing of Mime. In fact, Mime is himself contemptible and loathsome, but this does nothing to mitigate Siegfried's behaviour, and only increases observers' disquiet about their relationship. Siegfried's hatred is based not on what he knows about Mime (for he has not yet tasted the dragon's blood). Instead, Siegfried's violent reaction is instinctive: he recognizes Mime as physically different from himself. In turn Mime is presented as not only physically grotesque (as is his brother Alberich, too) but also, significantly, feeble. Siegfried derides him as 'shuffling and shambling, weak-kneed and nodding, blinking [his] eyes'. Clearly, Wagner intended Mime to be repellent in his deformity and frailty.

It has been argued that many of the physical and moral characteristics of Alberich and Mime would have been familiar to contemporary German audiences as key features of the vitriolic caricatures of Jews which were current in Wagner's time. Certainly, the Nibelungs' association with gold is a depressingly familiar aspect of antisemitic propaganda still. But even without this direct connection, the dynamic of the physically beautiful hero despising the weak and the ugly is, to a modern sensibility, acutely distasteful. And the insistence on physical difference as marking one 'race'

– the heroic Volsungs – from another – the despicable Nibelungs – quite plainly rests on theories of race which were held to demonstrate the supremacy of the tall, fair, civilized 'Nordic' peoples, and which came to be used as justification for the eradication from the Germanic *Volk* of not only Jews, but also those who were believed to be less than physically and mentally perfect. Having experienced Siegfried's response to Mime, it is almost impossible not to reflect back on the now sinister significance of the incestuous union of Siegmund and Sieglinde, and quite impossible to ignore the fact that when Siegfried wakes Brünnhilde from her sleep on the mountain top within the ring of fire, he supposes, from her resemblance to himself, that she is his mother. Her insistence that he is 'her own self' only reinforces this expression of physical unity, and their impassioned love duet is coloured through and through by a modern audience's hindsight.

In *Völsunga saga*, Odin occasionally appears to intervene directly in the affairs of humans, invariably disguised as an old man with one eye, hat pulled down low over his face. But although in the saga the Volsungs have Odinic blood in their ancestry, Odin remains a shadowy presence in the heroic poems of the *Edda*, and in the manuscript which contains the poems a clear distinction is maintained between the mythological poems, in which Odin features very prominently, and the heroic ones. In Wagner's *Ring* cycle, however, Wotan is the dominant presence throughout, and the relationship between the gods and the humans lies at the heart of the meaning of the whole drama, as Siegfried takes over the gods' role in recovering the Rhinegold, and Brünnhilde readily relinquishes her divine status in order to share her love with Siegfried. Nowhere is this connection between the human and the divine more crucial than in the final opera of the cycle, *Götterdämmerung* ('The Twilight of the Gods'). Wagner's original plan was to make the death of Siegfried a free-standing opera, and as we can see from the *Nibelungen-mythus*, the twilight of the gods barely features in it. But the triumph of the hero became indivisibly linked with the demise of the gods, Wotan in particular, and Ragnarök – an exclusively Norse concept – forms the powerful climax of the whole cycle.

The prologue to *Götterdämmerung* is wholly based on Old Norse myth. The three Norns of Snorri's *Edda*, and ultimately the poem *Völuspá*, are shown gathered together recalling the past (another re-capping device by Wagner). They recall the World Tree (in Old Norse, Yggdrasill), and how Wotan pledged one of his eyes to partake of the wisdom of its well.

In an imaginative extension of the original myth, Wagner has the Norns claim that Wotan fashioned a spear from a branch he broke off from the World Tree, and that this has caused the tree to wither and die. Wotan's spear – as the symbol and instrument of the oaths he swears – is a key motif in the *Ring* cycle. The image of Yggdrasill, which will, before Ragnarök, show signs of ageing as it shudders and creaks, an image of an organic cosmos nearing its end, is one of the most evocative in all Old Norse myth. The words of the Norns echo very precisely the sibyl's repeated, testy, rhetorical question in *Völuspá*, 'Do you know yet, or what?', and the Norns too, like the sibyl, sink down when their speech ends.

Following this prologue, the continuing story of Siegfried and Brünnhilde is picked up. Siegfried becomes involved with another heroic family, the Niflungar – here, the children of Gibich, and therefore known as the Gibichungs. The names of Gunther and his half-brother Hagen are borrowed from the *Nibelungenlied*, although there they are not brothers, unlike their counterparts in Old Norse, Gunnar and Högni. The essence of the next part of the narrative is that Gunther plans to marry Brünnhilde, but it is Siegfried, transformed by the Tarnhelm into a likeness of Gunther, who actually rescues her from the fiery mountain top. Brünnhilde, to whom Gunther is a stranger, is appalled by having to marry him, and is horrified by the belief that Siegfried has betrayed her. This basic story is elaborated in different ways in the various sources, German as well as Old Norse. Only in *Völsunga saga* is Sigurd (Siegfried) given a magic potion to make him forget Brynhild, and Wagner must have used the Old Norse as the source for Brünnhilde's dramatic claim that she never slept with the hero who rescued her from the flames, since he placed a naked sword between them in the bed. But by different routes, and for slightly different reasons, both the Old Norse and Wagner's libretto have Brynhild/Brünnhilde plotting the death of Sigurd/Siegfried.

The key figure in the death of Siegfried is Hagen, Gunther's half-brother. In *Götterdämmerung*, his father is the Nibelung dwarf Alberich, and although the motif of the half-brother is prominent in Old Norse sources, nowhere is a half-brother evil as here. In the Old Icelandic *Gisla saga*, the eponymous hero Gisli is involved in an extended blood-brotherhood ritual with his own brother and two brothers-in-law, his wife's brother and his sister's husband. The brother of a wife and the husband of a sister are actually very tenuously related, and in *Gisla saga* one brother-in-law refuses to take part in the ritual, for this reason. This scene seems very likely to have influenced Wagner in his depiction of Hagen's refusal to join in the oath of loyalty which Siegfried and Gunther swear. But Wagner's elaboration of this scene once again raises issues of blood and race: Hagen claims that his blood, cold and coagulating, will not mix with theirs. This is a clear physical sign of his racial otherness, as a half-Nibelung.

Hagen succeeds in his plan to kill Siegfried (just as, in various versions of the story, the Niflung brothers kill Sigurd). With the aid of a memory-restoring drink administered by Hagen (Wagner's own invention) Siegfried poignantly begins to recall his past, and dies as he remembers his first encounter with Brünnhilde. Her grief, just as in the Norse sources, is quite terrible; her unnatural laughter echoes in both opera and Eddaic poem. And in both, she commits herself to her lover's funeral pyre, in the opera having first restored the Rhinegold to its proper guardians, the Rhinemaidens. *Götterdämmerung* – and the whole cycle – ends as the flames from Siegfried's funeral pyre extend to Walhall itself. This climax, dramatic though it is, is quite different from the Norse myth of Ragnarök, with its grotesque encounters between gods and giants in monstrous form, as Thor meets the World Serpent, Odin, the wolf Fenrir, and Tyr, the dog Garmr. As always, Wagner carefully skirts around the more surreal aspects of Norse myth; he is not interested in sensation. But the Old Norse poem *Völuspá* does not end with this cosmic conflagration, but with a new world, a fresh, clean creation purged of its old horrors. And Wagner too conveyed this sense of regeneration, of hope: not through his libretto but through his musical score: *Götterdämmerung* ends with a return to the musical theme which has been identified as 'atonement'.

Wagner was to become, notoriously, Hitler's favourite composer. There is no doubt that his *Ring* cycle, in its transformation of Norse mythology into a German national epic, suited both the ideology of National Socialism, and the tastes of its adherents. And it is also evident that Wagner shared the widely held racist views of his time, and did little to moderate the potential of his source material to promote a supremacist message. The presentation of the inferior and yet threatening Nibelungs directly recalls antisemitic caricatures prevalent in Wagner's time.

Another work which Hitler was said to have admired greatly – to the extent of being moved to tears by it – was Fritz Lang's 1924 film *Die Nibelungen*. In two parts (the death of Siegfried, and the vengeance of Kriemhild), the work is based very closely on the medieval German version of the material, the *Niebelungenlied*. Siegfried's winning of Brynhild in place of Gunther is depicted as a tense sexual drama. There is no wall of flame to clear, but only the failure of Gunther to subdue – evidently, sexually – his new wife, who is his mate, but not his match. However, Lang uses Norse material to make some fascinating changes to his basic source. Unlike the *Niebelungenlied*, the film is set not in the high Middle Ages, in a courtly society, but in an evidently earlier period, a visually unforgettable richly decorated barbarian culture full of bold geometric designs and even some authentic copies of pre-historic Norse carvings. And most striking of all, Lang presents the villain, Hagen – Siegfried's murderer – as Odin himself, unmistakable with his one eye, his sinister presence, and a magnificent raven-winged helmet.

Lang's racial stereotypes, however, are entirely predictable. Siegfried is tall and blonde, with regular, chiselled features. Brynhild is dark, Kriemhild, fair. Siegfried's foster-father, Mime, is a grotesque, sub-human creature, a bent little savage. And the figure of Alberich is precisely modelled on the contemporary stereotypes of the despised Jew.

Norse mythology – not on account of its actual subject matter, but simply as a subject in itself – was (and is) held in high regard by those who want(ed) to claim a Nordic ethnic origin, and this in itself is a racist impulse. But its relationship with Hitler and the Nazis remained more incidental than formative – Hitler himself regarded Wotanists, those who followed what they believed to be a pre-Christian Germanic religion, with complete contempt.

I want to look at the history of another familiar aspect of Norse myth and culture – the runes – and at the part they too came to play in National Socialism. Runes are the characters of an alphabet used for inscriptions in Germanic languages throughout North Western Europe. There is no 'runic language' – the individual letters can be used to spell out words in different Germanic languages: Anglo-Saxon, Frisian, early Scandinavian and so on. There are even some inscriptions in Latin. The distinctively angular shape of the letters has been explained as a response to the practical problem of carving them on strongly grained wood, though inscriptions are found on other hard surfaces, most obviously stone and ivory. There is no agreement about the origin of the letter shapes, although derivation from Greek or Etruscan alphabets has been suggested. The earliest inscriptions have been dated to the first century AD, and from then until around 1500 AD, runic inscriptions were carved on all sorts of objects for all sorts of purposes. The simplest messages involve the name of the owner or maker scratched on to an object such as a comb, or piece of jewellery. More public runic inscriptions on monuments such as gravestones or stone crosses are common, and are not confined to the pagan period: there are plenty of Christian inscriptions. It is worth bearing in mind that the inscribed objects which have survived tend to be significant in themselves: precious, carefully crafted articles, or great monumental sculptures. This has tended to give the impression that runes themselves were in some way portentous, conferring gravity on the object. This impression was conclusively swept away only as recently as the second half of the twentieth century, when hundreds of runic inscriptions, mostly on bits of wood, were found in Bergen, in Norway. Most of these messages concern trivial domestic or commercial matters: business letters, prices, name-tags. Very many are more like examples of modern graffiti than serious inscriptions: *inkebjørkunimer þaerekuarisþa(fa)kri* 'Ingibjorg had sex with me when I was in Stavanger'. In short, in spite of the modern association of runes with magic and mystery, the vast majority of runic inscriptions are either secular – nothing to do with magic or religion at all – or straightforwardly Christian, such as the gravestones.

Magic almost always involves language – sometimes in combination with ritual action. One only has to think of spells, curses, or magic words such as 'abracadabra'. So given that any alphabet is a sign system for a language, it's not surprising that there are some runic inscriptions which do seem to be designed to perform a magical function. Sometimes, scholars have been over-imaginative in interpreting strange or repeated combinations of runic letters as magic words. It is likely that some otherwise indecipherable inscriptions are the result of an incompetent or apprentice carver: a botched job, or a trial piece. It is even possible that runes could have had a decorative function, rather than a meaningful one – in much the same way as Western fashion has from time to time decorated objects or fabric with invented Chinese or Japanese characters. But other inscriptions were plainly designed to have a magical function. Each runic letter has a name, often a common noun. Thus the first rune in the runic alphabet, or 'futhark', F, had the Scandinavian name *fé*, which means money, cattle or wealth, and the reason for repeated carving of this symbol on any object is easy to understand. Even more obvious is the repeated carving of the T rune on a sword, for the name of the character, as well as being the name of one of the most powerful of the Old Norse gods, Tyr, means 'glory' or 'renown' in both Old English and Old Norse. And just as Christian runic inscriptions may invoke God, or Christ, so inscriptions which date from the pagan period will occasionally make appeal to the heathen gods of Old Norse myth: the commonest formula is some variation on 'may Thor hallow these runes' (on a gravestone).

It is easy to see how these mysterious carvings – so very like a secret code – on evidently ancient stones throughout Europe caught the attention and the imagination of antiquarians. At the beginning of the seventeenth century, for instance, the British antiquarian Sir William Camden notes in one of the early editions of the *Britannia*, his great topographical and historical survey of the British Isles, that there is a carving on a stone cross at Bewcastle, in Cumberland, but that the inscription is unreadable. Later British historians consulted Danish scholars about it, but it was not until the beginning of the next century that this and other celebrated runic inscriptions in Britain – such as the Ruthwell Cross, in Dumfriesshire – began to be recorded and interpreted, again with help from the Danes. In Scandinavia itself, as I explained in the previous chapter, runic inscriptions were seen as the last surviving fragments of a great national literature created by the magnificent ancient Goths, ancestors of the modern Scandinavians, and the Danish historian Ole Worm – whom English scholars consulted about runes – believed that all Old Norse literature had originally been written in the runic alphabet. At around this time, runes were not in themselves associated with magic. They were merely understood as a distinctive alphabet, peculiar to the forebears of some European nations. But it was with the re-discovery and circulation of Old Norse literature – especially the mythological texts – that the connection between runes and heathen magic was made.

Surprisingly enough, a significant step was taken by an English scholar, Sir Henry Spelman. He suggested, boldly, to Ole Worm that the word 'rune' was not, as had been proposed, derived from the Scandinavian word for groove, or furrow, but was rather related to the Anglo-Saxon word *run*, meaning 'secret'. And once European scholars became familiar with the Eddaic poem *Hávamál*, and with the prologue to Snorri Sturluson's *Heimskringla*, the belief that runes were an invention of the arch-magician Odin quickly became established, together with the belief that runic characters must have had some supernatural power, which would explain why the alphabet was suppressed by the Christian Church, and fell into disuse. These two ideas remained at the heart of how runes were regarded, especially among later German mystical nationalists, as we shall see.

There are references to the use of runes for magical purposes in several Old Norse texts. In the Eddaic poem *Skírnismál*, for instance, the god Frey sends his messenger, Skirnir, to the giant maiden Gerd to cajole, bribe and ultimately coerce her into a sexual union with him. Skirnir's threats to Gerd include carving at, or on, her three 'Þ' runes. In the Anglo-Saxon futhark, 'Þ' was known as *thorn*, and was widely used as part of the Roman alphabet to represent the 'th' sound. But in older Scandinavian tradition, 'Þ' was called *þurs*, the word for an ogre, or giant. In a runic alphabet poem which plays on the names of the individual letters, 'Þ' – *þurs* – is called 'the torment of women'. No-one knows what, precisely, this refers to, but it is clearly meant to be damaging and injurious. That Skirnir threatens to carve it three times recalls actual runic inscriptions in which one character is carved repeatedly, apparently for emphasis. This reference in *Skírnismál* could then reflect some knowledge of the actual practice of using runes for magical purposes. Similarly, in another Eddaic poem, *Sigrdrífumál* ('The Words of Sigrdrífa'), there is a series of references to the magical properties of individual runes, including the recommendation that a 'victory rune' carved on a sword hilt could ensure success in battle, again recalling actual inscriptions from the Viking period.

But runic references in Old Icelandic sagas are more doubtful, and may betray nothing more than their authors' vague awareness of some authentic runic practice. In *Grettis saga*, for example, Grettir has taken refuge from his enemies on a rocky island off the coast of Iceland. Its cliff faces make it impregnable, but one of Grettir's enemies has an old woman carve a runic inscription on a log, and she reddens the inscription with her blood, and recites spells over it while walking around it backwards and withershins (in the opposite direction to the sun). As she throws the log in the sea, she curses Grettir, and prophesies that the log will float out to Grettir's island and cause him harm. As might be expected from such an overload of hostile magic, the log does indeed prove to be Grettir's downfall, but for an unexpectedly mundane reason: he chops the washed-up log for firewood, and cuts his leg as the axe glances off the block; his leg becomes (understandably enough) infected, and he is fatally weakened and hence unable to withstand when his enemies next attack. *Grettis saga* is full of different kinds of language: Grettir speaks skaldic verse, proverbs and riddles, and it is entirely fitting that he should seem to meet his death through the effects of curses and spells. But the saga author is careful to underpin this with a naturalistic explanation. Similarly in *Egils saga*, the fictionalized biography of the fearsome Viking poet Egill Skalla-Grímsson, the hero is called to the bedside of a sick child. He finds beneath her mattress a piece of whalebone, with runes carved on it, which he scrapes off, and replaces with better ones. The girl is cured. This episode is derived more from Christian miracle stories than from any real Viking-age event or practice, and no doubt the saga author, in his presentation of Egill as a pre-Christian poet, an acolyte of the god Odin, adapted a story from a saint's life to suit his Odinic hero, and this explains the rune carving. In both cases, the references to runes belong to the literary theme of the sagas.

It was knowledge of the Eddaic poem *Hávamál* ('The Words of the High One') that cemented the connection between Odin and runes for early modern scholars. *Hávamál* is a patchy collection of pieces of traditional wisdom attributed to the god Odin. At its climax, often regarded by scholars as a separate poem in itself, the god seems to describe a dramatic ritual of self-sacrifice – 'myself to myself' – from which the god is apparently resurrected, having acquired wisdom from the world of the dead. Disturbingly, there are several detailed parallels with the biblical account of Christ's crucifixion – hanging from a tree, being pierced by a spear, denied food and drink – as well as the central theme of death and resurrection. It may be that the author of *Hávamál* recognized the fundamental parallels between his material and the biblical account, and enhanced the similarity with the inclusion of these details – it is not likely that the sacrifice of Odin was wholly derived from Christian sources, not least because kennings in very early skaldic verse refer to it.

The first of Odin's gains after his torment hanging on the tree is apparently the acquisition of runes. The poem's expression is obscure, but the first-person speaker describes looking downwards, and then declares: 'I picked up the runes, screaming I took them'. This strange and opaque claim – supported by some Scandinavian runic inscriptions which

150

describe runes as 'divinely inspired' – became the basis of the generally held belief that Odin invented runes. But *Hávamál* continues with more mysteries. Odin relates how he has learnt 'nine mighty spells' from a giant called Bölthor, Odin's mother's brother, and also drank from the mead of poetry. What may be an interpolation into the poem speaks of very powerful letters, carved by Odin, and created by the mighty gods themselves. And then the Odinic first-person voice takes over again, to recount eighteen spells: healing charms; spells to blunt an enemy's weapons; to put out fires; to calm storms at sea. Some of them involve Odin's own characteristic activities: to speak to those who have died by hanging; for making himself irresistible to young women. It is not at all surprising that from the time that this text became widely known by European scholars, Odin was established as the creator of runes, the inventor of poetry, and the originator of magic. The connection between runes and the occult was secure.

In the nineteenth century, German nationalism harked back to an idealized Germanic past, and was preoccupied with the ancient roots of the Germanic peoples. It was inevitable that Norse mythology would occupy a large part of this self-image of the Germanic race, or *Volk*. The concept of the *Volk*, which was to become such a central element in later Nazi ideology, was always much more than simply 'the people' – it denoted an almost mystical racial identity, and for this reason, so-called *völkisch* thought concerned itself not only with history, but also with the more shadowy aspects of a supposed racial culture such as folklore, ancient wisdom, mysticism and magic. Runes, therefore, at the heart of all these issues, were an obvious focus for mystic nationalism and *völkisch* thought.

Interest in the occult was not of course confined to Germany, but was common throughout Europe. One of the most celebrated occult gurus was Helena Petrovna Blavatsky – Madame Blavatsky – who built up an immense (and immensely influential) occult system – theosophy – maintaining that all ancient religions contained enough of a fundamental spiritual truth to provide a basis for mystical union with the one true god. She believed that this esoteric wisdom had been, and could be, passed on by the initiated members of various secret societies. She traced the origins of the human races way back through a series of mythic pre-historical cycles, each cycle marked by the rise of a particular 'root race'. Each root race was to be greater than the one preceding it, and the

151

society of her time was witnessing the ascendancy of the Aryan race. Theosophical thought and German mystic nationalism were made for each other, and were brought together most cogently in the work of an Austrian nationalist, Guido von List, with his inspired blend of the two: 'ariosophy' – the occult wisdom of the Aryan people.

Von List's ariosophy was, like Blavatsky's theosophy, anti-modernist, racist and mystical. Von List dovetailed the accounts of created generations of giants in Norse myth with Blavatsky's great cosmic cycles, and argued that the original German pagans, worshippers of the gods of Norse myth, had been driven out of their homeland by Christians, to end up in Scandinavia and, eventually, Iceland. He published articles about Norse mythology, and a number of Norse-based works including a play called *Der Wala Erweckung* ('The Awakening of the Wala'), inspired by Odin's consultations with the sibyl of *Baldrs draumar*, and *Völuspá*. Although he was brought up as a Catholic, from an early age von List rejected Christianity and devoted himself to Wotan as the true god of the German people. Wotanism was the name given to the religion supposedly practised by these original Germanic people, and it too was based on a system of esoteric wisdom guarded by a secret Wotanist priesthood. (It should be remembered, incidentally, that Norse sources tell us practically nothing about actual forms of worship, doctrine or theology.) Towards the end of his life, he had developed the concept of this elite priesthood into a political idea: what he called the 'Armanenschaft' – a secret ruling elite of initiates who could preserve ancient Aryan wisdom, and guide lesser Aryan folk to a new society based on patriarchy, racial purity, a strict hierarchy (with a powerful leader at its head) and the union of Austria and Germany. Von List based the name 'Armanenschaft' on the name given by the Roman historian Tacitus to one of the chief Germanic tribes, the Hermiones.

Von List's ideas were eagerly adopted by German nationalists. In the early years of the twentieth century – before von List's death in 1919 – the von List society was set up, to discuss and promulgate ariosophy and the Armanenschaft. Von List's role in the development of Nazi ideology is evident. But what of the runes? In 1902, von List suffered a period of blindness. Recovering from an eye operation, he spent long hours pondering theories of Aryan languages and especially the function of magical symbols and runes. His nationalist interests in German prehistory swung towards the mystical, and he came up with an extraordinary, and at the same time obvious, idea. The number of characters in the runic alphabet varied during the history of rune use; the shortest alphabet amounted to 16 characters, the longest (and oldest) to 24. But von List claimed that the authentic number of characters was 18 – precisely the number of Odin's spells in the poem *Hávamál*. It was obvious: each of the runes which Odin had picked up represented in itself a magical charm or spell. Each runic character was a powerful site of ancient Germanic wisdom. Runes as magical symbols encoded this wisdom from the past. Von List's nationalist ideals and passion for the occult were fused in this insight.

Von List and his followers saw runes – and therefore the encoding of ancient Germanic wisdom – everywhere. The heraldic devices of Austrian aristocratic families (themselves the carriers of the race wisdom, for which reason Guido List added the aristocratic marker 'von' to his real name) were runic shapes in cunning disguise. The patterns of wooden beams on the outside of half-timbered houses secretly expressed Aryan esoteric wisdom. Runic characters – now, symbols – had become powerful icons of German, Aryan identity. Incidentally, the swastika itself was not a Norse character, but originally a Hindu symbol for good fortune, and was adopted because of its association with what were believed to be the ancient roots of the Aryan race, in India. (This perhaps surprising bit of racial myth allowed the Germanic race to dissociate itself once and for all from any suggested origins among the Semitic peoples of the Middle East.) However, the double 'S' rune was to become very familiar as part of the symbolic regalia of the SS, Heinrich Himmler's elite secret para-military organization.

Many of von List's followers went on to form or belong to societies which became progressively more racist, and explicitly antisemitic. Often under names borrowed from Old Norse – the Edda Society, the Thule Society – and in the guise of scholarly societies investigating such topics as Old Norse mythology, they became influential forums for the discussion and spreading of Nazi ideology. With scientific advances concerning radio waves and electromagnetic fields came a bizarre new refinement on the idea that runes could be the vehicles of ancient wisdom. Rudolf John Gorsleben founded the Edda Society, and had for a while been a member of the Thule Society, which had direct links to the forerunners of the National Socialist Party. But he had left politics to devote himself to writing: he translated the *Edda*, and derived from it yet another version of a mystic Aryan ancient religion, one that was explicitly racist, and incorporated new theories about eugenics and racial mixing. Many of his ideas were based on von List's theories about runes, but he went a step further still. He claimed that the universe was permeated by an invisible energy emanating from the ancient and powerful god of the purest Aryan people, and that runes could attract and channel this energy, forming a quasi-electrical link between each individual Aryan man and the creator of the universe Himself, and thus a quasi-scientific union with God. One of the periodicals he set up in his political phase came to be called *Hagal*, the name of one of the runic characters, believed by adherents to be the most powerful of all.

Heinrich Himmler was much influenced by occult ideas – hence his adoption of runic symbols for SS uniforms. Supporters of the Nazi regime were often devotees of Norse myth, and the story of Ragnarök, with its final battle, the many reverses for the gods, and the eventual triumphant establishment of a wholly new world order, became for some a metaphor for the progress of the Third Reich, and the course of the Second World War itself. But if Norse myth was part of a nationalist package, it was not the defining element of Nazi ideology, especially in its occult forms. Such ideas remained on the fringes of Nazism. Himmler involved himself in occult circles, but Hitler dismissed Wotanists as no more than despicable play-actors. Occult theories about runes, always tangential to actual Nazi politics, continued a life of their own outside the doctrines of racial purity and antisemitism. Friedrich Bernhard Marby developed Gorsleben's theory of runes as conduits of divine energy into the cult of *Runengymnastik* – rune gymnastics, which involved participants holding yoga-like poses in the shape of runic letters, in order to attract to themselves this energy, which took the form of cosmic waves or rays. Different runic characters could attract and transmit different kinds of powers and qualities. Siegfried Kummer added to this a practice called rune-yodelling (*Runenraunen*), in which various kinds of humming, supplemented by mystic paraphernalia such as magic circles, and the performance of runic exercises, could draw down these mysterious forces.

Marby and Kummer were denounced by the Nazis; Marby was accused of making the 'Holy Aryan heritage' look silly, and ended up in Dachau. In fact, the man who criticized them, Karl Maria Wiligut, a special advisor to Himmler on all things mystical, had plenty of strange ideas of his own. He believed that his family were the survivors of a Germanic super-tribe of ultimately divine origin, the Irminists. Their chief prophet was called Baldur/Chrestos, and he had been crucified by Wotanists. The Irminists had been additionally successively persecuted by Catholics, Masons and Jews. Wiligut wrote under the name Jarl Widar; readers with long memories will remember the name Vidar as that of the god who was destined to tear apart the jaws of the wolf Fenrir at Ragnarök. It is striking how neatly these fantasies align with modern popular psychology – persecution complex, megalomania, and so on – and no surprise, perhaps, that Wiligut was in due course certified insane.

The theories of von List, Marby and Kummer have continued to be propagated, and a quick search on the web will bring up a number of sites devoted to rune gymnastics and similar practices. They belong, along with a great deal of other runic lore, to the wide spectrum of New Age activities, and their original connection with racism and the Third Reich is hotly disavowed by their practitioners. Revivals of Germanic paganism will form part of the next chapter, the reception of Old Norse myth in modern times. Before moving on to that, however, we need to look at such interest in Old Norse myth as there was in Britain in the nineteenth century.

In the British Isles, as explained at the beginning of this chapter, attitudes to romanticism, nationalism and paganism were quite different from what was happening in Germany. High Romantic poets never latched on to Norse mythology with the same engagement that authors such as Thomas Gray and William Blake had shown, and mythology faded as an artistic subject. Political circumstances, far from fostering Romantic nationalism, tended rather to suppress it. Norse mythology in Britain never achieved anything like the role in national politics that it came to assume in Germany and Austria. Interest in Old Norse literature tended to focus on what passed for historical actuality, and its main mythic dimension was the mental image of the brave, male, bearded, fair or red-haired Viking warrior – often represented in art or drama with his horned helmet, although there is no justification for this in any of our texts. These horns may originally have been a theatrical brainwave which caught on and has never died out. From time to time, major literary figures made use of Norse mythology, but always in an oddly marginal way. I want briefly to consider three of them: Thomas Carlyle, Matthew Arnold and William Morris.

Thomas Carlyle was a Victorian political philosopher, born in Scotland in 1795. In 1840, he published what came to be one of his most popular works, a series of lectures *On Heroes, Hero-Worship, and the Heroic in History*. The title of the first of these lectures was 'The Hero as Divinity. Odin. Paganism. Scandinavian Mythology'. Carlyle, who had abandoned his Christian beliefs, wrote in prophetic mode, denouncing what he saw as the ills of contemporary society and proclaiming the need for strong, inspired, leadership (the most famous, and influential, Carlyle quotation is that 'the history of the world is but the biography of great men', taken from the lecture on Odin). Carlyle, as is evident from all this, was greatly influenced by German philosophers and political thinkers, and his essentially (and increasingly) anti-democratic position has sealed his reputation as one of the forerunners of fascism. His line on Norse paganism, and on Odin, was very far from mystical, however. He begins the lecture by urging his listeners to see the natural good in paganism, as an untutored religion which tended, to its credit, to wonder at God's creation, and worship the most impressive aspects of it. One of these objects deserving of 'transcendent wonder', as Carlyle put it, was 'the great man', and thus it was, according to Carlyle's brief summary, that Odin as leader of the ancient Scandinavians came to be worshipped as a divinity. It was by a similar process, according to Carlyle, that the figures of Norse myth, originally natural phenomena such as flame, or storms at sea, or thunder, were turned into gods, and worshipped. The narrative surface of Norse myth, as Carlyle concedes, can seem like the merest nonsense: 'A bewildering, inextricable jungle of delusions, confusions, falsehoods and absurdities!' How could anyone take it seriously? And yet there was, even for Carlyle, something seductive about its images – of the World Tree, Yggdrasill, Carlyle writes 'the rustle of it is the noise of Human Existence'.

Carlyle was enormously influential in his own time, but soon went quite out of fashion: his social criticism was topical rather than timeless. And some of his formulations – for instance, his celebration of hero-worship as 'heartfelt prostrate admiration, submission, burning, boundless, for a noblest godlike Form of Man' – are hard to admire today (though ironically, Carlyle was here characterizing Christianity). The rise of fascism certainly threw a harsh backward light on his writings. But he incorporated the god Odin – whose divine status arose only through the natural ignorance of his human followers, however – into a political philosophy, and forced Norse mythology into the popular consciousness.

156

Carlyle was also a major influence on the Victorian poet and critic Matthew Arnold: though their political and religious positions were very different, Arnold was also a fierce critic of what he saw as the ills of contemporary society, and there are even verbal echoes of Carlyle's *On Heroes* lectures in Arnold's poetry. Arnold was a classicist by training and inclination, but he came to Old Norse myth, like so many of his literary predecessors, through Mallet's *Northern Antiquities*. Moreover, a contemporary critic, J.A. Froude, had complained that Arnold's poetry was too narrowly based on classical themes and models – interestingly, Froude recommended taking up Germanic myth, as material which for British poets embodied 'the inheritance which has come down to them of the actions of their own race'. The resulting poem, *Balder Dead*, is based on Snorri Sturluson's story of the death of Baldr as it appeared in *Northern Antiquities* – and as Carlyle paraphrased it in his lecture on Odin. But few critics found themselves sympathizing with the 'actions of their own race'. One contemporary reviewer dismissed Norse myth as a subject precisely 'too remote to arrest sympathy', though Arnold himself wrote in his letters that he was pleased with and proud of the poem.

In *Balder Dead* Arnold re-told Norse material in classical tradition: he applied the poetic techniques of Homer and Virgil to Old Norse myth. He had been reading Homer's *Iliad* and *Odyssey* alongside *Northern Antiquities*, and in terms of poetic style, he writes that he had succeeded in giving the poem a distinctively Virgilian 'propriety of diction and rhythm' and 'tenderness and pathos'. As one might expect, then, all the wild and colourful elements in the original – for instance, the gods' playful hurling of missiles, the bizarre congregation at Baldr's funeral, including a giantess mounted on a wolf with snakes as reins, Freyja riding her cats, and god Thor kicking a dwarf into Baldr's funeral pyre – are discreetly omitted. But the dignified and solemn stance can seem flat and even bathetic, and the opening line of the poem 'So on the floor lay Balder dead' is more comic than arresting. However, both the powerful pathos of the gods' loss – commended by Carlyle – and their doomed determination to overcome it are well conveyed by Arnold, and the power of the story carries his stately, Miltonic blank verse along. In fact, Arnold was urged to write another long poem explaining the back-story to the events of *Balder Dead*, just as Wagner began what was to be his *Ring* cycle with the death of Siegfried, and then worked on the prequels, *Die Walküre* and *Das Rheingold*. In the end, Arnold made do with an introductory note taken from the *Northern Antiquities* version of Snorri's *Edda* story, but it is strong testimony to the drive and cogency of the original Norse narrative that the need for such extensions was felt.

In *Balder Dead* the Norse setting is completely unrecognizable; Arnold has replaced Asgard with a classically inspired and architecturally elegant city; characters wander 'the streets of Asgard' and Balder's house there is on the harbour, next to the city wall. The Norse gods are replaced by dignified human figures from classical tradition. Frigg's hall, with its 'lighted windows' and 'open doors', is peopled by

> The Prophetesses, who by rite eterne
> On Frea's hearth feed high the sacred fire
> Both night and day; and by the inner wall
> Upon her golden chair the Mother sate,
> With folded hands, revolving things to come –

These prophetesses are more vestal virgins than valkyries. The most distinctively classical – and by the same token, un-Norse – elements in the poem are the so-called Homeric similies, lengthy and elaborate comparisons which are often hugely inappropriate to the Norse subject matter. Thus, for example, Balder's brother Hoder, miserably wandering the streets of Asgard after Balder's death, fortuitously comes across Hermod (who is destined to ride into Hel in the hope of reclaiming Balder) in the dark:

> …Hoder touched his arm.
> And as a spray of honeysuckle flowers
> Brushes across a tired traveller's face
> Who shuffles through the deep dew-moistened dust,
> On a May evening, in the darkened lanes,
> And starts him, that he thinks a ghost went by –
> So Hoder brushed by Hermod's side…

Nothing could be less like the Norse original, in either literary form or individual detail, though the simile itself is a touching one. Hermod's journey to the goddess Hela, in Hel, to reclaim Balder, is only a partial success – he returns to Asgard without Balder, but with Hela's offer to give up Balder if the gods can make everything weep him back to life. Arnold's Lok (the malicious half-god, half-giant, Loki) compares Hermod, with astonishing inappropriateness, to a farmer who has lost his dog at market. The lost dog itself occupies the bulk of the simile; again, touchingly, the dog is described as

> With flanks a-tremble, and his slender tongue
> Hangs quivering out between his dust-smeared jaws,
> And piteously he eyes the passers by...

In fact, it might be argued that these very attractive nuggets of pastoral description are the best bits in the poem, even though they are so anomalous. Perhaps the most bizarre example comes as Arnold describes Hermod's perilous journey to the underworld. For nine days and nights Hermod gallops Odin's horse Sleipner (its eight legs tactfully not mentioned) through a wild and mysterious landscape. He comes to the bridge over the great river Giall; guarded by a strange giantess, Modgud, it is the last barrier before the gates of Hel itself. Arnold compares Modgud blocking Hermod's way to a charming rustic traffic jam:

> ...as when cowherds in October drive
> Their kine across a snowy mountain-pass
> To winter-pasture on the southern side,
> And on the ridge a wagon chokes the way,
> Wedged in the snow; then painfully the hinds
> With goad and shouting urge their cattle past,
> Plunging through deep untrodden banks of snow
> To right and left, and warm steam fills the air –
> So on the bridge that damsel blocked the way...

By contrast, Arnold's account of how (almost) all created things weep for Balder shows, in its use of an extended comparison, how sensitively he develops the implications of the mythology. Snorri tells how all things – except, of course, the giantess Thökk – were persuaded to weep Baldr out of Hel – 'just as you must have seen that these things weep when they move out of frost and into heat'. Snorri's deft rationalization of this mythical event has been echoed by mythographers who identify the story of Baldr's death as a vegetation myth; the god might be resurrected in spring, when the world thaws out. Arnold's simile captures this perfectly:

> And as in winter, when the frost breaks up,
> At winter's end, before the spring begins,
> And a warm west-wind blows, and thaw sets in –

> After an hour a dripping sound is heard
> In all the forests, and the soft-strewn snow
> Under the trees is dibbled thick with holes,
> And from the boughs the snowloads shuffle down;
> And, in fields sloping to the south, dark plots
> Of grass peep out amid surrounding snow,
> And widen, and the peasant's heart is glad –
> So through the world was heard a dripping noise
> Of all things weeping to bring Balder back.

The spring thaw is evoked very exactly and vividly, but the simile is not merely decorative, but delicately suggests a deeper meaning to the myth. Arnold's reading of *Northern Antiquities* was careful and scholarly; his allusions to other events in the mythology are impressively accurate and well worked into the narrative. Balder's passionate closing speech, in which he foresees the coming of a new world, 'more fresh, more verdant than the last', after Ragnarök, is strikingly in tune with the mood of the Norse original. But Arnold's attempt to classicize a Norse myth was not, in the end, a success. One contemporary critic could not resist an obvious joke: 'Balder Dead is Balder dash'.

As a committed socialist, the writer William Morris also felt himself to be at odds with the prevailing social ethic of his time, and he too turned to the medieval period as an inspiration for both his creative writing and his politics. Like Arnold, he was influenced by Carlyle, though he was even more unlike Carlyle in his view of the world than Arnold was. Morris had developed a passion for Iceland and all things Icelandic, and in 1870 he and the Icelander Eiríkur Magnússon translated *Völsunga saga*, together with some of the Eddaic poems it was based on: essentially, the same material Wagner used for the *Ring*. Six years later, Morris completed *Sigurd the Volsung*, a stately poetic version of the same material, four times as long as the original, in long alliterative lines. Morris could not have been more in sympathy with his material. He knew the original well. He admired the spirit and values of the Icelandic people, which he thought were reflected in the Sigurd material. He believed that in the Middle Ages – in depressing contrast to his present day – there was a more natural and productive relationship between the individual and society. His Sigurd was not a heroic bully, like Wagner's Siegfried, but, improbably, a just and humane ruler, whose political dictum, like Morris's

THE RISE OF RACISM

own, was 'that the sheaf shall be for the plougher'. In fact, Morris detested Wagner and his work.

Contemporary critical opinion was divided about *Sigurd the Volsung*. George Bernard Shaw called it 'the greatest epic since Homer', praise which would have been especially pleasing to Morris because he felt so strongly that the original material was 'a story which should be to all our race what the Tale of Troy was to the Greeks'. Again, racial ties were an important issue: other critics reviewing Morris's work denied the special relationship between England and Germany – 'it does not follow that because we speak a German tongue we must be a German people. Language is not a final and absolute test of race' – and felt the Norse material to be alien and unappealing. Reference was often made to Carlyle's lecture on Odin, as if the understanding of Norse myth had not moved on at all for the last three or four decades. Morris was sometimes praised for his achievement in making his recalcitrant material at all palatable: 'To make the Eddas interesting is no easy task'. Words used of the original material were 'crude', 'primitive', 'incoherent' and even, iron-ically, 'deficient in heroes'. Plainly, these heroic myths had not been taken to heart as they had been in Germany. They were dismissed as 'too much the outcome of a transient vogue in sentiment to insure a very long remembrance'. At best, enthusiastic reviewers suggested the possibility of a vogue for Norse myth being kicked off by Morris's work. But the prevailing opinion was that the perceived 'foreignness' of the material, which 'may be admired and applauded by the lettered few', was a grave handicap to any popular acceptance of it. The poet Swinburne wrote scathingly of 'all that dashed and blank Volsungery'.

Morris made some careful improvements to his original material. Like Wagner, he drastically simplified the repetitive and episodic prehistory of the Volsungs, and he ironed out some of the inconsistencies in *Völsunga saga* which arise from the fact that the prose saga is a compilation of separate poems which did not necessarily take each other's version of events into account. The major stumbling-block here was the attitude of the Norse Gudrun to her brothers: in some poems they were responsible for the death of her beloved Sigurd, while in others she gladly took revenge on her husband Atli (Attila the Hun) and, indeed, her children by him, in order to avenge her brothers' death at his hands. Morris's characterization of Gudrun as a traumatized, almost catatonic, victim of the violence is both in keeping with the original, and at the same time unexpectedly modern. His Atli, too, is a wonderful villain.

Morris's poetry, with its slow, long alliterative line, and its many archaisms, met with a mixed reception. But at its best, it has a grandeur which rises to match the awesome grandeur of creation and apocalypse in the Norse sources. Gunnar, Gudrun's brother, has been sentenced to death by Atli. He is to be killed in a snake pit. His slow death is the occasion for a poetic speech describing creation:

> So perished the Gap of Gaping, and the cold sea swayed and sang,
> And the wind came down on the waters, and the beaten rock-
> walls rang;
> Then the sun from the south came shining, and the Starry Host
> stood round,
> And the wandering moon of the heavens his habitation found;
> And they knew not why they were gathered, not the deeds of their
> shaping they knew:
> But lo, Mid-earth the Noble 'neath their might and their glory grew,
> And the grass spread over its face, and the Night and the Day were
> born...

This is a remarkable re-telling of *Völuspá*. Like the classical harpist Orpheus, Gunnar charms the snakes in the pit into quiescence –

> – All save the Grey and Ancient, that holds his crest aloft,
> Light-wavering as the flame-tongue when the evening wind is soft:
> For he comes of the kin of the Serpent once wrought all wrong to
> nurse,
> The bond of earthly evil, the Midworld's ancient curse.

Here Morris pulls together the dragon slain by Sigurd (who cleared the wavering flames to win Brynhild), the biblical serpent from the Garden of Eden, and the mighty Miðgarðsormr, the World Serpent of Ragnarök. But Morris's conception of Norse myth stretched to the new world which would arise from the ashes of the old one, 'when the new light yet undreamed of shall shine o'er earth and sea'. Like Carlyle at the beginning of the century, Morris despaired of the modern world, and both saw in Norse myth the heroes and values which matched their own vision of a better one. Their visions could not have been more different, and yet the mythology served both their purposes.

CHAPTER 8

Contemporary Myths

The celebrated literary critic Northrop Frye has insisted that all kinds of texts are linked in a chain of influence, an unbroken line of descent: 'Poetry can only be made out of other poems, novels out of other novels... Everything that is new in literature is reworking of what is old'. And so it is that various reworkings of Old Norse themes in the nineteenth century have given rise, in their different ways, to the subjects of this final chapter on present-day responses to Norse myth. In many cases, the line of descent is clear and evident. The dominant literary reworking of Old Norse myth in the twentieth century is J.R.R. Tolkien's *The Lord of the Rings*, whether in print or on film. Its legacy from William Morris's quasi-medieval fantasy writing is plain, and its reaction against Wagner almost equally so, as I shall show. The political writings – in print, again, or, more commonly, online – of the neo-pagan or white racist groups, especially those based in North America, with their enthusiastic focus on Old Norse mythology and culture, echo (though they rarely develop) the *völkisch* mysticism of such as Guido von List, and, sometimes, the brutal racism of National Socialism.

But it is also true to say that at the beginning of the twentieth century there were some radically new departures. The literary movement which came to be known as modernism, and which encompassed all the great literary figures of the period, such as Virginia Woolf, James Joyce, W.B. Yeats and T.S. Eliot, is actually defined by its self-conscious dissociation from the literary, philosophical and political assumptions of the previous

163

century, and in turn a search for new systems of belief. As a result, many writers turned to myth as an alternative framework of ideas. However, only in special cases was their mythology culture-specific; it was more often a vague distillation of traditional ideas of rebirth and cycles of nature and the seasons. James Joyce's *Ulysses* might seem from its title to draw explicitly on Homer's *Odyssey*, but the novel is actually a deliberate burlesque, even a rejection, of its classical precursor, and certainly not a re-telling in any straightforward sense. None of the canonical figures of English literature drew directly, even in such perverse ways, on Old Norse myth.

Although the First World War naturally dampened enthusiasm for Old Norse myth as the precious legacy of a pan-Germanic 'race' including the British, right up until the Second World War themes of Nordic racial supremacy are still occasionally evident in literature, as we shall see. But the open celebration of Norse-inspired heroism, based on Wagnerian power and strength, went to ground, understandably, and resurfaced in the unexpected form of fantasy comics and games, and children's literature. In fact, the line between adult and children's fiction has become increasingly blurred – as *The Lord of the Rings* itself demonstrates. The suitability of Norse myth as a subject for children's stories was, however, a direct legacy from the Victorian popularity of Viking stories of courage and heroism for budding empire-builders. Finally, one new development at the end of the nineteenth century became a very important factor in the twentieth-century reception of Old Norse mythology in all cultural fields: the inception of Norse studies as an academic discipline, a subject studied in universities. This status did not, of course, protect it from the prejudices of its practitioners, but it meant that there could be a politically, and at least to some extent aesthetically, disinterested dissemination of Old Norse myth, which formed another route into popular (and elite) culture, particularly the literary world. In the twenty-first century, then, there are many ways of coming to Old Norse myth, and even more ways of using it.

Some twentieth-century poets had a special relationship with Old Norse literature because of their origins – or at least, their perception of them. George Mackay Brown, for example, who lived and worked all his life on Orkney, immersed himself in the Icelandic literature about the Norse settlers of the islands, which had an enormous influence on his own work. But though he was deeply interested in the local Norse-derived folklore, as a devout Christian he concerned himself more with the Viking history of Orkney, and the texts which contained it, than with Norse myth. He particularly deplored any glamorizing of Viking violence, and despised claims to racial purity or superiority made by those who thought themselves Norse-descended. W.H. Auden's special relationship was less clear-cut. He believed himself to be of Icelandic extraction – partly because he thought, like his father before him, that their surname was derived from the Icelandic name Auðunn, or even Odin, and partly because he identified in himself what he thought were typically Nordic physical characteristics: blond hair, pale eyes and a fair skin. Auden, who had studied both Old Norse and Old English, translated, with the help of Paul Taylor, a medieval academic scholar, the mythological poems of the *Edda* – and dedicated the volume to J.R.R. Tolkien. But his few references to Old Norse myth, especially as revealed in his and Louis MacNeice's travel journal, *Letters from Iceland*, were quirky and academic, and it plays relatively little part in his poetry, although work has been done recently on Auden's interest in, and use of, words of Anglo-Saxon and Old Norse origins, as a reaction against the Latinate rhetoric of other modernists such as Eliot and Pound.

It was perhaps the racial connotations of Old Norse myth, together, paradoxically, with its re-tellings as children's literature, which precluded its reworking by even Norse-inclined writers such as Mackay Brown and Auden. But some poets have been able to take the central symbols of Old Norse myth – if not the narrative exploits of Odin and Thor – and build them into the new, alternative structures which modernist writers and thinkers sought at the beginning of the twentieth century. The Scottish poet Hugh MacDiarmid, in difficult, obscure verse, often in broad Scots dialect, used the Norse World Tree Yggdrasill, and the World Serpent, as symbols of mankind and the cosmos. In MacDiarmid's celebrated long visionary poem *A Drunk Man Looks at the Thistle*, published in 1926, the drunk in the gutter gazes up at 'this sorry weed' – a symbol of Scotland itself – and sees himself in it, and therefore the potential of all mankind to connect with the Infinite. From his perspective, the humble thistle towers above him, and becomes in his eyes, ironically, the World Tree, a 'michty trunk o' space' with centuries for rings, and comets for fruit. It takes a drunk man to make this transformation, and MacDiarmid's drunk is a version of the visionary poet, an identification again drawn from Norse myth, with its insistent linking of poetic inspiration and the mead of Odin. But in the original myth, Yggdrasill signals the end of the world: it shudders as Ragnarök approaches. MacDiarmid's thistle shudders too, and with two reductive comparisons it, like Yggdrasill, is shown to reflect the real world's capacity for decay and degeneration: MacDiarmid likens it to a dried-out herring, and its terminal shivering to the twitching of a horse's hide in response to the bite of a horsefly. Mysteriously, the thistle also stands for the poet himself, just as in Norse creation myths the humans originate as animated pieces of driftwood, and in skaldic verse the commonest kennings for men and women are based on tree words. In one final playful comparison, the drunk man's Adam's apple is described as slower to bob up and down 'like a squirrel' than it was in his youth – a clear reference to the squirrel in Old Norse which scuttles up and down Yggdrasill's trunk.

The figure of the Miðgarðsormr, the giant serpent of Old Norse myth, also stirred MacDiarmid's poetic imagination. For the drunk man, feeling his age, the sea-serpent is way beyond his reach: unlike the ambitious young god Thor, who is obviously recalled here, he has no ambitions to land the serpent, remaining 'content to glimpse its loops'. Or perhaps the poet imagines himself as unwilling to disturb the mystery of the distant deep sea creature, a symbol of God's creative ability which can be admired but not reduced by explanation. In 'The Sea-Serpent', MacDiarmid again calls up the image of a monstrous serpent, its endless coils filling the whole sea, and the universe besides, and thrilling even God himself with its power and joyous writing. In this poem, the sea-serpent seems to represent God's first creative act, its protean shape unlike the fixed forms of mankind and the rest of the animal kingdom. MacDiarmid has created his own creation myth.

Hugh MacDiarmid was very conscious of the partly Viking origins of the Scottish nation. He contributed in a characteristically learned and passionate way to the often bitter debate between those Scots who celebrated Celtic roots and those who looked to the North, writing movingly of an Icelandic saga character, Aud, nicknamed 'the deep-minded' for her wisdom, a fitting matriarch for the Scots, since she was of mixed Hiberno-Norse origins. And like Auden, MacDiarmid loved Iceland, and drew much inspiration from it. But later poets too came to draw on Norse myth, not because they sensed or paid homage to any special relationship with Old Norse culture, but because a knowledge of Norse myth became part of some poets' literary and historical education.

Thus, for example, Paul Muldoon, in a poem from the collection teasingly entitled *Quoof* (apparently a private family term for a hot-water bottle), published in 1983, describes a strange tree in a northern landscape which the poem's speaker climbs in pursuit of wisdom. Muldoon is renowned as a deliberately puzzling poet; and the poem's title helps only those well versed in Norse myth. 'Yggdrasill' (the title, with significant scholarly rigour, spelt in exactly the correct Icelandic form) is a poem which works with the idea, advanced by academic mythographers, that the World Tree might have formed part of a shamanistic ritual, which the Norse perhaps learned from their neighbours the Saami, or Lappish, people. But the ascent of Muldoon's Yggdrasill does not result in wisdom; in true post-modern style, at the top of the tree there is only an insignificant scrap of paper, a cheap fragment of the truth. *Quoof* is packed with allusions to many mythologies (including personal ones); Old Norse myth simply takes its place among them.

These allusions do not reflect a general knowledge of or interest in Norse mythology: on the contrary, they serve to make the poetry 'difficult', to underpin Muldoon's pervasive urge to challenge or mystify the reader. Muldoon's use of Old Norse allusions actually furthers his character-istically modernist purpose of making a single, absolute reading of his work as unlikely as possible, precisely because so few readers of his poetry will be equipped to unravel the references. There is a very striking example in one of Muldoon's more recent collections of poems, *Hay*, published in 1998. The poem entitled 'Rune' was originally written for an anthology of riddles. It follows the traditional form of the riddle: a first-person speaker describes his/her/its experiences, and the poem ends with an invitation to the reader to guess the speaker's identity. Elsewhere in Muldoon's work, he has associated runes with secret knowledge, and quoted the *Oxford English Dictionary*'s definitions of runes, including 'any song, poem or verse', so that 'Rune' would seem to be an obvious title for his riddle poem. But this is all too obvious. There is, characteristically, a riddle buried within the riddle. The speaker of the poem boasts of having 'cut a figure', ostensibly in the colloquial sense of having made a visual impact, as in 'to cut a dash'. But the phrase is also a direct translation of the technical term for carving a rune. Muldoon is not using the word 'rune' loosely, to mean a mystery poem, but pointing to a piece of wordplay even deeper in the poem. The speaker of 'Rune' is a mystery figure, just as each runic character is, in the alphabetical sense, a figure, and the verb 'to figure' is the one Muldoon uses at the end of his poem to invite the reader to solve the puzzle: 'Go figure'.

In theory, the visual arts ought to be another area in which elements of Norse myth might be freely re-worked and imaginatively recreated. However, apart from the offensive iconography of Nazi propaganda, which often incorporated images from Norse myth or Viking culture into its depiction of blond-haired German soldiers who matched the supposed Nordic racial ideal, the influence of Norse myth on the visual arts in the twentieth century was very limited. Two exciting exceptions are, interestingly, works of art not by painters or illustrators, but by artists working in two media characteristic of the Viking age itself: tapestry and jewellery. Towards the end of the twentieth century, the Danish artist Bjørn Nørgaard created a set of tapestries for Queen Margrethe of Denmark which now hang in the royal reception rooms in Christiansborg Palace in Copenhagen. The centrepiece of the full tapestry is a stylised representation of the World Tree, Yggdrasill, and the panels are filled with visual references to Old Norse myth, often echoing the images of actual Viking age carvings or tapestries. In the field of jewellery, Lori Talcott is an American artist who has produced a series of elaborately crafted neck pieces inspired by the Old Norse story of the necklace of the Brisings. As Talcott herself points out, there are no descriptions of this mythic treasure in any of our sources, so Talcott's new treasures are works of art in their own right, and not in any sense replicas, or even re-interpretations of the contents of the texts. But the actual texts play an important part in Talcott's work, because she has inscribed each piece with one of the seven medieval literary references to the treasure, taken from the manuscripts themselves. Remarkably, the very language of Old Norse myth has been transformed into art.

To return to the world of more conventional literary texts, it is of course much easier to give the great symbols of Old Norse myth a vital, working significance in poetry than in prose fiction. Allusions to Norse myth in novels abound, from the nineteenth century until the present day, but often have little more significance than the learned classical allusions they stand in for. So, for instance, in Thomas Hardy's 1887 novel *The Woodlanders*, a character steps out into the dark night, which is likened to 'an absolute void, or the ante-mundane Ginnung-Gap believed in by her Teuton forefathers'. Behind this comment is a typically Victorian assumption about 'Teutonic' – that is, pan-German – culture, held to include Norse myth, but the allusion is little more than a minor didactic aside by Hardy, and one which, significantly enough, he felt the need to explain quite carefully. A good example of more extended reference to Norse myth is A.S. Byatt's recent novel *Possession*, in which the protagonists are aspiring academics researching the life and works of a Victorian poet, appropriately named Randolph Ash, given that the title of his magnum opus is 'Ragnarok'. Here, the Norse references are at one remove: they add historical colour to the young researchers' subject, a literary figure who might well, in his time, have been directly influenced by Norse themes, although, as we have seen, a poet in Ash's time would have been more likely to engage with heroic legend or saga narrative than with the myths themselves. Byatt even produces a pastiche of Ash's verse, and she explains exactly why contemporary audiences would have found a full-blown reworking of pagan mythic themes uncomfortable. Ash's poem 'Ragnarok' was controversial: 'some saw [it] as the Christianizing of Norse myth and some trounced [it] as atheistic and diabolically despairing'. Ash himself is presented as recognizing, and developing, the parallels between Norse myth and Christian tradition. He defends his poem against the charge of having caused Christabel LaMotte – who is to become Ash's lover – to doubt her Christian faith:

> I meant ['Ragnarok'] rather as a reassertion of the Universal Truth of the living presence of Allfather (under whatever name) and of the hope of resurrection from whatever whelming disaster in whatever form. When Odin, disguised as the Wanderer, Gangrader, in my Poem, asks the Giant Wafthrudnir what was the word whispered by the father of the gods in the ear of his dead son Baldur on his funeral pyre – the young man I was – most devoutly – meant the word to be – *Resurrection*. And he, that young poet, who is and is not myself, saw no difficulty in supposing that the dead Norse God of Light might prefigure – or figure – the dead Son of the God Who is the father of Christendom.

Possession reworks its Norse themes at one and then two removes, depicting fictional scholars who are researching a fictional author himself engaged in that reworking. Otherwise, for myth to be used by prose writers in an active, productive way, the author must almost always abandon naturalism – that is, narratives which depict an apparently real, recognizable world, filled with similarly plausible characters and events.

For this reason, then, we must look at literary genres such as science fiction, fantasy, the supernatural and magic realism to see Old Norse myth being reworked in significant ways.

Literature in the style known as magic realism, with its incorporation into otherwise naturalistic narratives of elements of often disturbing fantasy – sometimes derived from myth or fairy tale – is an obvious site for Old Norse mythic elements. It can be difficult, however, to recognize these elements, because there may be no very evident connection between the overall narrative and the Norse motif or episode in question. Günther Grass's novel *The Tin Drum*, published in Germany in 1959, is a fantastic chronicle of a Polish–German family from the beginning of the twentieth century to the period following the Second World War. The novel is narrated from the very singular perspective of Oskar Matzerath, speaking from a mental institution in Düsseldorf: he made the decision at the age of three to mature no further, and refuses to be separated from the tin drum of the novel's title, which he beats incessantly. *The Tin Drum*, as Oskar's strange autobiography, inevitably concerns itself with the history and politics of twentieth-century Europe, and, especially, nationalism. For instance, Oskar's mother's husband is an enthusiastic Nazi; her lover (and perhaps Oskar's father) is a nationalist Pole. Given this historical setting, and the strong links we have already explored between German nationalism and Old Norse myth, it is perhaps not surprising that Grass's novel draws so copiously on Old Norse. Some of the echoes are faint. Oskar's drumming is reminiscent of the rituals of Lappish shamanism, in which a drum is beaten to summon spirits – especially given that the drumming is Oskar's own way of summoning memories and the inspiration to tell the story – and this is a ritual which seems to have influenced accounts of magic practices in Old Norse. The love triangle theme which centres on Oskar's mother and her husband and lover also recalls the various relationships in *Völsunga saga*, and there is even a curious little scene in which spitting into sherbet powder is associated with procreation – just as the Old Norse gods are said to have mixed their spittle to create Kvasir. One of the most powerful scenes in the novel describes a strange fishing expedition: on the end of a long line, hauled up with great effort by an old man in a distinctive hat, is 'something heavy and dripping, a great living lump of something'. It is a horse's head, used as bait to catch eels; Oskar's mother is violently sick at the sight of it. This is an unmistakeable reference to Thor's encounter with the World Serpent, but it is the very quantity of the other, fainter references which alerts the reader to Grass's allusive practice.

On the face of it, it is more surprising to discover elements from Old Norse myth in the work of perhaps the most celebrated magic realist, the Colombian writer Gabriel García Márquez. And yet his short story 'A Very Old Man with Enormous Wings', set somewhere in Central America, at some unspecified time in the past, is clearly based on the figure of the Norse smith Völund in the *Poetic Edda*, who escaped his mutilation and imprisonment by King Nidud by assuming a bird coat and flying away. In Márquez's story, the mysterious incomer has clearly fallen to earth: 'it was a very old man, lying face down in the mud, who, in spite of his tremendous efforts, couldn't get up, impeded by his enormous wings'. These wings are squalidly realistic: 'huge buzzard wings, dirty and half-plucked…forever entangled in the mud'. The villagers take him for an angel, but the local priest establishes that he can't be an angel because he can't converse in Latin, 'the language of God'. Márquez offers a couple of clues to the Völund connection. The old man is at first said to speak 'in an incomprehensible dialect' but later became 'delirious with the tongue-twisters of an Old Norwegian'. Eventually, he flies away again, 'with the risky flapping of a senile vulture'. It is very curious that Viking-age carvings in Britain persistently link depictions of the Völund story with Christian iconography, as if they too saw an unlikely parallel between this bird-man and one of God's angels. And to go by a brief mention in Anglo-Saxon elegiac poetry, for those Anglo-Saxons who knew the story of Völund, his flight might have been seen not simply as a triumphant escape, but as the beginning of a weary and interminable exile for a creature now belonging to neither earth nor sky – the very old man of Márquez's story. Perhaps Márquez has simply picked up a very vivid image from Norse myth, and used it without regard to its original context or modern connotations. Or perhaps there is more: the story offers a bizarre twist on the coming of the Norse to the New World.

I want now to turn to non-naturalistic literature which does have a clear ideological reason for drawing on Old Norse myth, and to take as my example two novels by David Lindsay, a writer of Scottish descent who wrote before the Second World War, and whose use of Old Norse myth is vividly brought to life because of the extraordinarily explicit doctrines of racial supremacy and purity which inform his characters' world-view.

Lindsay's novel *A Voyage to Arcturus*, published in 1922, is essentially science fiction. It begins with a séance, which sets the scene for strange happenings, and rather perfunctorily brings together the main characters, who then travel together to the star Arcturus. In fact, the space travel is passed over very swiftly. The rocket is powered by 'back rays' which, having emanated from Arcturus, have a natural and unstoppable propensity to boomerang back there, and can somehow (no technical details are given) be harnessed to propel the space vehicle. Once on Arcturus, the protagonist Maskull (whose improbable-sounding name seems to be built out of 'mask' and 'masculinity') begins his real voyage, which takes him through a fantasy land where even the colours are different from those on earth. Arcturus is peopled by characters whose physical strangeness (they have all sorts of different protuberances and extra limbs, and even tentacles) is matched only by their moral and philosophical idiosyncracies. Much of the novel is taken up with discussions between Maskull and his fantastic interlocutors. Lindsay himself read a great deal of German philosophy, and it is therefore no surprise that the themes which are explored include the necessity of sacrifice, the abnegation of individuality, the acceptance of fate and the role of suffering as a means to recover what Lindsay saw as mankind's 'original sublime nature'. Interestingly, Thomas Carlyle was an important influence on him.

Explicit Norse references are deceptively few. Maskull goes in search of a mysterious figure called Surtr – the name of the fire-giant who according to *Völuspá* commands the troops from (or of) Muspell in the last great war against the gods at Ragnarök. Muspell itself is described by Snorri as the realm of fire on one side of the *ginnunga gap*, facing and opposing the icy world of Niflheim, but in the poetry the name is given to a shadowy but powerful figure, himself a giant like Surtr. In *A Voyage to Arcturus* the significance of Muspel as a place is only made clear at the very end:

Muspel was no all-powerful Universe, tolerating from pure indifference the existence side-by-side with it of another false world, which had no right to be … Muspel was fighting for its life … The moral combat was no mock one, no Valhalla, where warriors are cut to pieces by day and feast by night; but a grim death struggle in which what is worse than death – namely, spiritual death – inevitably awaited the vanquished of Muspel.

Lindsay has not simply borrowed strange-sounding names from Norse myth to label his alternative world; he has engaged with Norse creation and apocalypse myths to create not only his own physical universe, but a whole alternative moral order.

Devil's Tor, published ten years later, is a very different novel, but it develops in a remarkable way the ideas touched on in *A Voyage to Arcturus*. In *Devil's Tor*, Norse myths are boldly connected to the actual beliefs of Lindsay's apparently naturalistic human characters – and, one fears, Lindsay's own. Its main characters are, as was Lindsay himself, of Scottish descent, and extremely proud of it. But to this national heritage is added a vibrant racial dimension: they have not only Scandinavian names – Ingrid, Helga, Magnus – but also supposed Nordic racial characteristics. Ingrid, indeed, the novel's heroine, is physically perfectly Nordic, with her pale hair, skin and blue eyes. Her cousin, red-haired Hugh Drapier, is evidently a despised Celt, and Lindsay, speaking through Ingrid, contrasts the two 'races': Ingrid, 'though English born, of English parents, was accustomed to insist in her mind on the distant Norse descent which she fancied was her peculiar personal heritage, whereas Hugh Drapier, like his father before him an outsider to the family, was obviously a Gael, a Highland Scot, whose nameless ancestors had been unbreeched savages when Kolbiorn the Marshal, from whom the Colbornes (her own kin) derived, was already subduing peoples and framing laws under the great King Olaf Tryggveson, nearly a thousand years ago'. Historical scholarship has moved on since Lindsay was writing, however, and it's no longer taken for granted that Highlanders are Celts – or even that 'Celtic' is a meaningful label anyway.

Magnus Colborne's great work is called *Racial Derivations*. We can infer some idea of its contents from discussion throughout the novel of racial theories. 'No dark skinned race,' explains one character, 'has yet achieved a philosophy'. And 'even the grander monuments of Egypt seem difficult to account for, considered as the handiwork of a sun-baked race'. It is clear that we are in Aryan supremacy territory here: what Lindsay calls 'the old, conquering Aryans' as against the 'pitiless, mercenary Semites'. Much of this polemic is familiar from eighteenth-century treatises on the relationship between a bracing climate and the supposedly essential qualities of the Nordic people, who are warlike and freedom-loving. The conclusion is inescapable: 'the blood-descendants of that northern stock not only built all the noblest edifices of Greece

and Gothic Europe, but created the dream-like Hellenic mythology ...'
and so on. This is all ultimately derived from early pseudo-historians like
Johannes and Olaus Magnus, who claimed similar cultural superiority
for the supposed ancestors of their own nation, the Goths. Such views are
not merely the background to the action of the novel. They are integral to
the plot, which centres on possession of a mysterious holy stone originally
looted from a Lama monastery in Tibet (held by some, it will be remembered, to be the ancestral home of the superior Aryans). Northern blood
has been diluted, and has degenerated – giving rise to such inferior
European peoples as the Spanish and Italians. It must be renewed, and it
turns out that the stone – a meteorite fallen to earth – is to be the means
to this. And Ingrid – that perfect Norse type – is to be its sacred vessel.

This all sounds like entertainingly preposterous – if nastily racial –
whimsy. But Lindsay backs up the plot with an elaborate 'explanation'
given by a professor of languages and antiquities, and his theory involves
a detailed and radical re-interpretation of Norse myth. Eddaic accounts
of the creation of the cosmos – 'the sparks and flakes that flew into
Ginnungagap from Muspellheimr' – really recount the falling to earth of
a sacred stone from outer space, a blazing meteorite. The earth also
received at the same time 'a female visitant' – the Great Mother. She was
allegorized by the simple Norse myth-makers as the cow Audumbla; the
stones she licked were the shattered fragments of the meteorite. The life
forms which arose from the licked stones were Odin's father and the
'giantess' Bestla, who '(to omit an obviously falsely inserted generation)
were the chosen individuals from a pre-existing barbarous tribal forest
folk. Odin himself was the resulting god-man.' Thus it was, as the myth
explains, that a darkish Northern people were mystically translated into
the highest race on earth; the divinity of the Aryan people came about
because of an intervention from outer space. Subsequent Old Norse
sources encode this occult wisdom, insistently recording the differences
between the dark and the fair. Lindsay's professor offers a telling example
of the contrasting dark/fair pairing from the Icelandic *Egils saga*, in which
Egill, dark and difficult, is contrasted with his successful, popular and
fair-haired brother Thorolf. He goes on to explain the origins of another
fundamental opposition. The giant Ymir is hard to place in this re-reading
of Snorri's *Edda;* he is nourished by Audumbla's milk, but is mentioned
before her in the text. But Professor Arsinal, as is the way with professors,
has an answer to this: 'the myth must somehow have been corrupted'.

His explanation is that the creative Great Mother is matched by an equal and opposite evil principle, 'a sinister "infra" force…whose strength and malignity were those of death itself'. Unable to grasp the philosophical subtleties of this, the myth-makers represented it as the giant Ymir, from 'another myth system altogether, crudely welded to the first at a later date'. Arsinal's confident identification of interpolation and transformation in order to reach down to the underlying meaning is not too far from the actual practice of academic mythographers.

Lindsay does not confine his re-interpretation to creation myths. He also re-interprets the Norse apocalypse in his distinctively racialist reading. Surtr and 'the sons of Muspellheim' figure large, as they did in *A Voyage to Arcturus*: they 'stand for the archetype of the yellow-haired men of the north', and their role at Ragnarök is 'the destruction of the old order' and 'the second coming of the power of the lith [the sacred stone] raising those yellow haired ones to new and sublimer and final splendours'. Lindsay has brilliantly, if malevolently, united racial theories current in some circles in the real historical world with Norse myth. The mythology does not function simply as a cultural mark of Northern-ness, but is presented as a system which, as the occult racists, especially in Germany, were claiming when Lindsay was writing, encoded truths about the real world. These truths are universal, common to all racist writings: they concern the origins of the claimed race; its superiority and, somewhat paradoxically, its struggle for survival; and finally, its apocalyptic triumph. Such hidden knowledge may have been forgotten, suppressed or dismissed. But it can be accessed and recovered by assiduous academics, by an initiated elite, or simply by a respectful return to the old ways by ordinary people. Since the Second World War, the use of Norse mythology for explicitly racist ends has naturally all but disappeared from cultural productions such as books or films (though the ideology of hidden knowledge and how to access it has remained extremely popular, as witnessed by innumerable adventure films, conspiracy theories and most obviously the success of Dan Brown's thriller *The Da Vinci Code*). Nearer the end of this chapter, I will examine how successfully Norse myth has been used by writers whose aim seems not to be the promotion of any racist agenda. But first, I must turn to the area in which some or all of the collection of ideas which might be called a modern racist myth is still expressed: the political writings of the far right in Europe and North America.

The various ideologies of the many groupings which lay claim to or are informed by Norse myth are a shifting blend of nationalism, racism, neo-paganism and mysticism. Only the most extreme far-right groups can be said to promote unchanged the beliefs and aims of National Socialism, but aspects of ariosophy, notably its anti-Christian, occult, racial supremacist and *völkische* ideas, can be traced very widely. Groups such as Wotansvolk, Odinic Rite, Ásatrú and Forn Sed, while being very different in their beliefs and presentation, are all based on some sort of Nordic or Germanic nationalism. The core of their nationalist conviction is that their members belong to a community which once had true cohesion – a 'golden age', when ideals and practices had not degenerated, which has been lost and must somehow be recovered. For all of them, Old Norse literature is the ancient expression of this imagined community, hence its importance. To go back to 'the old ways' (a literal translation of the Swedish name Forn Sed) or to worship the Æsir (Ásatrú means 'the faith of the Æsir') is to reconnect with one's supposed ancestral origins – or race.

Some organizations, especially Forn Sed and the various splinter groups with Ásatrú in their name (the Ásatrú Alliance, the Ásatrú Folk assembly, and so on), vehemently reject the accusation that they are racist. The Northvegr Foundation, for example, advertises itself as an educational resource: in the words of its website, it is 'Dedicated to Bringing Knowledge and Understanding of Northern European pre-Christian History, Culture and Spiritual Values'. Technically speaking, what they all so insistently disavow is white supremacism. They simply claim the right to cultivate their own, and, as they see it, racially inherent, culture. Their mission statements typically accord other racial groups the right to do as their respective ancestors did – and indeed, encourage it. They may for example support the rights of indigenous North American peoples – particularly in opposition to multinational companies charged with exploiting 'homeland' resources. It is easy to see this sort of reversion to racial, or even tribal, structures, as a reaction to what might loosely be called globalization: the assertion of a more sharply defined and therefore more secure identity than the phrase 'citizen of the world' might offer. In the United States, such groups are presented as the natural ancestral home of Americans of northern European ancestry. The reality of mixed ancestry, however, challenges the definition of this group, and is often a topic of debate online. Significantly, the relatively liberal group The Ring of Troth cites Old Norse mythology itself in order to denounce ideals of racial purity insisted upon by other groups. It points out that the Norse gods themselves were of mixed ancestry: Odin's mother was a giantess, after all, and Frey was the son of the god Njörd and the giantess Skadi.

The more 'folkish' groups also strongly oppose the anti-democratic, fascist ideals of organizations such as Wotansvolk, which advocates the institution of societies ruled by initiated elites, an idea borrowed directly from Guido von List. Wotansvolk also clearly promotes white supremacism, including the old ideas that the Aryan peoples (itself an old idea) are semi-divine, and were responsible for the founding of all the great civilizations. The Australian Rud Mills, the founder of the Angelcyn Church of Odin, pulled together a number of racist beliefs in one defiant condemnation of the present state of affairs: 'once-glorious Nordics, builders of the noble civilizations of Sumeria, Egypt, Persia, Greece and Rome, [have] weakened due to foreign immigration and miscegenation'. As was the case with occult Nazism, advances in science have been called in to support and elaborate old mystical ideas. Race is re-defined genetically, and this is mystically extended to include religion itself; as one social scientist has mockingly put it, 'somehow, gods and goddesses are encoded in the DNA of the descendants of the ancients'. Nordic people and their descendants are thus genetically programmed to worship the Norse gods. This is a striking pseudo-scientific twist on Carl Jung's theory of the collective unconscious, in which archetypal symbols reside. In 1936, Jung wrote an extraordinary piece called 'Wotan' in which he claimed that the spirit of the Norse god Odin lurks deep in the collective unconscious of Germanic people, whether or not he is worshipped or believed in. In the early part of the twentieth century, this dormant spirit was somehow awakened, and the rise to power of the National Socialists was the devastating result. Jung's theory has been seized on by the further right groups, not as a way of explaining recent history, but as a means of manipulating the future: if only the descendants of Germanic people can be persuaded to worship the old gods again, the spirit of Odin may be again re-awakened, and National Socialism re-kindled.

Worship of and belief in the Norse gods obviously makes Norse mythology valuable and significant to nationalist groups. The relationship between Germanic paganism (often called 'heathenism') and the embracing of Germanic or Aryan ancestral identity has often been uncertain, however. Nazis were not necessarily pagan – as we have seen,

177

in spite of Himmler's interest in it, Hitler himself derided Wotanism. Wagner's opera *Parsifal*, its hero a Germanic knight in search of the Holy Grail, demonstrates just how Christianity might be appropriated by Germanists, and with a little ingenuity, Christ can be reclaimed for white racists. The doctrine of an 'Aryan Christ', espoused by groups such as Christian Identity in the United States, denies that Christ was Jewish – part of an elaborate and extreme project to expunge the apparently Semitic origins of Christianity. Groups such as this naturally dismiss neo-pagans as ungodly. By the same token, heathens, who take Norse myth to be the holy lore of their religion, need not be either racist or supremacist, although non-Nordic individuals (at least, to judge from their surnames, a rather rough and ready identifier) enquiring about heathenism are usually advised to turn to their 'own ancestral' beliefs. However, the fundamental weakness of the heathens' position is that, as we have seen, the Norse myths offer very little if any guidance about how the gods were worshipped, and certainly no liturgy or doctrine. On the other hand, this lack does give welcome scope for imaginative recreation of congenial rituals.

Immigrants from Britain, Germany and Scandinavia have constituted a large and influential section of North American society, and just as in northern Europe and the British Isles, some North Americans have liked to trace their ancestry back to the supposedly original Germanic peoples. That so many neo-pagan groups grew up and now flourish in North America must also be in some way related to the politics and geography of the United States and Canada, to the way smaller communities – comfortingly and tellingly called 'hearths' or 'kindreds' – offer definition and security to those who find themselves part of a huge and dazzlingly multi-ethnic nation. But there is another powerful reason why the North American descendants of northern European emigrants celebrate their ties with familial origins: the belief that the first white settlers of North America were the Norse.

According to such thirteenth-century works as *Eiríks saga rauða* ('The Saga of Eirik the Red') and *Grœnlendinga saga* ('The Saga of Greenlanders'), from the tenth century onwards there were a number of Viking voyages to the New World, and few serious scholars now doubt the general veracity of these accounts, which are additionally sub-stantiated by the otherwise extremely reliable twelfth-century Icelandic historian Ari the Wise, who makes the earliest Norse mention of Vinland

– the name given to North America, meaning either 'vine-land' or 'meadow-land' in Old Icelandic. According to *Grœnlendinga saga* the discovery was accidental: Bjarni Herjólfsson, an Icelandic merchant on his way to Greenland in around 986 AD, was blown off course southwards, and overshot Greenland altogether. He continued westward until he sighted what must have been America. He did not land, but sailed north along the coast until he judged that turning back would put him back on course for Greenland – which it did. Not long after this, Leifr Eiríksson, the son of Eirik the Red, made a determined attempt to explore this new land, and he and his companions spent the winter in Vinland, sailing back home the next spring. So it is that Leifr Eiríksson has been celebrated by some as the European discoverer of North America, anticipating Christopher Columbus by several centuries. Several trading voyages followed Leifr's initial exploration, some involving violent encounters with indigenous peoples the Norse texts call 'skrælingar' (saga descriptions of these people identify them very clearly as Inuit). Modern archaeological excavations have uncovered what are apparently sites of Norse settlement along the Canadian east coast, and Norse artefacts have also been unearthed.

Not everyone has accepted the truth of these accounts, however. Some of the voyages, as described in the sagas, involve clearly sensational or fantastic elements, and the name Vinland, understood as 'vine-land', has been held to undermine the credibility of the Norse discovery of America because of scepticism about the possibility of grapes growing at such a northerly latitude, though the case against either more northerly grapes or more southerly landings than hitherto supposed has not been sustained. Very damaging, paradoxically, has been the 'discovery' (the circumstances of which have been kept suspiciously secret) in the 1950s of the so-called Vinland map, which purports to be a medieval representation of the world, showing North America as a large island in the north-west, and annotated with references to Bjarni and Leifr. It has even been suggested that this map helped Columbus on his seventeenth-century voyage of exploration. Many regard the Vinland map as a hoax, although scientific and cartographical experts have been unable to bring the debate to a conclusion. Perhaps the strongest reason for not accepting the map as genuine is, ironically, the evident and compelling desire on the part of some North Americans of northern European descent to reinstate Scandinavians as the 'real' discoverers of their country. Few, one hopes, would put it in such extreme terms as one Ásatrú spokesman – 'if any white men should be credited as founders of America it should be Viking heroes and not a Catholic who lost his way to India'. 'Leif Erikson Day' (October 9), instituted by US President Bill Clinton, and such celebrations as commemorative voyages and exhibitions of replica Viking ships are of course not the sole province of Scandinavian nationalist groups. On the other hand, the story of the Norse discovery of America has been used by such groups as welcome ammunition against the claims of 'Mediterranean Catholics' to a special place in the history of North America. And the Vinland map (though not the by-and-large dependable saga accounts) should be seen in the context of a whole series of hoax pieces of 'evidence' of Scandinavian settlement of North America.

One of the most high-profile of these is the so-called Kensington Runestone: a flat rock, apparently inscribed with medieval runes, 'discovered' at the end of the nineteenth century in Minnesota – an area of especially dense Scandinavian settlement in that century. In a language which has been claimed to be 'Old Swedish', the runes describe a party of Vinland voyagers who travelled much further west, and there met with a disaster which left only a few survivors: the rune-carvers themselves. Very few Norse runologists are inclined to take the stone at face value, and an impressively tactful speech by the American ambassador to Sweden in 2003 avoided passing judgement on its authenticity, while being clear about its cultural significance: 'it has become part of the history of the state of Minnesota … a story of longing for contact with the Swedish homeland, a tale of ethnic pride amongst Minnesota's early Scandinavian settlers … and evidence of the strong identification … with Sweden and the Nordic region'.

More politically controversial – and even less tenable – have been the claims of white nationalist groups to the remains of the so-called 'Kennewick Man', a prehistoric skeleton found in Washington in 1996. Though it was at first thought that the remains were relatively recent, scientists soon established that the skeleton was very old indeed, and were keen to analyse what might prove to be the oldest human remains in North America. Native Americans, on the other hand, insisted that the remains of what was likely to be one of their own ancestors were sacred, and that it was not respectful to treat them like a scientific exhibit. However, it was far from clear exactly which Native American tribe could prove a direct link to Kennewick Man. But there was another twist: the earliest anthropologists to look at the skull identified it as Caucasoid, and a digital reconstruction of the face produced distinctly European features. The extreme antiquity of the skeleton, established by radiocarbon dating to be around 9,000 years old, had been highly significant to Native Americans since it endorsed their nationalist oral history and mythology in dating their settlement of North America way back in prehistoric times. But the possibility of Old World origins for Kennewick Man (now, in fact, discredited) was a bombshell, and eagerly seized on by the Ásatrú. Was North America perhaps first settled by Europeans eight centuries or so even before Leif Erikson? The connection between North Americans of northern European descent and pagan Scandinavians would then be a matter neither of modern emigration, nor even of early medieval Norse settlement. An Ásatru spokesman, using the familiar terminology of white nationalists, summed up their case: 'Kennewick Man is our kin, forged by the same powers that made us'. The Germanic pagan gods of Norse myth become, at one stroke, the earliest ancestral spirits of the whole nation.

The place of the ancestral gods of any one group in a multi-ethnic, multicultural nation such as the United States is precisely the subject of the novel *American Gods*, published by Neil Gaiman in 2001, but itself reworking many of the Old Norse-derived themes Gaiman experimented with in his long series of graphic novels, *The Sandman*. Gaiman himself is Jewish by birth, born in England, educated in Church of England schools, and now living in the United States. He does much of his writing in Ireland. *American Gods* sets Norse mythology alongside the very many other 'ancestral' beliefs of the various ethnic groups in America, and contrasts them all with what he sees contemporary society putting its faith in. The novel opens with the story of Shadow, facing his last few days in an American jail, looking forward to being reunited with his wife Laura and making a new life by picking up the threads of his old one. News that his wife has been killed in a car accident casts him completely adrift, but he is approached almost immediately by a mysterious old man with a glass eye, who offers him a job. Terms and conditions are not specified, but the old man – who cheerfully and readily admits to being a liar – tells Shadow that the rewards could be immense: 'You could be the King of America'. And Shadow notices his tie-pin: 'a tree, worked in silver: trunk, branches, and deep roots'. Although the atmosphere and naturalistic details of the novel's opening pages are in the distinctive hard-boiled style of American crime fiction, and Shadow's subsequent journey across America suggests the familiar form of the road novel, it is clear from the outset that his mystery companion is to some extent based on the Norse god Odin, and this is confirmed when he calls himself Mr Wednesday. But *American Gods* is neither crime fiction nor road novel: it is mythic fantasy, and Mr Wednesday is not merely reminiscent of Odin – he is the god himself. The job he needs help with is the gathering of all the old gods of America to take part in a great battle against the new deities: a modern Ragnarök.

So what has happened to the gods now that no-one believes in them any more? Mr Wednesday has resorted to making a living as a second-rate confidence trickster, and many of the gods and spirits that he and Shadow meet in the course of their journey across America are in similarly straitened circumstances. Abandoned fertility goddesses have turned to prostitution. The Slavic gods Bielobog and Czernobog live in a down-at-heel tenement block in Chicago which smells of boiled cabbage. Much of the fun of *American Gods* lies in identifying individual deities from Gaiman's often witty Americanization of their names (a technique which mirrors the way in which the names of actual immigrants were Americanized). Shadow's ostensibly helpful cell-mate is Low Key Lyesmith – 'a grifter from Minnesota' – but Gaiman's smart transformation of the name of the Norse half-god Loki warns the alert reader of betrayal to come. One of Mr Wednesday's many pseudonyms (in itself, an echo of Odin's many different names in Norse myth) is Emerson Borson, a cleverly disguised allusion to the ancient genealogy of Norse creation myths, in which Bor is the father of Odin, and Ymir his primordial ancestor. The new gods of America – including the geeky boy-god Internet, and a seductive goddess called Media – allow Gaiman free rein in his social satire of present-day American beliefs and ideals.

Who, then, is the oddly passive, taciturn Shadow? Although his name gives no obvious clue, given that he is from the outset an acolyte of Mr Wednesday he is relatively easy to identify as Baldr, Odin's son in the original myth. Gaiman may have based his characterization of Shadow on Snorri Sturluson's description, in the *Prose Edda*, of Baldr as a god whose words nobody takes any notice of. Of course, recognizing Shadow as Baldr has dramatic consequences for the reader's anticipation of the end of the novel, since Baldr was sacrificed by his father Odin in the hope of a resurrection which is not immediately fulfilled. *American Gods* is not merely a comic novel, a witty satire on modern America; it uses Norse (and other) mythology to explore serious issues of mortality, illusion and religious belief. The one immigrant religion which is not taken issue with is Christianity; presumably, this is because its gods have not been discarded in America. But just as the depiction of Baldr in Norse myth shares, disturbingly, some elements with the story of Christ's crucifixion, so Gaiman hints at features which Shadow shares with Christ. Not for nothing, for instance, is Shadow said to be aged thirty-two at the novel's opening.

Gaiman's kaleidoscopic vision could not be further from the narrow racism of some of the political groups discussed earlier. But it is worth pointing out here that, remarkably, his ideologically very different stance and his use of a particular fictional vehicle reflect nonetheless the same preoccupations as does all of the material, political as well as literary, which takes Norse myth as its inspiration. There is often some perceived or actual personal connection with Scandinavia on the part of authors or adherents (Gaiman was inspired to write *American Gods* after a visit to Iceland; Lindsay and MacDiarmid were Scots, conscious of the Norse settlement of Scotland; nationalist groups celebrate their claimed descent from Northern Europeans). The mythological stories about the gods are less congenial material than the great mythic symbols: the World Tree Yggdrasill, or Ragnarök, feature in many guises. Norse mythological names are a source of inspiration, and often the subject of wordplay. The distant past – generally, a better place to be – is the lens through which to view the special circumstances of the present, which is often despaired of, or condemned, or satirized: something has somehow gone wrong with it. There is an awareness, whether anxious or excited, of impending catastrophe which must be met with a cataclysmic battle or struggle. The interface with Christianity is uneasily evident. And finally, there is an air of mystery, of the possibility of initiation into academic or pseudo-academic wisdom and learning. As one of Neil Gaiman's fans put it online, 'What I love about Neil Gaiman's stories is that you always feel you are being imparted with some long-forgotten, secret knowledge, and that even the most ordinary places and events are infused with a sense of the magical'.

Though *American Gods* has become a cult novel in the United States, and has won several literary prizes, by far the most successful and cele-brated literary work to draw on Norse myth has been J.R.R. Tolkien's

The Lord of the Rings. With enormous and extended sales, many citations in favourite or best-loved book polls, influence on a whole genre of fantasy novels and games, and, finally, a highly successful series of recent films, and even a musical, *The Lord of the Rings* has been called the most popular novel of the twentieth century. A trilogy, over one thousand pages long, *The Lord of the Rings* is not easy to summarize, but its setting is as celebrated and significant as its plot, for the action takes place in an elaborately detailed fantasy world, peopled by fantasy creatures with invented names and addresses who speak languages created for them by Tolkien, and pause between their many arduous journeys and battles only to recount the long, ancient histories of their respective cultures. At the centre of its byzantine (if episodic, rather than many-stranded) narrative stands the ring itself, a symbol of absolute power, with the power to corrupt absolutely. The influence of Norse myth is pervasive and everywhere apparent: in the names, the characters, individual scenes such as riddle contests or monster killings, in magic objects and in weighty symbols such as the broken sword. Tolkien's most obvious debt is to Norse heroic legend: the stories of the Volsungs and Sigurd the Dragon-Slayer which Wagner drew on for his *Ring* cycle. But there are no gods.

Tolkien himself hated comparisons between *The Lord of the Rings* and Wagner's *Ring* cycle. With an asperity some have found suspicious, he once wrote that 'both rings were round, and there the resemblance ends'. This is not strictly the case. As might be expected from the fact that he and Wagner drew on the same Norse material, the resemblances between the two works are striking. In both, the cursed ring is the key symbol, and the fight for possession of it drives on the narrative and motivates the central characters. The origins of this powerful, iconic treasure belong to a time before the narrative proper begins, and it is fought over by two brothers with echoing names: Wagner's giants, Fasolt and Fafner, and Tolkien's Deagol and Smeagol. One brother kills the other, and ownership of the ring transforms the victor into a loathsome, miserly monster. The subsequent history of the ring demonstrates its power to corrupt its owner; and it can confer both invisibility and unlimited domination. This history is set against a great conflict which signals the end of the old order of things. Such similarities seem irrefutable. But Tolkien's disavowal of Wagner's *Ring* as a model for his work is entirely explicable if we see *The Lord of the Rings* as a purposeful countering of

Wagner: the thrust of Tolkien's narrative undermines and deliberately reverses what happens in Wagner, while at the same time drawing on the same sources.

Frodo Baggins, the hero of *The Lord of the Rings*, is not so much an anti-hero as a sympathetically comic inversion of what heroism is usually taken to mean. He is a hobbit, one of Tolkien's imaginary races. Tolkien's hobbits are home-loving, rustic and simple in their pleasures. Their homeland, the Shire, is presented by Tolkien as an English rural idyll, untouched by modernity, whose inhabitants live together in harmony, merriment and self-deprecating contentment with their lot. The values and virtues prized by hobbits are homely ones: friendliness, loyalty, cheerfulness and honesty. Frodo (whose first name, perhaps derived from the Old Norse name Fróði, which is also the adjective meaning 'wise', is in sharp contrast to his unprepossessing and irresistibly comic surname Baggins) is thus a most unlikely hero, and as un-Wagnerian as one might imagine. His ascent to the stature of hero and ring-bearer does not necessitate a transformation of his inherent characteristics, however: they merely deepen into steadfastness, courage, integrity and pity. And Frodo's great quest is neither to possess nor recover the ring. His mentor, Bilbo Baggins, Tolkien's original hobbit, came upon it apparently by accident, and the ultimate anti-Wagnerian twist is that Frodo's epic struggle is to destroy it, to return it to the flaming Crack of Doom, the terrifying chasm in which it was first forged.

It is clear from several references in his letters that Tolkien profoundly resented the racist appropriation of Norse material (material which he himself knew well, valued and admired), which Wagner's work had come to represent. There have been questions raised about possible racism in *The Lord of the Rings* itself, and some white supremacist groups have tried, to the fury of Tolkien's devoted fans, to adopt the novel as a new epic mythology for their cause – because, one assumes, of its basis in Norse myth. It is true that many of the evil beings in *The Lord of the Rings* are said to be dark in colour, while the forces for good are often fair-haired and blue-eyed. Some of the more monstrous enemies of the Fellowship of the Ring have physical features which recall traditional Western xenophobic caricatures: the so-called Half-Orcs, for instance, are 'swart' and 'slant-eyed', and invading armies from the east and south have long black hair and dark complexions, carry scimitars and ride elephants. But there are telling exceptions. The arch-villain Saruman is a pale, even radiant, figure, and Tolkien is quoted as identifying the elves – the most gifted and civilized of the peoples in *The Lord of the Rings* – with the Jews, pointing out that his invented Elvish tongue is clearly a Semitic language. It is not unlikely that Tolkien unconsciously reproduced some of the prejudices of the twentieth century, while at the same time purposefully opposing the supremacist agenda of right-wing ideologues. *The Lord of the Rings* has been interpreted as a coded polemic against fascism, and the sinister thugs who take over the Shire in Frodo's absence, held to be reminiscent of right-wing groups such as the blackshirts in Britain and Italy, are sometimes cited in support of this. But it is equally possible to read the unwelcome transformation of the Shire as its ideological opposite – a communist takeover. Hob Hayward's complaint, when asked about the hobbits' harvest – 'We grows a lot of food, but we don't rightly know what becomes of it. It's all these "gatherers" and "sharers", I reckon, going round counting and measuring and taking off to storage' – sounds more like a veiled reference to Soviet collectivism.

Tolkien's most memorable monstrous creation is Gollum, 'a loathsome little creature ... with his large flat feet, peering with pale, luminous eyes and catching blind fish with his long fingers'. His name has been explained as being onomatopoeic – that is, it echoes the sound of a revolting gulp or swallow. Gollum, like almost all Tolkien's villains, is repulsive to the senses – to look at, to smell, or, most particularly in his case, to hear. Gollum's most distinctive feature, apart from his appearance, is his voice. It is characterized not only by a persistent hissing noise, but also by its speech patterns and idiom: Gollum habitually talks to himself, often referring to himself in the third person, and punctuating his sentences with the repeated endearment 'my precious', addressed to the ring. In conversation with Frodo, he swings abruptly between ingratiation, self-pity and vicious aggression. In all these respects, his speech is unmistakably reminiscent of Charles Dickens's notorious representation of the Jewish villain Fagin in *Oliver Twist*. This association is at best unfortunate, and in fact the film of *The Lord of the Rings* highlighted the connection, because the actor who provided Gollum's voice also played a memorable Fagin in a film of *Oliver Twist*.

But Gollum's name, in addition to its onomatopoeic origins, has a curious and positive relationship with actual Jewish tradition. The name is very like that of the figure known from Jewish folklore as a 'golem'. A golem – meaning, in modern Hebrew, 'fool' – is a creature shaped out of mud, and then animated, in order to serve its creator in some way. In the Talmud, for instance, Adam is described as the first golem. Some later stories recount the use of a golem for defensive purposes, as a mindlessly loyal bodyguard. This recalls, unexpectedly, an episode from Norse mythology. According to Snorri in his *Prose Edda*, the giant Hrungnir is to fight a duel against the god Thor, and his fellow giants are afraid that he will not be strong enough to win. They therefore create for him a helpmate, an enormous figure made out of clay to stand at his side. But this creature, named *Mökkurkálfi*, or 'Cloud-Calf', has been given the heart of a mare, an animal synonymous with cowardice in Old Norse tradition, and is easily dispatched. It is likely that this episode from Snorri's *Edda* derived from Jewish traditions which were circulating among Christian scholars in the thirteenth century, when Snorri was writing. It is tempting, then, to believe that Tolkien recognized the connection, and was intrigued by this unexpected link between Old Norse myth and Jewish traditions. It may even have persuaded him to give Gollum a voice borrowed from a celebrated literary representation of a Jewish villain, Dickens's Fagin. What is not in doubt is that Tolkien's personal distaste for and opposition to racism, especially antisemitism, is clearly documented in his letters.

Everything so far noted about *The Lord of the Rings* matches those recurrent features, mentioned earlier, of works which draw on Norse mythology. Tolkien had a very particular personal relationship with Norse culture: actually a professional one – as a professor of medieval language and literature at Oxford he had immersed himself in Norse literature and myth. He re-uses Norse names, or elements of them, throughout *The Lord of the Rings* – the list of dwarf names in the poem *Völuspá*, for example, is a very productive source for him, and the name of Gandalf, Tolkien's immensely wise and knowledgeable wizard, can be found there: in Old Norse, Gandálfr. This is a particularly evocative name in the original, a combination of the Norse world *álfr* ('elf', but in Norse tradition a powerful and revered spirit) and the mysterious word *gandr*, tentatively defined by the standard Old Norse dictionary as 'anything enchanted or an object used by sorcerers' – most familiar to Old Norse scholars as part of an alternative name for the World Serpent, Jörmungandr, 'the world's magic thing'.

The hobbits' home, the Shire, is plainly an evocation of an England of the past, a countryside without any sign of modernity: no machines or technology, no trace at all of the twentieth century. It is, perhaps for this very reason, a sort of rural paradise. Middle Earth itself is presented without reference to any actual history: the only clue to its situation in the far distant past is Gandalf's prediction that the time of the dominion of men is approaching. But apocalypse awaits – the great battle which forms the backdrop and climax to the action of *The Lord of the Rings* heralds the end of one cycle of Middle Earth history, and a new one is about to begin. Nevertheless, it has been noticed that Tolkien, a committed Catholic, recreates every aspect of the cultures of the many peoples of Middle Earth with the exception of religion; there are no gods and no theology of any kind. So his hobbits are not Christians, or even crypto-Christians, and his dwarves and elves are not heathens. Unlike his colleague C.S. Lewis, Tolkien did not build any coded religious message into his narrative. But it is worth mentioning briefly here that Lewis himself wove Norse references into his religious allegory, *The Lion, the Witch and the Wardrobe*: the Witch whispers into the ear of the dying Aslan, as Odin whispered into Baldr's ear; the dominion of evil in Narnia is represented by an endless winter with no summers in between, like the *fimbulvetr* in Norse, and after the final great battle, the cricket ball the children had been playing with before it all began is re-discovered, like the chess pieces dropped by the Norse gods before Ragnarök.

Perhaps the most striking example of conformity with so many other Norse-influenced works or systems is the potential of *The Lord of the Rings* to offer readers access to an (in this case, immense) body of arcane knowledge. Gandalf himself might be read as an idealization of a medievalist scholar, with his all-encompassing knowledge of ancient scripts and languages, and his mastery of the most esoteric wisdom and distant history. Tolkien's work is so far unparalleled in its amassing of names and details, and his other works, and his many pseudo-scholarly appendices, extend an already hugely extensive and elaborate system. Its fictionality is immaterial; *The Lord of the Rings* meets a need for its devotees to become initiates.

It is relatively easy to 'place' Tolkien's work in a line of descent, from the utopian fantasy writing of William Morris, and his evident reaction against Wagner's *Ring* cycle, on the one hand, and, on the other, and most markedly, the innumerable ensuing fantasy novels with a Norse or at least vaguely medieval theme and setting which involve dwarves and giants, and highly symbolic dangerous rings and broken swords which need mending. Other developments, such as computer games, and make-believe tabletop role-playing games like 'Dungeons and Dragons', also clearly owe a good deal to Tolkien. The most striking similarities – apart from the symbolisms, and the various races of warring creatures, including dwarves, elves and orcs – are the creation of a whole world, or vast landscape in miniature. Again, this offers an enormous amount of detail which devotees can immerse themselves in. Some computer games are derived directly from Old Norse myth, and, like the comics which I shall discuss shortly, base their appeal not only on the alternative world they offer but also on the opportunities for sensational but unserious violence inherent in the medium, as enemies are bloodlessly zapped, and whole armies wiped out.

As the quotation from Northrop Frye at the beginning of this chapter implies, it is characteristic of authors to be influenced, to a greater or lesser degree, by what has gone before, and of texts in their turn to influence what comes after. But what has been called 'the Grand Narrative' of literary culture has its own *raison d'être*: prestigious forerunners are bound to be influential not only because they have the sheer quality to impress themselves on the authors who come after them, but also because of their very status as high culture, as part of the academic, literary and cultural heritage of society. This is where *The Lord of the Rings*, and the derivatives of it outlined above, can be seen to have a problematic relationship with this line of descent.

Firstly, and ironically, the immense popularity of *The Lord of the Rings* has in itself – especially in the higher reaches of academia – called into question its literary quality, or seriousness, in the great tradition of critics such as the poet T.S. Eliot, who influentially maintained that worthwhile literature was 'difficult', or inaccessible. And secondly, *The Lord of the Rings* raises awkward questions of audience. Is it a book for adult readers? Clearly, *The Hobbit* is a children's book. Equally, *The Silmarillion*, published posthumously, is not a work many young readers would find accessible (an early draft was rejected by publishers as being too abstruse). But *The Lord of the Rings* itself – and the films and games based on it – somehow defy categorization, and of course their *actual* audience has been restricted to neither young people nor adults. And related to the age of the audience is the issue of what might be called the literary experience, or even the academic status of the audience. How much difference does it make to our individual experience of any works which draw on Old Norse myth if we do, or don't, know the original material? And what if the implied or the actual audience is precisely one which is least likely to be familiar with the original sources? The medieval references in *The Lord of the Rings* clearly have the power either to delight or to irritate those who are familiar with Old Norse or Old English, but they function only as a marker of strangeness or exoticism for those who don't; the narrative line does not depend on them. But the issue of how far prior knowledge of the mythic background either adds to, or, indeed, detracts from, one's enjoyment becomes really critical with works which closely follow the actual narratives of the myths.

I want to end this chapter by looking at more works, in very different genres – children's literature, comics and music – which also appeal to an audience extending well beyond the limitations of high culture. Interestingly, this new audience is also defined to some extent by age, insofar as it is not confined to adults, though it may well include them. I begin with a book which is explicitly categorized by its publishers as 'teenage fiction', and which also follows its Norse model so closely that it therefore almost predicates a 'double' audience: for those who know 'what happens' and those who don't, reading Melvyn Burgess's *Bloodtide* is a completely different experience.

Bloodtide, published in 1999, is set in a post-apocalyptic London which has been transformed into a barely recognizable wasteland, where there are 'cows tethered to parking meters... pigs scavenging for rubbish in the streets'. At first, readers might assume a catastrophe such as a nuclear strike, but it gradually emerges that this dereliction is a result of a social breakdown; parts of Britain, largely the inner cities, have been given up by the authorities, and are barricaded against the Outside: 'Beyond the Wall, dappled in the distance, lay the halfman lands... After that, the World began.' This looks very like a knowing inversion of typically Middle Earth geography. Inside, London is ruled by two rival ganglords, Val Volson and Conor. Volson children include Signy and Siggy: evidently, *Bloodtide* is a re-writing of the Old Norse *Völsunga saga*, the story of the Volsungs. Specifically, it relates to the opening parts of the saga, which recount the story of Sigmund the Volsung, and his twin sister Signy: Wagner's Siegmund and Sieglinde. *Bloodtide* is not just a modern-day version of *Völsunga saga*; the story is updated right into the distant future.

Norse references include a number of very subtle allusions which seem to function as in-jokes for the eavesdropping specialist reader. Thus for instance, one character remarks, 'We all have to make sacrifices'; another mutters, 'Oh Hel'; the street term for gold jewellery is 'dripping'. Some of these references are so slight that it's not clear that they are actually intended by Burgess himself: either his own familiarity with the sources might lead to unconscious allusions to them, or the reader sensitive to *Bloodtide* as a reworking of *Völsunga saga* might read them into the prose. They certainly add an element of fun to the narrative, whether for the author's or the informed reader's benefit. In the same way, there are some extremely imaginative and sharp transformations of motifs and episodes in the original saga. One of the best is the presentation of the *barnstokkr* – the great tree which grows in the centre of the Volsungs' hall – as a mighty lift shaft, made of some futuristic adamantine material, rising up to the now-derelict roof of the city tower block which the Volsons use for their formal feasts. As in the saga, Odin puts in an appearance at the hall, here a figure made mysterious by his ability to evade the heavy security the Volsons think they have put in place. Echoing the saga, he plunges a blade into the great shaft, and only Siggy Volson can pull it out.

There are – as in *The Lord of the Rings* and the many fantasy novels inspired by it – a number of extremely inventive and often quite disturbing monsters, especially the so-called halfmen: weird combinations of human and sometimes multiple bestial elements which Burgess cleverly explains as the products of genetic engineering, 'mix 'n' match with genes and chromosomes'. They are effective on two distinct levels: both as monsters in their own right, with horrific charisma and a plausible futuristic origin, and as witty updates on their medieval or immediate predecessors in fantasy and science fiction. But the effect of prior knowledge of 'what happens' in *Völsunga saga* is very marked when it comes to the actual course of the narrative. Signy, married off to the rival warlord Conor, naively looks forward to meeting up again with her twin – 'I'll see him when they come to visit'. For readers familiar with any number of works based on Germanic legend, the mention of this forthcoming visit is grimly ominous.

Apart from the odd eavesdropping specialist, the overlap between *Bloodtide*'s teenage readership and those familiar with the original material is likely to be fairly limited. So if we can discount offering readers the pleasure of recognizing correspondences between *Bloodtide* and its source, why might an author like Burgess base a teenage novel on Old Norse mythic sources? Possible answers to this question rest, I think, on two contrasting aspects of the original material: its suitability for a modern teenage audience, and, paradoxically, its *un*suitability.

The story of the Volsungs is potentially full of what have come to be the staples of serious fiction for teenagers: human interest matters such as divided family loyalties, young people faced with the responsibilities adults have left them with, sex with a partner you don't love, the opportunity to prove oneself and show courage, and even controversial 'problem' issues such as incest. The ethos of the saga is at the same time a very fruitful one for shocking a new audience, with its harsh violence, its monsters, and its often vicious amorality. In both of these respects, *Völsunga saga* is ripe for re-telling to a modern audience used to emotional empathizing as well as horror and excitement. In addition, there is a very particular significance and indeed urgency in basing a science-fiction novel – that is, one set in the future – on a medieval source. The implication is that the strangeness of the alternative world – especially if it is a dystopia, that is, a nightmarish vision of the future – is not simply the product of the author's imagination, but part of the history and heritage of its contemporary readers: in all its barbarity and violence it is what we have emerged from, and, crucially, what social breakdown (or, for instance, nuclear catastrophe) might return us to. Burgess uses religion to make this point clear: Christianity, in the London of the future, has long since died out, and the old gods, led by Odin, have returned.

The *un*suitability of *Völsunga saga* takes us back to a wider consideration of reworkings of Norse myth. As this and the previous chapter have shown, some of those who have based their literary or political writings on Old Norse myth have had a specific and more or less discreditable ideological reason for doing so – usually, a racist agenda. One of Burgess's achievements in *Bloodtide* is to engage with racism, and to use the Norse myth to expose and oppose, rather than advance, it. This is a remarkable act of recuperation for a present-day audience – to make the myth new, and to make the new narrative work against those aspects of the old which would call it into question for a modern audience. The sub-human halfmen in *Bloodtide* function at first simply as grotesque and diverting monsters. But gradually, Burgess exposes the prejudices of the ruling humans – which are uncomfortably reminiscent of contemporary racial prejudices – and eventually the warlord Conor is demonized as a Hitlerian tyrant, a racial purist whose policy is a Nazi-like rooting out of physical difference. This policy eerily echoes white supremacist rhetoric about the supposedly divine origins of the Aryan races: 'Only the races the gods had made must walk the earth. Anyone with even the slightest trace of animal blood in them was all beast – dirty, foul and monstrous.' And these halfmen are even said to be sterile.

Basing the novel on a text from the past also enables Burgess to present a new way of reading characters in the original who are otherwise hard to understand, let alone sympathize with. Thus a great deal of narrative space in *Bloodtide* is given over to analyzing the feelings of Signy, who has such a commitment to her brothers, especially her twin, Siggy, and yet has a child by the enemy her father has married her off to. There is an interesting comparison to be made here with William Morris's depiction of Gudrun in his long poem *Sigurd the Volsung* – Morris does not attempt to explain or understand Gudrun's divided loyalties, presenting her instead as catatonic with grief and resentment, an inscrutable, half-insane figure. Burgess similarly makes no attempt to recuperate Sinfjötli, in *Völsunga saga* the child of the incestuous union of the twins, and thus the epitome of racial purity. In *Bloodtide*, his equivalent, Styr, has been grown in a 'womb-tank', a monstrous, genetically engineered hero who (like Odin's son Vali in Norse myth) reaches maturity in an unnaturally short time, and though artificially equipped with the outstanding physical attributes of the hero, has not been provided with normal human feelings – another way, perhaps, of understanding a traditional, but unattractive, hero figure like Wagner's Siegfried.

At the end of *Bloodtide*, Burgess specifies his source as 'the first part of the Icelandic Volsunga saga'. This is vital information on one level, because *Bloodtide* ends very abruptly: it does not stand independent of its source, and the opportunity – not to say necessity – for a sequel (published in 2005 as *Bloodsong*) is obvious. But directing readers to the source of the material has an important function in that it suggests not so much the double audience – the teenage reader and the eavesdropping specialist – as the possibility of a double reading: that one might return to *Bloodtide* ready to see the correspondences and get all the in-jokes. This is one strategy for countering the double audience problem. Diana Wynne Jones, in a book aimed at younger readers still, has devised another.

Eight Days of Luke, published in 1975, is an altogether more traditional children's novel. It is set in the slightly old-fashioned present characteristic of many children's books, and derived more from literary predecessors than actually reflecting contemporary life. The hero, a boy called David, is home from boarding school for the summer holidays. He lives with uncaring relatives, but their careless cruelty to him is a comic rather than distressing matter. The summer stretches tediously ahead for David; the nearest children to his foster home have just moved house, and he has only books, and the memory of the recent cricket season at school, to sustain him. But his life improves dramatically when he accidentally conjures up a mysterious companion, Luke, who claims that David has released him from a prison. Luke is Loki from Old Norse myth, meant to be bound until Ragnarök as a punishment for his part in the killing of Baldr. As the holidays go by, Norse gods in various guises turn up to recapture Loki. Mr Wedding, with a glamorous 'lady chauffeur', is Woden with one of his valkyries; Frey and Freyja are Mr and Mrs Fry, the new neighbours; the sinister gardener Mr Chew is the god Tiw; and so on. As is evident from this list, the names of the gods are in their Anglo-Saxon, rather than Norse, forms, though the storyline is straightforwardly Norse, involving not only the death of Baldr and the binding of Loki, but also the loss of Thor's hammer. There are allusions to Norse myth in the novel's place names, such Ashbury, or Wednesday Hill, just as there are elements of the Norse gods – which may have been common to the pre-Christian Anglo-Saxons – in actual English place names. The days of the week are of course the most celebrated survivals of the pagan gods in the English language.

Interestingly, Luke as Loki is shown as having a special relationship with fire. David can summon him by lighting a match, and he himself loves to start fires, and burns the hated housekeeper's food to amuse David. But in the original myth, Loki is not especially associated with fire. The purely formal correspondence between his name and the Old Norse word *logi* ('flame') is played on in Snorri's *Prose Edda* in order to point out a crucial difference between the two: in an eating competition, Loki cannot be expected to prevail against Logi, because though Loki can stuff himself with meat at a remarkable rate, Logi can devour the trough as well. But Wagner in his *Ring* cycle creates a figure who combines both Loki's unscrupulous cunning and Logi's elemental nature, in Loge, who can transform himself in the fire which surrounds Brünnhilde and eventually burns up Valhalla itself. Diana Wynne Jones has based Luke not directly on Norse myth, but on a celebrated derivative of it. Luke frightens David with his amorality (he starts a fire in a building which threatens the life of its occupants, and enjoys the flames more than he cares about the victims). But Wynne Jones, as Burgess was to do, opens up the possibility of a new understanding of a familiar mythic figure – here Loki, who is known simply for his mischief and untrustworthiness. The killing of Baldr, 'the greatest misfortune ever to befall gods and men', is reduced, by Luke's account, to a schoolboy prank gone wrong: 'But it was a mistake, an accident! ... I meant it as a joke – I didn't think for a moment it would kill him.' Loki meets *Just William* in a remarkable and unexpectedly entertaining reworking of the original.

In *Eight Days of Luke*, Wynne Jones addresses the issue of the double audience in an ingenious way. David himself comes to work out what is going on in his life because he remembers the original myth from his own reading (and helped out by Mr Wedding, appropriately god of wisdom and knowledge). Knowledge of the myths is not external to the narrative, a readership issue, but an integral part of the narrative itself. This allows a certain amount of explanation of the background – just as, for instance, in David Lindsay's very different novel, *Devil's Tor*, a professor in the narrative can explain to the other characters – and therefore the audience – the significance of a myth that Lindsay's actual readers may not know.

As well as recognizing its place in the great tradition of children's literature (a parallel universe is actually accessed through the back of a cupboard) we can see in *Eight Days of Luke* a number of correspondences with other reworkings of Norse myth. Wynne Jones – as Neil Gaiman was to do – explores the role of the Norse gods in our own, near-contemporary, world. As Mr Wedding explains, without Thor's hammer, the gods have lost their power, and 'other beliefs have conquered us'. Mr Wedding is pleased that the recovery of the hammer will enable the gods to get back their full strength 'for the final battle', which some readers will know the gods are destined to lose. Ragnarök itself, we are left to suppose, will take place in mythic time, in a mythical parallel universe. As we might expect from a novel aimed at younger readers, there is, in *Eight Days of Luke*, little of the implied or explicit criticism of contemporary society which I have argued is a common thread in re-workings of Norse myth, and certainly no sense that Ragnarök is a cataclysm which may overwhelm the real world.

An extreme case of fierce dissociation from the past, and determined rejection of the present, while at the same time drawing on a traditional cultural heritage, is the work of rock bands in the recent genre known as 'Viking metal'. Viking metal is a development of the original heavy metal music, which was characterized by its noisy distortion, aggressive lyrics – sometimes howled or screamed rather than sung – and heavy amplification. There are an astonishingly large number of heavy metal derivative genres – black metal, doom metal, thrash metal, grindcore metal and so on – but what distinguishes Viking metal music is its dependence on Viking themes and mythology. Its immediate predecessor, black metal, originated in Norway, so the evolution of Viking metal is perhaps not surprising, though the band usually credited with starting the Viking metal trend is a Swedish group called Bathory. Black metal music in Norway was from the first characterized by violent anti-Christian sentiments, and was associated with a wave of arson attacks on churches in Norway. Black metallists, in their music and in their stage present-ation – lots of fake blood and corpse-like make-up – have tended to promote themes of violence, death and murder, and occasionally this spills over into real life: the Norwegian musician Varg Vikernes is at present serving a jail sentence for the murder of Euronymous, the nickname of a member of the black metal band Mayhem.

Viking metal draws on Norse themes not in a strictly musical sense – the work of such groups as Bathory is not by any means a mock-up of medieval music. Rather, it is in the band names, album titles, artwork of album covers and, especially, in the song lyrics that Viking themes are so evident. The first album released by Bathory which critics came to label 'Viking metal' was *Blood, Fire, Death*, but their next album, *Hammerheart*, has the Victorian painter Frank Dicksee's *A Viking Funeral* as its sleeve illustration, which neatly ties together the central themes of death and Vikings. The title of the third album, *Twilight of the Gods*, is completely transparent in its debt to Norse myth. The lyrics of individual tracks endorse this debt: one song from *Hammerheart* is addressed to Odin: 'Odin in the sky up high, let the ravens of yours fly'. Another song, 'Valhalla', describes how a Viking warrior expects to be welcomed into Valhalla. There are no twists or variations: the myths are represented entirely straightforwardly.

Bathory have been quoted as saying that for Scandinavian metallists, the move into Norse mythological themes was inevitable and natural, given their nationality and ethnic roots. And certainly, the themes of death and violence inherent in many of the myths make them ideal subject matter for rock music derived from black metal. But we should also take into account the anti-Christian perspective of neo-paganism (and remember that Varg Vikernes was an Ásatrú member). In fact, the full spectrum of black metal music, including Viking metal, is very like that of the neo-pagan groups discussed earlier on in this chapter: we find, for instance, plainly neo-Nazi beliefs in what has been called 'National Socialist Black Metal', and to a lesser extent in 'pagan metal' and 'satanic metal'. Even the more mainstream music has lyrics which promote the idea of a racial nationalist culture, and its connection with the Norse gods: 'After the sound of my hammers beat upon the anvil...Never lose the values I have taught you, Always keep your morals and ideals, Do never bring your flag disgrace.' And there is even a gentler folksy (if not folkish) strand to some of this music.

Viking metal of course has a cult following, rather than any appeal to popular culture. Popular appeal would probably be accounted artistic failure. But it is firmly in the tradition not only of Norse myth itself, but also of the subsequent popular reworkings of it. Thus Varg Vikernes took his stage name, Count Grishnakh, from a minor character in *The Lord of the Rings*. And there are two metal bands called after Tolkien's Isengard – the 'circle of sheer rocks that enclose a valley as with a wall, and in the midst of that valley is a tower of stone called Orthanc'. One band is Norwegian and the other Swedish, playing Viking metal and power metal, respectively. Isengard is also the name of a number of computer games based on Norse mythic themes.

Another major area of what might be called 'alternative culture' to draw on Old Norse themes is the domain of comics and graphic novels. Here, as with science fiction and magic realism – with which comics and graphic novels share many features – there is scope for representing the bizarre and the grotesque, the magic and the supernatural, unconstrained by the limits of naturalism. The visual iconography of Norse mythology – Thor's hammer, Odin's ravens, and so on – is also good material for illustrators, though there are few illustrations which feature runic decorations, perhaps because of their association, in the United States, with white supremacist organizations. The hallmark of all comics aimed at younger readers is violence made entertaining – dramatic but essentially unserious and undisturbing physical encounters between figures exhibiting almost humorously excessive physical strength. It is no wonder, then, that one of the most successful and long-running series has been Marvel's *The*

Mighty Thor, published by DC Comics using a number of different writers and illustrators, and varying enormously in quality. Thor is an improbably highly muscled superhero, his costume owing more to the conventions of science fiction films than to any Norse iconography, but he is easily recognizable by his mighty hammer, named in the text as Mjolnir, and represented as a very large mallet. He wears a winged helmet reminiscent of Fritz Lang's Odin, but is usually blond and clean-shaven, rather than red-haired and bearded. The narratives do not follow actual Norse stories (though many feature his delinquent 'half-brother', Loki), but involve successful battles against a number of enemies from outer space, the underworld, or simply the writer's imagination. As the series progressed through the second half of the twentieth century, Thor came to be represented as speaking in a strange half-Shakespearian idiom, presumably to suggest some sort of antiquity.

The background to Thor's exploits is very often modern-day America, because the figure of Thor is a transformation (one might say, a shape-shifting) of a modern human – specifically, a disabled medical student called Donald Blake, who once lashed out with his walking stick and transformed himself into Thor with Mjolnir. Thor is confidently labelled 'our guy', and like so many other superheroes, acts alone to defend 'our' world from the various forces which arise from time to time to threaten it. The political ideologies which Norse myth has so often been used to underpin seem to be almost completely absent. Thor's power is crudely physical, and in no sense political. The contemporary world is by implication worth defending, and not the object of complaint or scorn. According to some storylines (and one of the features of comics is the lack of concern for consistency over a long period) Ragnarök, as a cataclysmic battle, took place, with due visual drama, and Asgard was wiped out – Thor being the only survivor. This explains why Thor is continuing his superhuman battles on earth, and why there is no ominous feeling of impending doom. Strict censorship regulations have ensured that the Thor comics, aimed at a teenage or younger audience, never engage with seriously anti-religious, occult or sinister themes. But adult comics, and graphic novels, have reworked the darker side of Norse myth. For example, Grant Morrison's disconcerting graphic novel *Arkhan Asylum* is set in the eponymous mental institution familiar from Batman narratives, and features Batman himself, impaled on a spear, crying out in despair: 'I am Christ on the Cedar. Odin on the World Ash,' and quoting fragments of the Old Norse poem *Hávamál*: 'Hung on the windy tree for nine whole nights wounded with the spear. Dedicated to Odin. Myself to myself.' Motifs from Norse mythology, stripped bare of both medieval context and later political connotations, have become part of the repertoire of adult horror literature. And the influence of Norse myth has moved back into the realms of the cult audience, the secret society, the literary coterie, and the learned antiquarians with which its post-medieval reception began.

Epilogue

yths have no beginning, no evident point of origin. What we call 'Norse mythology' is an extensive compilation of ideas, beliefs and stories from different periods and different peoples. It is largely based on Snorri Sturluson's thirteenth-century gathering – and, some would say, elaboration – of earlier material from many sources. Some of Snorri's stories find echoes in pre-Christian carvings or sculpture, or in poems we attribute to pagan poets, though they were not written down until after Christianity had brought literacy to Iceland. Others echo narratives from quite other locations: Jewish legends, Bible stories, Christian saints' lives, or classical texts. The Norse myths must have held special meanings for Snorri's thirteenth-century audience, but these meanings may not all have been intrinsic to the myths themselves – rather, they may have belonged to what the myths represented: traditions from a valued, indeed cherished and romanticized past. From as near as we can get to the beginnings of Norse myths, then, their significance has been as a voice from the past, a past to which the present has always had its own reasons for harking back.

For Snorri's contemporaries the myths represented the cultural inheritance of their own people, and were the precious product of their precocious democratic republic, Iceland. In the Nordic renaissance of the seventeenth century, Norse material provided the northern European nations with evidence of impressive antiquity – with myths of origin. This was particularly important in Britain, where, in the early Middle

Ages, Scandinavians – the Vikings – had settled widely and permanently. In the eighteenth century, the same material fed the fashionable literary taste for romantic incident and sublime emotion. But most of all, an emerging German nation was coming to regard Norse myth as its own cultural inheritance, as the beliefs of its ancestors, as encoding the primeval history and religion of all the Germanic peoples. In North America, too, the knowledge that the Norse were the first Europeans to arrive has always lent the mythology a very special cachet for those Americans who have believed they could trace their ancestry back to northern European roots.

The adoption of Norse mythology as a badge of supposedly racial identity has often led to its being associated with pernicious racial doctrines. This, however, is entirely incidental to the substance of the myths themselves. Those who do not have or claim an ethnic connection with Old Norse myth have been equally drawn to it. Norse mythology comprises a great pantheon of gods, a huge variety of incident, and the irresistible lure of secret knowledge, knowledge hidden from the world for centuries, but available to those who apply themselves to ancient texts and strange alphabets. The earliest sources of Old Norse myth – the poetry, the narratives, the sculpture – are full of drama, on both a human and a cosmic scale, and also subtlety, poignancy and unexpectedly engaging wisdom. Cultural giants (so to speak) in the fields of opera, poetry, film-making or novels have produced their own versions of Old Norse myth, and these have in their turn influenced later artists. Norse myths have functioned both as a marker of cultural familiarity – the beliefs of 'our' ancestors – and also as a source of arcane allusion, available to those who pride themselves on their ability to deal in difficulty and strangeness.

And like all myths, Norse mythology offers any audience a perspective on the fundamental issues of human life: from its beginnings, to its last things, and beyond. For all these reasons, there can be no end – just as there are no discernible beginnings – to the representation of Norse myth in our cultural life.

TIMELINE

AD

700–1015	the Old English poem *Beowulf* was written sometime between these two dates
793	Vikings sack Lindisfarne – conventional opening of 'the Viking age'
c. 850	composition of the earliest surviving skaldic poetry, attributed to the Norwegian Bragi Boddason
870–930	settlement of Iceland
999/1000	conversion of Iceland to Christianity
1016	accession of the Danish King Canute (Knútr) to the throne of England
1066	William the Conquerer establishes Norman rule in England
1178/9–1241	life of Snorri Sturluson, author of the *Prose Edda*, *Heimskringla* and perhaps *Egils saga*
c. 1220–25	the *Prose Edda*
c. 1230	*Heimskringla*
c. 1270	compilation of the *Codex Regius* (manuscript of the *Poetic Edda*)
1262	Iceland loses independence to Norway
1550	Jón Arason, last Catholic bishop in Iceland, executed
1593	Arngrímur Jónsson's *Crymogæa*, a history of Iceland in Latin
1665	an edition, with a Latin translation, of Snorri's *Prose Edda* by the Danish scholar Peder Resen
1768	Thomas Gray's *Norse Odes* (written in 1761) published
1770	Bishop Percy's *Northern Antiquities* (a translation of Mallet's *Introduction à l'histoire de Dannemarc*)
1790	Fuseli paints *Thor Battering the Midgard Serpent*
1797–1804	William Blake's *The Four Zoas*
1876	first complete performance of Wagner's *Ring* at Bayreuth
1908	founding of the von List society
1920	David Lindsay's *A Voyage to Arcturus*
1921	Hitler becomes leader of the National Socialist German Workers' Party
1932	F.B. Marby's book (in German) on runic gymnastics
1954	Tolkien's *The Lord of the Rings* first published
1962	first appearance of *The Mighty Thor* in Marvel Comics
1996	discovery of 'Kennewick Man' in Washington
2001–3	*The Lord of the Rings* film trilogy released

BIBLIOGRAPHY

Old Norse primary sources in translation

Heimskringla, by Snorri Sturluson, trans. L.M. Hollander (Austin, TX, 1964)

The Poetic Edda, ed. and trans. Ursula Dronke (Oxford; vol. I, 1969, vol. II, 1997, two further volumes forthcoming)

The Poetic Edda, trans. Carolyne Larrington (Oxford, 1999)

Scaldic Poetry, E.O.G. Turville-Petre (Oxford, 1976)

Snorri Sturluson: Edda [*The Prose Edda*], trans. Anthony Faulkes (London, 1987)

The Vinland Sagas, trans. Magnus Magnusson and Hermann Pálsson (London, 2003)

The Saga of the Volsungs [*Völsunga saga*], trans. Jesse Byock (London, 1990)

Primary texts in English

Arnold, Matthew, *Poems*, ed. Kenneth and Miriam Allott (London, 1979)

Blake, William, *Complete Poetry and Prose*, ed. David V. Erdman (Berkeley, CA, 1982)

Burgess, Melvin, *Bloodtide* (London, 1999)

Byatt, A.S., *Possession: A Romance* (London, 1989)

Carlyle, Thomas, *On Heroes, Hero-Worship, and the Heroic in History*, ed. Michael K. Goldberg (Berkeley, CA, 1993)

Gaiman, Neil, *American Gods* (London, 2001)

Grass, Günther, *The Tin Drum*, trans. Ralph Manheim (Harmondsworth, 1965)

Gray, Thomas, *Complete Poems*, ed. H.W. Starr and J.R. Hendrickson (Oxford, 1966)

Heaney, Seamus, *North* (London, 1975)

Lindsay, David, *A Voyage to Arcturus* (London, 1920)

Lindsay, David, *Devil's Tor* (London, 1932; Edinburgh, 1992)

MacDiarmid, Hugh, *Complete Poems*, ed. Michael Grieve and W.R. Aitken, 2 vols (Harmondsworth, 1985)

Márquez, Gabriel García, 'A Very Old Man with Enormous Wings', trans. Gregory Rabassa, at http://www.geocities.com/cyber_explorer99/ garciamarquezold man.html?200626

Morris, William, *The Story of Sigurd the Volsung* (London, 1887)

Muldoon, Paul, *Hay* (London, 1998)

Muldoon, Paul, *Quoof* (London, 1983)

Scott, Walter, *The Pirate*, ed. Mark Weinstein and Alison Lumsden (Edinburgh, 2001)

Scott, Walter, *Poetical Works*, ed. J. Logie Robertson (Oxford, 1904)

Tolkien, J.R.R., *The Lord of the Rings* (London, first published 1954; one-vol. edition, 1968)

Wynne Jones, Diana, *Eight Days of Luke* (London, 1975)

Secondary literature

Bailey, Richard, *Viking Age Sculpture in Northern England* (London, 1980)

Björnsson, Árni, *Wagner and the Volsungs* (London, 2003)

Clunies Ross, Margaret, *Prolonged Echoes: Old Norse Myths in Medieval Northern Society*, vol.I: *The Myths* (Odense, 1994)

Clunies Ross, Margaret, *The Norse Muse in Britain 1750–1820* (Trieste, 1998)

Farley, F.E., 'Scandinavian Influences on the English Romantic Movement', *Harvard Studies and Notes* IX (1903)

Gardell, Matthias, *Gods of the Blood: The Pagan Revival and White Separatism* (Durham, NC, 2003)

Goodrick-Clarke, Nicholas, *The Occult Roots of Nazism* (London, 2004)

Karlsson, Gunnar, *Iceland's 1100 Years: The History of a Marginal Society* (London, 2000)

Lindow, John, *Norse Mythology* (Oxford, 2001)

Loyn, H.R., *The Vikings in Britain* (Oxford, 1994)

Mallet, Paul Henri, *Introduction à l'histoire de Dannemarc*, trans. as *Northern Antiquities* by Thomas Percy (London, 1770)

McKinnell, John, and Rudolf Simek, with Klaus Düwel, *Runes, Magic and Religion: A sourcebook* (Vienna, 2004)

Omberg, Margaret, *Scandinavian Themes in English Poetry, 1769–1800* (Uppsala, 1976)

Orchard, Andy, *Cassell's Dictionary of Norse Myth and Legend* (London, 1997)

Page, R.I., *Runes* (London, 1987)

Roberts, Michael, *The Swedish Imperial Experience 1560–1718* (Cambridge, 1979)

Roesdahl, Else, and P.M. Sørensen, *The Waking of Angantyr: The Scandinavian Past in European Culture* (Aarhus, 1996)

Seaton, Ethel, *Literary Relations of England and Scandinavia in the Seventeenth Century* (Oxford, 1935)

Spencer, Stewart, and Barry Millington, *Wagner's Ring of the Nibelung: A Companion* (London, 1993)

Turville-Petre, E.O.G., *Myth and Religion of the North* (New York, 1964)

Wawn, Andrew, ed., *Northern Antiquity: The Post-Medieval Reception of Edda and Saga* (Enfield Lock, 1994)

Wawn, Andrew, *The Vikings and the Victorians* (Woodbridge, 2000)

Wilson, David, *Anglo-Saxon Paganism* (London, 1992)

Wilson, David, *Vikings and Gods in European Art* (Moesgård, 1997)

Websites

There is a vast amount of information about Old Norse mythology on the Internet. Not much of it is scholarly, and not all of it is reliable. Some neo-pagan or 'New Age' websites have very useful information, however. The following list is no more than a short sample of what is available, and I cannot vouch for the content's accuracy or political correctness.

www.vikinganswerlady.com/index.shtml

www.aswynn.co.uk

www.hrafnar.org

www.geocities.com/heatheneurope

www.irminsul.org

www.thetroth.org

www.ugcs.caltech.edu.~cherryne/mythology

www.northvegr.org

www.immortalthor.net/

www.sunnyway.com/runes/stadha.html

www.viking-society.group.shef.ac.uk (the scholarly society of academics teaching Old Norse)

and of course, the entry in Wikipedia:

http://en.wikipedia.org/wiki/Norse_mythology

INDEX

The index is divided into two sections, first a general index, then an index of Norse names.

GENERAL INDEX

King Ethelred 86
King of Northumbria, executed
  Ragnar Lothbrok 87
Kipling, Rudyard, *Just So Stories*
  76

Lang, Fritz, director of 1924 film
  Die Nibelungen 145–6, 198
Larkin, Philip 7: and the 'myth-
  kitty' 7
Latin 97, 106, 114–15, 117,
  119–20, 146, 171
Leifr Eiríksson, Icelandic explorer
  179–80
Lévi-Strauss, Claude 3
Lewis, C.S., *The Lion, the Witch
  and the Wardrobe* 188
Lindsay, David, 171–5, 183: *A
  Voyage to Arcturus* (1922)
  171–3, 175; *Devil's Tor* 173–5,
  195; racial dimension of novels
  173–5

MacDiarmid, Hugh, 165–6, 183:
  'A Drunk Man Looks at the
  Thistle' (1926) 165–6; 'The Sea-
  Serpent' 166
Macpherson, James, *Fragments of
  Ancient Poetry* 111–12
magic 147–50, 152
magic realism 170, 197
Magnus, Johannes 107–8
Mallet, Paul-Henri, 110–11, 118,
  122, 125, 157
Marby, Friedrich Bernhard 154
Márquez, Gabriel García, 'A Very
  Old Man with Enormous Wings'
  171
Marvell, Andrew 109
Marvell Comics' *The Mighty Thor*
  197–8

Mesolithic hunter-gatherers in
  Europe 21
Michelangelo 121
Milton, John 116, 157
modernism 163–4: and myth
  163–4
monastic settlements 94
monks 87, 91, 98: East Anglian
  98; Frankish 87; Irish 87
Montesquieu, Baron Charles de
  125
Morris, William 155, 160–3, 188,
  193: *Sigurd the Volsung* (1876)
  160–2, 193; translation of
  Völsunga saga (1870) 160
Morrison, Grant, *Arkhan Asylum*,
  graphic novel 198–9
Muldoon, Paul 167–8: *Hay*
  (1998) 167; 'Rune' 167–8;
  Quoof (1983) 167: 'Yggdrasill'
  167
music 190
mysticism 76
myth: and belief 1, 3; and classical
  allusion 7; and escatology 4; and
  'gods' 1–2; and literature 4; and
  the modernist movement 163–4;
  and psychology 3–4, 6; and
  racial purity 52, 175–6; and
  ritual 2, 3; and science 4; and
  society 3; and the supernatural 2;
  and truth 2; as a means of
  cultural preservation 7; as
  recorded, retold or reworked
  6–8; as sacred 2; as 'story' or
  narrative 1–2, 3; as universal 3;
  books on 1; collecting mythic
  sources 6, 7; definition 1, 6;
  derivation 1; endurance of 8; in
  history 1; of poetry 28–33, 100;
  power of 6; present usage 1;

'teenage fiction' 190–2, 198
Temple, Sir William, writer of *Of Heroic Virtue* and *Of Poetry* 109
theosophy 151–2
Thorkelin, Icelander, first editor of *Beowulf* 90
Three Fates: in classical tradition 115; in Old Norse tradition 120
Tolkien, J.R.R. 35, 163–4, 183–91: *The Hobbit* 189; *The Lord of the Rings* 35, 163–4, 183–8; *The Silmarillion* 189
Torfaeus (Þormóðr Torfason) 107, 112
Tower of Babel, the 107
tragedy 93
travel writing in Europe in sixteenth century 106; Iceland becomes a subject for travel writers 106
Tristan and Isolde 65

Uggason, Ulf: *see Húsdrápa* in index of Norse names
Ulysses, character from Homer's *Odyssey* 6
Uppsala temple, Sweden 65–6, 69

vegetation myths 21
Venerable Bede, the 56, 61, 64, 73: connection with Norse saga 61; *History of the English Church* 61
Verstegan, Richard 109
Viking age, the 68–9, 88, 150, 168
Viking-age England and Norse mythology 97
Viking-age runic inscription 98
Viking-age sculpture 88, 94, 95, 96

'Viking metal', music 196–7: Bathory 196
Vikings 64–5, 85–9, 109, 127–9, 131, 149, 164, 180: commemorations of 180; representation of in Victorian Britain 128–9, 164; Vikings' gods 88; Viking kingdom of York 88; Viking raids 85–7 ('sack of Lindisfarne' 86)
Vinland, Old Icelandic name for North America 104, 178–9
Virgil 157
visual arts 168: tapestry and jewellery alluding to Norse mythology 168
von List, Guido, Austrian nationalist, devised ariosophy 152–5, 163, 177: *Der Wala Erweckung* 152
Vita Waldevi, Latin account of the life of Waltheof 98

Wagner, Richard, composer 6, 7, 50–1, 53, 132–45, 157–8, 160–1, 163–4, 178, 184, 188, 193–4: Brünnhilde 133, 137, 139–44; *Das Rheingold* 51, 53, 134–7, 140, 143, 158; *Der Nibelungen-mythus* 133–7, 139–41, 143; *Der Ring des Nibelungen* 51, 132–3; *Die Walküre* 137, 139–40, 158; German audiences of Wagner 142; *Götterdämmerung* 133, 143–4; Jewish caricatures in operas 142; *Parsifal* 179; *Ring* cycle 6, 132–8, 143–4, 157–8, 160–1, 184, 188, 194; *Siegfried* 140–2, 144, 146; *Siegfrieds Tod* 133, 137; 'translation' of Norse characters into characters in *Ring*

219

INDEX OF NORSE NAMES

poetry 17; sexual prowess of 29; sleeps with Gunnlöd for three nights 29; source of wisdom in giant Vafthrudnir 13; symbolised in skaldic verse 33; wisdom contrasted with Thor's foolishness 40–1; Woden, Anglo-Saxon name for 63–4; worship of 62; *Valföðr*, alternative name for 12

Ragnarök 4, 23, 24, 25, 32, 36, 42, 67, 72–3, 76, 77–81, 93–6, 109, 116, 118, 133, 143–5, 154–5, 160, 166, 172, 175, 182–3, 188, 194–5, 198
Ragnarsdrápa 25, 35–6: *see also* Bragi in general index
Rerir 51–2
Rind 30

Sæhrimnir 71
Saint Olaf 58–9
seiðr 30–1, 40–1, 42
Sessrumnir 48
Sigi 51
Sigmund the Volsung 50, 52–3, 190: *see also* Fafnisbani
Signy 52–3, 190, 193
Sigrdrífumál 149
Sigurd 50–1, 95–6, 113, 140–142, 161, 184: *see also* Fafnisbani
Sigyn, loyal wife of Loki 76, 95
Sinfjötli 52–3, 193
Skadi 43–5, 99, 177
skáld 28
Skáldskaparmál 28, 43, 101
Skírnismál 45–7, 149
Skirnir 45–7, 149
Skrymir: *see* Utgarda-Loki

Sleipnir 48, 53, 117, 159
Son, Bodn and Odrœrir 28
Sonatorrek 17: *see also* Egils saga in general index
Snæbjörn 101
Starkad 53–4, 75
Surtr 15, 78–9, 172: *see also* Muspell
Suttung 28, 29
Svadilfæri 48

Þórsdrápa 33–4
Þrymskviða 39–40, 48

Thjazi 44
Thjodolf 44
Thökk 159
Thor 23, 33–42, 48, 49, 53, 57–60, 62, 65, 76, 78, 93, 95, 121, 123–4, 135, 145, 148, 157, 165–6, 170, 187, 198
Thorgerd Hölgabrud 59
Thorgrim 60, 69–70
Thorolf 57, 174
Thridi 15
Thrudgelmir 14
Thrym 39–40, 48
Tyr 78, 79, 90, 145, 148

Utgarda-Loki/Skrymir 37–9, 41

Vafþrúðnismál 13–14, 70, 141
Vafthrudnir 13–14, 16
Valföðr 12: *see also* Odin
Valhalla 25, 33, 41, 59, 70–2, 99, 101, 109, 114, 118, 120, 126, 134, 139, 172, 194, 196
valkyries 33, 52, 71–2, 76, 97, 113–15, 120, 133–4, 139, 140–1, 158